How to Be Your
Own
Therapist

How to Be Your
Own
Therapist

A Step-By-Step Guide to
Building a Competent,
Confident Life

Patricia Farrell, Ph.D.

McGraw-Hill
New York   Chicago   San Francisco
Lisbon   London   Madrid   Mexico City   Milan
New Delhi   San Juan   Seoul   Singapore
Sydney   Toronto

The *McGraw-Hill* Companies

Library of Congress Cataloging-in-Publication Data has been applied for.

1 2 3 4 5 6 7 8 9 0   DOC/DOC   0 9 8 7 6 5 4 3 2

The purpose of this book is to educate. It is sold with the understanding that the author and publisher shall have neither liability nor responsibility for any injury caused or alleged to be caused directly or indirectly by the information in this book. While every effort has been made to ensure the book's accuracy, its contents should not be construed as medical advice. Each person's health needs are unique. To obtain recommendations appropriate to your particular situation, please consult a qualified health care professional.

ISBN: 0-07-138733-1

 This book is printed on recycled, acid-free paper containing a minimum of 50% recycled de-inked fiber.

The journey toward writing this book began with a wish, in adulthood, but it truly began in childhood when a sister I cherish, Dolores Gross, saved silver pennies as a coming-home-from-the-hospital gift and a mother, Pauline, showed me I could be independent. My mother understood the need for independence at an early age. At twelve she had to work in a factory to help support her parents and three sisters.

These two women and my dear friend, Dr. Rita Posner, have been an inspiration and an endless source of encouragement for me; I could have done little without them.

CONTENTS

ACKNOWLEDGMENTS

The thoughts, beliefs and values in this book—and the belief in myself that translated these things first into ideas, and then into words upon a page—are deeply rooted in my past, and nowhere more so than in my family history. Although my wish to share the powerful beliefs that I hold became more developed and more conscious in my adult years, I knew early and with certainty that I had things I wanted to say. The faith and belief in myself that convinced me that I had something *worth* saying was fostered and reinforced by three remarkable women. For as long as I can remember, my sister, Dolores Gross, has been an example and a friend to me. One of my earliest memories comes from when I was only six; Dolores gave me the treasured silver penny collection she'd saved for herself as a welcome-home gift when I returned from the hospital, just a scared and hurting six-year-old child, after facing the near-amputation of my leg. It was one unselfish act among many that made me feel loved. Like my sister, I cherished my brave, independent and adored mother, Pauline, who taught me that I could be strong, successful, independent and loved. She taught by example, helping to support her parents and three sisters from the time she was twelve by working long hours in a factory, and yet always finding the time and love, throughout our lives, to let us know that we were cherished. Along with my mother and sister, my dear long-time friend, Dr. Rita Posner, has been there in the good times and the not-so-good. She has always been a source of support, bringing her terrific wit and an unbeatable combination of "book" intelligence and "heart" smarts to my life. These three women have formed a circle of inspiration around me with their endless encouragement and love. Little that I've done could have happened without them believing in me and cheering me on.

Like any book, *How to Be Your Own Therapist* was the result of a collaborative process, with many people taking part in the creative effort. Three people, in particular, helped to bring this book to life. The ideas for the book were shepherded into reality through the unparalleled talent, commitment and dedication of my agent-extraordinaire, Jeff Kleinman at Graybill & English. My editor at McGraw-Hill, Nancy Hancock, is a magician who time and again proved her powerful skill in always knowing exactly what should stay and what had to go. She performed her magic with graciousness, humor and an infallible sense of just the right word or phrase. The third member in our collaboration, writer Laura Joyce, translated my ideas and beliefs onto the page. She brought an indispensable sense of humor and an unerring gift for "voice," a love of words and a willingness to do whatever needed to be done to help create not just any book, but the *right* book.

Along the way, I've been encouraged by more people than I can count, but I want to offer special thanks to several in particular. My appreciation goes out to McGraw-Hill's Vice-President of Marketing and Communications, Lynda Luppino; the marketing manager, Eileen Lamadore; and the publicist, Lizz Aviles, each of whom has treated the book with energy, enthusiasm and excitement. A special thank you, also, to Maury Povich, who is committed to his work as few are—and who is also the person who gave me my start in television. Similarly, words can't cover my appreciation for the estimable Nancy Grace of Court TV, a feisty, insightful and delightful woman; her last name says it better than I ever could. Mike Stanton also deserves a big thank you: he produced my audition reels one after another without once asking how many more I would need—and without once asking for a dime, for that matter.

Finally, I'd like to thank my clients over the years; they'll stay nameless but they know who they are. I have had the good fortune to be invited inside of many lives, often at times of great vulnerability. I have seen courage, strength and unwavering honesty, even in the most difficult moments of life and even when it might have seemed easier to accept mediocrity or avoid reality. My clients have left me with a permanent sense of awe at the power, resiliency and majesty of the human spirit. It is in honor of this spirit that I wrote this book.

A Call to Sanity:
Coming Home to Yourself

SANITY IS A MADNESS PUT TO GOOD USES;
WAKING LIFE IS A DREAM CONTROLLED.

George Santayana

I was six years old and small for my age. No bigger than a preschooler, I lay shivering in the chilled hospital room. A huge, fluid-filled knot on my leg throbbed painfully. I had been throwing a baseball in my family's tiny cold-water flat in Queens—something I shouldn't have been doing at all. In a fluke accident, the ball hit the wall and came flying back at my thigh, badly bruising my tendons and muscles. We were too poor to go to a family doctor, and, as many people do even today, we used the hospital emergency room when we needed medical care. An intern sent me home, assuring my parents that I would improve quickly if they applied hot wet towels to the injury—as hot as I could tolerate. The treatment was pure torture, and instead of healing me, it caused the injury to become badly inflamed, leaving a lump in my leg that grew more and more painful and large. Soon I was rushed back to the same hospital, but this time a more experienced doctor intervened. Not only was he better informed, but he was gentle with me and a master at handling scared, hurting children. The nurse who assisted him was nothing less. I was quickly taken into surgery in order to save my leg where a broken vein was bleeding badly.

Unfortunately, as a charity patient I ended up experiencing something far more frightening than the injury or the surgery. On that second trip to the E.R., the kind nurse and doctor, both of whom were well-intentioned, involved a social worker in my care. The social worker was a woman who spoke to me in syrupy tones at first, although her voice changed as the hours went on. She called herself a "helper" and asked questions one after another as she relentlessly tried to get me to admit the "truth" about my injury—that I'd been abused. Remember, I was little—only six—and although I didn't understand much of what was happening, I did know one thing: she wanted me to say something bad, something untrue, about the parents I loved. The doctor's early concern had been turned into an assumption by the misguided social worker, who just assumed that my parents had injured me, perhaps by throwing me against a wall, certainly by scalding me with hot water.

It was the doctor who finally intervened, putting a stop to the overzealous questioning by the social worker. I pleaded with the doctor just as I had pleaded with the social worker, insisting that I was telling the truth. The difference was that he listened, while she merely seemed to grow more displeased with my answers. I didn't know enough to understand that my family's poverty, our lower social status when compared to the professionals in the room, and who knows what other socioeconomic factors, weighed heavily against me, at least with the social worker—and it also weighed heavily against my parents. What I did understand were bits of the discussion that went on just above my head: casual talk, guided by the strong opinions of the social worker, about taking me away from my parents. I remember the banter that flowed between the grown-ups as they casually debated my future, and the false sympathy of the social worker—a woman who had just pronounced my parents unfit (another term that was new to me, but one whose meaning I grasped instantly).

To my parents' great relief, the doctor had more authority, and the hospital finally allowed me to go home. I'm certain to this day that the social worker remained fully convinced that I was returning to yet more abuse.

For me, the scars ran deep. My leg may have healed quickly, but for many years I looked upon "helpers" with a sense of confusion: there were helpers like the doctor, who had literally and figuratively saved me, and then there were helpers like the social worker. I didn't know whether to feel gratefulness or fear and mistrust. Somehow I did know, though, even at six, that I had been both totally powerless and ultimately powerful in that hospital room. Even as the helper with her own agenda questioned me, intent on "saving" me and disbelieving my heartfelt responses, I stuck to the truth—*my* truth—and it saved the day. I've relearned that point countless times since: *telling your truth*—whether it's about how someone is treating you or what you need to do to be successful or something else—*will always save the day.*

Although I wouldn't understand most of the dynamics of that day for many years to come, I did learn two important lessons. One was about other people: that there are good people, people who don't see your poverty or your neighborhood or any other surface feature when they look at you; they see the real you, in this case a scared, hurting little girl. At the same time, I learned that there are powerful people who will pretend to be saving you even as they take you far from home. But I also learned a lesson about myself: I came to realize that if you know yourself, trust yourself, and live according to your truth, no one can ever take you away from your home. Your real home will be within yourself: powerful, safe and constant.

That experience in the hospital was my first encounter with the strange world of therapists, and it colored my views of the helping professions for many years. In some dark, hidden recesses of my mind, it probably still does. I went into my own work believing that other professionals had beliefs similar to mine: that we were all there to help our clients grow in power and self-determination as they made progress in their search for competence and confidence. Certainly many other professionals *do* feel this way; I've had the pleasure of working side by side with some gifted, wonderful professionals, many of whom have taught me new ways to help my own clients without stripping them of their power. I think of the nurse and doctor who were gentle and kind, tending to my needs, trying to protect me when they thought I was in danger. At the same time, I can't help but remember the social worker who was so intent on seeing what she wanted to see, regardless of what was real or true for me.

Undoubtedly, this incident contributed to my views about the potential positives *and* pitfalls in the world of professional helping. I learned fast and early that any number of factors, including an individual therapist's foibles, enter into any interaction between a "helper" and a person seeking help—and this can be a good thing or a bad thing. I've seen the healing and grace that can result when two people sit down to tackle a problem together—and I've seen the Pandora's box that can be opened if one of those two people is wielding power for power's sake.

It was in part because of the distrust and frustration that grew out of my encounters with healers like the social worker—people who needed to heal themselves—that I began to develop the ideas and tools in this book. At the same time, I was hearing stories from people who'd been in therapy and hadn't found what they were looking for. I heard from others who had never considered being in therapy—and never would, for a multitude of reasons—yet had certainly faced challenges that affected relationships, work, or other areas of their lives. I couldn't help but notice that some were developing competence and confidence *despite* their bad experiences and *despite* the lack of therapy. Faced with challenges, and unable or unwilling to get the answers from a professional, these people were stumbling along—and eventually stumbling upon their *own* answers. Maybe it doesn't sound like rocket science to you, but to someone trained in a field that requires Arrogance 101 as basic course work—instilling in therapists the belief that their very existence is critical to the well-being of the universe—it was mind-blowing. As you can imagine, any beliefs I'd had about the essential nature of my field were turned upside down. Talk about a blow to the ego!

As a result, I rethought my field, and my role in it, and now I feel fortunate that I did it sooner rather than later. It's given me 20-some years of the magical experience of watching my clients make their own discoveries, rather than handing them solutions on a silver platter—solutions that will as often as not be unworkable, unreliable, or just plain rejected since they come from me, not them. It's the difference between teaching a class and giving someone the answers to an exam. If you've ever cheated on a test—and I'm sure you haven't, but try to imagine for a moment—you know just how much benefit you gained from the class.

For most of my professional life, then, I have practiced and refined a kind of therapy that recognizes and builds upon several truisms I've just discussed. First, *you must be aware of others' agendas when they offer to help you,* whether they've got professional credentials or not. Second, whether you *can* rely on someone else or not, *you may not choose to involve someone else in solving your problems*—and that's all right. And, finally, *the best kind of help is often the help you give yourself.*

Fair enough, right? But where do you go, then, when you face a daunting challenge in your life?

Bottom line: except in certain circumstances, which I'll discuss soon, *you go on a journey to the center of yourself.* To do this, you don't need a "helper" standing above you dispensing advice or pills or observations. Even if others have accused you of being repressed or emotionally uninformed, the fact is that *you know your own emotional terrain better than anyone on this earth.* What you *could* use is a tour guide to point out a few of the highlights along the journey. A good tour guide can help get you where you want to go faster, with fewer detours, and with a better sense of the surrounding countryside than if you go it alone.

This book is your tour guide, your tools for the trip. Think of it as a map and a compass and a bunch of road signs all rolled into one: pressed between the covers of this book are the tools that will keep you from running off the road or ending up in some godforsaken little place like Confusion or Hysteria. I can't promise that we'll only go to pretty places—the inside of every life is filled with the good, the bad, and the downright ugly—but these tools will help get you there and back safely.

As we set out, and along the way, one of the things I want to do is help you be able to discern those who are helping you and those who aren't, both in the helping professions and out. Whether the "helper" is in a therapy room or your living room, if the agenda isn't about your confidence and your competence, the outcome won't be helpful. In the field, these people cause what I term "professional pollution," and out of it, they cause "interpersonal pollution." Either way, I want to enable you to heal yourself even in the presence of false claims or broken promises from the very people you should most be able to trust—those who are offering to journey with you through your most intimate challenges.

Self-Therapy

Over the years, while developing my approach to helping others create confidence and competence in their lives, I came to believe that therapists aren't absolutely essential. I also developed the even stronger belief that people can be their own therapists. The vast majority of people who face life challenges could do far better for themselves—whether mentally, physically, emotionally, or financially, and often all four—by avoiding the cumbersome process of traditional therapy altogether. Instead, using "self-therapy" is the shortest, fastest, most effective, and least expensive approach to answering the challenges they face.

Perhaps it seems odd that I'd say this. After all, each patient who doesn't enter therapy is one more patient I can't treat—or bill an insurance company for. The fact is, though, my criteria for success, both professionally and personally, isn't about how many people I treat, how much I earn in a given year, or how much power I wield over people who seek help at a vulnerable time. I like to think I got into this field for all the right reasons, and I fervently hope that the day I start caring more about my paycheck or my power is also my last day in the field. It should be, and that's true for anyone providing therapy.

You can help yourself more powerfully, more rapidly, and more permanently, in almost any situation in which you might normally turn to a therapist (or in any situation in which you wouldn't but others might agree you should!) by instead serving as your own therapist. If this belief cuts into my patient roster, so be it—in fact, I genuinely hope it does. I hope it empties out psychotherapy offices across the land as if it is forever August in New York City, when most of the therapists flee to the Hamptons or Cape Cod and mental health is on hiatus—and perhaps better than ever.

If this should happen, even as my own practice shrinks I will have the satisfaction of knowing that you're out there, facing your problems and challenges head-on, using the techniques and skills I'll discuss and avoiding the pitfalls of traditional therapy, which we'll discuss in Chapter Two. That's more than enough consolation for me.

The idea that you could possibly better heal yourself than a therapist could heal you won't endear me to many of my colleagues, I suspect. The same needs and desires—some valid, some less so—that I have rejected are of nearly primal importance to some of my fellow practitioners: after all, each client is part of what keeps us solvent, whether the solvency is financial or emotional. Each unquestioning client is also what helps to keep the helpers perched upon pedestals of power, handing down diagnoses and brilliant insights like sages from ancient times. I'm going to stick to my guns, though, even if my colleagues come out gunning for me because of my beliefs. What I have learned about power and empowerment, confidence and competence, and the self-determination that can take you to places you want to go, is too big to keep quiet and too effective to keep to myself. The incredible power that self-therapy offers you is simply so remarkable that it deserves its place at the table.

Tools for a Lifetime

Perhaps you've heard this bit of folk wisdom: if you give a man a fish, he eats for a day; if you teach a man to fish, he eats for a lifetime. This has always been one of my favorite quotes—and a foundation belief in my approach to life. It doesn't matter whether I'm teaching a class, or responding when someone requests that I "save" them, or posting a response to a question on a message board on WebMD, where I serve as a psychological consultant. Regardless of context, this belief reminds and encourages me to *empower others rather than enable their ineffective behaviors or choices*— and empowerment is what this book is about.

As you read on, you will see that much of what I object to in traditional approaches to problem solving—whether or not the problem solving occurs in psychotherapy—is that dependency is so often created as a result. My objections to dependency are clear in the tools I provide you: self-therapy is all about personal choice, personal effectiveness, personal power, and personal responsibility.

Even as you're exploring your own power through reading this book, I want to emphasize that there are situations in which you should seek help from a professional. In Chapter One we'll address what types of situations warrant professional intervention, but for the moment, the point I want to make is that when therapy *is* indicated and appropriate—and there is no doubt that it can be a highly effective, life-changing process at certain times and with a good therapist—it should *never encourage or create dependency.* What any type of professional intervention *should* do is help you develop the innate skills—the tools I share with you in this book—that you can use over a lifetime to face the challenges of life.

As the book guides you behind the scenes of therapy, your insider's view will help you begin to realize that self-therapy isn't quantum physics—whatever that is. In fact, self-therapy isn't a science at all. Instead, healing is about compassion for yourself, hopefulness for your future, and faith that not only *can* you overcome your challenges, but you *will.* Healing is not only *possible,* but highly probable. I am confident that you have these traits—compassion, hopefulness, and faith—in spades, or will discover them soon enough as you move ahead into the learning that awaits you.

Preparing to Embark on Your Journey

In Section I, "The Myth of Psychotherapy and the Promise of Healing," we will examine the process of self-therapy. We'll consider whether it's appropriate for you, how to prepare yourself, and other issues that will affect you as you begin to apply the process to your own life challenges. You will also learn about the influences that others have on you as you face your challenges, and how that influence can impact the outcome of your self-therapy. After examining the myths that further influence your beliefs about therapy, change, and challenges, we'll look at three elemental factors that influence your beliefs and behaviors. And finally you will determine your personality type and what impact that has on the outcome of your self-therapy.

At the end of the first section you will be on the brink of embarking on your journey of discovery. Armed with new information, and possessing a better understanding of the power of your beliefs about your ability to take full responsibility to learn, grow, and change, you will be well-equipped to move on to the second section of the book, "Discoveries from the Toolbox.".

In this section we'll discuss the 10 practical tools that make up my approach to self-therapy, which will help you make the changes you want in your life. Each tool gives you methods for understanding your motivations and for meeting your needs as you deal with the impact others have on your journey—and thus each will be a powerful companion on your journey of growth.

In using these tools, I believe you will discover, as I have, that much of what you might otherwise seek from a professional is already available to you—at no cost, and with all the gain imaginable. Even if you've never considered seeking professional help, you'll discover that the 10 tools in this book are powerful adjuncts for or replacements to the mechanisms you've already developed for handling your life and its challenges. And if you're already working with a therapist, I believe you'll discover that these tools can further empower you: they can take you inside of the process of therapy and can give an added positive kick to that therapy.

The goal here is to find approaches to change that meet *your* needs in the most immediate, effective, and powerful way possible—without taking you to the poorhouse or to the brink in the process. I believe that the best, fastest, and most exciting way to do this is through self-therapy: I've seen it work, and I know you'll find the results you want if you put your energy and commitment into these tools.

If you're ready, then, let's not delay; it's time to lay the foundation for a new understanding of therapy—and most important, for the growing sense of confidence and competence that will help you to find your new, more powerful self.

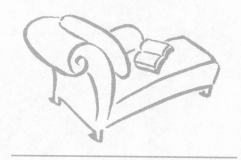

THE MYTH OF PSYCHOTHERAPY
AND THE PROMISE OF HEALING

Seeking the Answers Within or Without

THINGS DO NOT CHANGE; WE CHANGE.

Henry David Thoreau

What's been on your mind lately? Has something been bugging you, tugging at you, getting stuck in your consciousness and refusing to let go? Maybe something's getting to you about a relationship you're in: you're tired of the craziness of being with someone who doesn't seem to want to be with you— you're at the point where you want a partner who really wants *you*. Or perhaps you're tired of taking care of someone when what you really want is a true equal who can meet the ups and downs of life head-on with you.

Maybe you're ready for a change in the communication, the conflict, or the chaos in the relationship. Then again, perhaps it's work that's getting to you. You no longer feel like tolerating a boss who talks down to you, takes credit for your work, chastises you like a toddler when you make a mistake, or simply ignores your contributions—and you're fed up with yourself because you *do* tolerate it. You know you could be more successful, yet every time you seem close to that big achievement, somehow *something* goes wrong. It might be your family, a great bunch of people, but too close for comfort; or they're more distant than you'd like. Or maybe they're mixed-up, a crazy collection of oddballs who would never have chosen to know each other if your parents hadn't gotten together all those years ago (and then there's *that* whole area, one you're not even going *close* to!).

Here's the reality: I can't know what's going on in your life, but I can be pretty sure of one thing. You want a more satisfying life, happier or easier or more successful relationships, a better job or a greater sense of accomplishment

3

from the work you already do, and less stress or more pleasure in your family life. In other words, *there's something about your life that you want to change.* Let me reassure you that if anything I've just said rings true for you, it doesn't signify a problem. Instead, it just makes you like 99 percent of the rest of us.

You're not misguided, you're not bad, and you're certainly not crazy. In fact, I'd guess that your life is even working out pretty well—if not in general, at least in some important areas. And by the way, if it's not—if things are feeling too crazy for comfort—that's okay too. You can't expect a smooth ride all of the time when you're dealing with reality. There are going to be times when it seems that everything might come crashing down around you, and there will be other times when you feel on top of the world, in control, and taking life's challenges and difficulties in stride like the champ you are.

But you're *ready for a change.* You're ready to take charge of your own life and quit complaining. You've had it with feeling dissatisfied and wishing things were different, even as your life continues to roll along, the same as yesterday. You might not have admitted it to yourself yet, but you've made a decision: no more standing by shaking your fist out of a sense of futility or frustration because your life isn't turning out the way you want it to.

This life is the only one you've got, the single chance you have to get it right, and the fact that you've picked up this book and started to read sends a signal that can't be missed. You're *going* to get it right, and you're going to get it right for *you*—not to please your parents, not to be more successful than your siblings, not to keep your boss happy and quiet. The key to getting your life right lies, first, in recognizing that it's your life, and, second, on accepting the fact that there's only one person who can define "right" for you: *you*. Defining "right" and getting it "right" are exactly what this book is going to help you do.

Before you can do either, though, it's essential that you accept that there's nothing wrong with you because you now feel the way you do. On the contrary; it's a good sign! When the day arrives that you discover yourself ready for "out with the old and in with the new," it means you're *stronger than you've ever been,* whether you feel it yet or not.

Part of what's happening to you—part of what caused you to pick up this book, in fact—is that you've outgrown your old coping mechanisms, the ones you developed years ago. You're also facing new challenges, as everyone does throughout life, challenges for which you haven't yet had a chance to develop coping mechanisms. Think of it as if you're wearing clothes from the 1960s or early '70s. Not only do they not work in today's world—those red vinyl go-go boots are particularly awful—but they *don't even fit you anymore.* You've grown, you've changed; your *life is different now.* It's no wonder that you sometimes feel frustration, irritation, confusion, or even despair.

You're trying to make a date with someone at a new millennium party—while you're wearing a white leisure suit. What are your chances for success?

Lugging around your set of old behaviors, some of which work and some of which don't, and facing frustration when they don't, you fall into one of three groups of people. In the first group, you'll find the people who have considered seeking professional help but haven't done so for a variety of reasons. In the second group—which contains an estimated 20 plus percent of the population—you'll find those who have tried therapy or some sort of professional mental health care. Then, there's the third group: it is comprised of the people who haven't given professional help a second thought (or even a first thought, for that matter!). The members of this group would no more consider therapy than they would an elective amputation.

It truly doesn't matter which group you're in when it comes to dealing with day-to-day life and the frustration and confusion it can sometimes bring. I'm here to tell you that not one of the groups I've mentioned corners the market on the "right" answer to facing life's challenges: professional help, self-therapy, coffee, and deep discussions with a neighbor, or any other approach. The fact is, there *isn't* a single correct answer that applies to everyone. The question of how or even whether you should make changes to your life is highly individual, and the answers in most cases are even more difficult to generalize. You'll discover *the right answers for you* in this book, even as you see that the answers you come up with are right in large part because of how very individual they are.

In Chapter Three we'll discuss the generalities that do apply—and that might mean you should seek professional help. I strongly urge you to make note of them. Although it's unlikely that you'll see your own life struggles and challenges reflected in any of these generalities, it's critical that you be aware of the distinctions. It would be irresponsible of me—and irresponsible of you toward yourself and your own well-being—to ignore the fact that there are certain instances in which professional intervention is warranted. In most situations, it is unnecessary or optional, but we'll specifically address the distinctions that identify the types of problems that call for the help of a qualified mental health professional.

TAKING ON LIFE'S CHALLENGES

For the moment, though, there *is* a question that applies to everyone: When the challenges of life feel like they're catching up with you, or when you're ready to change a part of your life for the better, what is the best way to go about it?

This question addresses a number of factors: whether you need professional intervention, what types of help are available (including self-therapy), how the assistance is offered (including how you go about helping yourself), and what kind of beliefs and behaviors influence your potential for success.

That there are options available is a positive sign, an indication of how much our society has changed its views toward mental health and personal growth. Until the mid-1960s, mental health was typically something that only psychiatrists and embarrassed families talked about, and then only in the context of sanity and insanity. Mental health was thought of as the reflection in a mirror of a dirty little phrase—"mental illness"—which was cloaked in shame, secrecy, and stigma. For most of us, mental illness isn't the issue; at times we have problems or challenges, and we always have psychological needs. But in the past, conventional wisdom, pride, and self-esteem contributed to the belief that life's problems or challenges were best addressed in the privacy of your own home or, in a pinch, over coffee with a trusted friend. Better yet, you would deal with whatever needed attention without breathing a word of it to anyone. That tough, pioneering spirit, the pull-yourself-up-by-your-bootstraps philosophy, prevailed.

Fortunately, as our society became more open and emotionally aware, the stigma surrounding mental health issues began to fade. In fact, in some circles a stigma developed if *you weren't in therapy!* It became hip to get help; if you didn't have an analyst, who were you? Think Hollywood, think midtown Manhattan. The pendulum has swung back and forth plenty of times since, adjusting itself to the tenor of the times. Unfortunately, with each sweep of the pendulum, the most important point about seeking help, *wherever* you might seek it, seems to get buried deeper.

The real point is that it doesn't matter what's hip, what's in or out or today's newest trend; *what really matters is how you can create the best life possible, the life you want and deserve.*

Can you create this life in a therapist's office, or can you find it over dinner with a friend? Can you get what you need by letting off steam with strangers in a chat room on the Internet? What about helping yourself? Is it possible to arm yourself with a toolbox of methods for taking on the ups and downs of life and emerge stronger, better, healthier?

You've read this far, so you know my answer by now, but indulge me as I repeat it once more in case there's any confusion. You know yourself better than anyone else knows you. With few exceptions, *that makes you the best candidate for the living room couch* —instead of the therapist's couch—when you're seeking someone to help you face current difficulties, or when you simply want to learn new ways of coping with the inevitable challenges that arise in life.

THE NEED FOR PSYCHOLOGICAL INTERVENTION

Over the 20-plus years I've spent in the field of mental health , I've developed and refined my belief in the power of what I call "self-therapy," the practice of serving as your own therapist. My early personal experience with a "helper," for instance, was one of the foundations of this practice. Personally, through my work, and more theoretically, through research, I have come to believe in the benefits of and need for self-therapy up close. I have seen firsthand the profound need for the ready availability of psychological intervention of *some* kind in our world today.

One reputable estimate finds that approximately 20 percent of all Americans have a mental disorder of some type, and nearly one-third of those people are turned down for treatment, typically because of the refusal of insurance companies to pay.[1] Other research shows increasing rates of depression,[2] with almost 10 percent of the adult population suffering from depression[3] and an estimated 16 million Americans from 18 to 54 years of age experiencing anxiety.[4] Psychological problems are costing the United States as much as 148 *billion* dollars annually.[5] These statistics alone indicate a clear and significant need for mental health treatment that is easy to access, affordable, and comprehensive. This has perhaps never been truer than it is today, given the increasing stress of living in such uncertain economic and political times. In fact, research shows that rates of anxiety, depression, insomnia, and other mental health disorders and symptoms have more than doubled since the 9/11 attacks on the United States.[6]

Obviously, the reasons people seek help vary drastically, from depression and anxiety to relationship problems, self-doubt, or an inability to make satisfying or successful choices about jobs, friendships, or other areas of their lives. The reality is that for every person who is *in* therapy, *considering* therapy, or simply feeling dissatisfied or frustrated with some aspect of his or her life, there is a highly personal, wholly individual motivation for seeking change. In your case, that motivation led you to a book about changing your life, in ways both large and small. It could be the beginning of the most important journey of your life.

What you do with the contents of this book will determine the extent of change you experience. If your life just needs a little fine-tuning here and there, that's what you'll get. If you're looking for a sweeping change, a "make-over" that transforms you into the person you've always imagined you could be, you'll find that too. You are the driver here, in charge of determining the starting point, the destination, and which stops to make along the way.

PROFESSIONAL INTERVENTION

Before we continue, a few points should be made about professional intervention. Earlier, I said there are three groups of people—or kinds of approaches—when it comes to dealing with the challenges of life. There are those who will go into therapy, those who will consider it but decide to take a shot at developing answers on their own, and those who wouldn't dream of seeing a professional to discuss their life issues or challenges. Although I'm a strong proponent of self-therapy—a process I've created, in which individuals define and solve their own problems—I want to emphasize that I am *not* antitherapy. There are many for whom "traditional" therapy has led to wonderful, life-changing and affirming experiences. I applaud the therapists in those cases, *as I applaud the clients*; both are responsible for the positive outcome.

At the same time, I have seen and heard much about unethical therapists, inflated fees, breaches of confidentiality, and therapists who were more concerned with power, sex, or their own emotional shortcomings, among other things, than they were with their clients' problems. I've had dinner where the background noise was the voices of a group of psychiatrists at the next table over, gossiping about their famous clients' peccadilloes. Once, I nearly lost my lunch overhearing the angst of two therapists trying to decide if it was wrong for one of the therapists to be "dating" a client's spouse.

I mention this—the helpful therapists as well as the unethical ones—because to make an informed choice about self-therapy, you need to be aware of the advantages and disadvantages associated with traditional therapy.

What follows are some factors that led me to develop self-therapy as an alternative or adjunct to traditional therapy:

- My own early experience with a therapist who was misguided.

- The many accounts I've heard about therapists and approaches to therapy that were about something other than the client's best interests.

- The economics of therapy: for many people the expense of professional intervention is simply prohibitive.

- Confidentiality: I have seen client's anonymity destroyed and their confidentiality breached too many times to trust the process entirely.

- The powerful effects that insurance and managed care can have on the process, confidentiality, and outcome of therapy.

- The labeling that can be a by-product of traditional therapy, and that can follow you into your workplace or elsewhere.

- The time commitment that some therapists expect from their clients: implying or stating outright that the therapy will not be successful unless it takes place weekly or even more often, involves an additional meeting in a group therapy setting, and the like. All of this, of course, also adds to the expense. Similarly, professional intervention can often move at a crawl, turning change and growth into long-term goals instead of immediate, workable solutions.

- My ongoing concern about the professional qualifications—or lack thereof—of some of the people providing therapy. The variation in the requirements for licensing and qualifications from state to state is far too great for my comfort.

- The "one-size-fits-all" approach to therapy that some therapists use, which doesn't quite fit and may not focus well enough on your individual situation.

- The questionable or downright atrocious ethics practiced by some therapists, including intimate involvement with clients, using interventions that are not quantified by research—and may even be dangerous—and breaking client confidentiality by ""telling tales out of school" to colleagues or friends.

Considering the above, you might think I advocate the self-therapy approach because I believe that traditional therapy is *always* harmful or unnecessary in some way. In fact, what I am opposed to is not therapy as a field or therapists as a group; I am instead opposed to the *largely unregulated brand of therapy prevalent today*. I call this type of professional intervention "vending machine therapy." It's the type of "help"—a misnomer if ever one existed—that is provided by charlatans or "gurus" who are more concerned with getting your quarters (or just about anything else) than with the quality of what they give back. Here's what you can be sure of: *it's not about you*. It is because of the prevalence of vending machine therapy that I advocate the alternative of self-therapy; it gives you the tools you can use for a lifetime of positive outcomes, and it does so while ensuring that the focus remains on you.

I encourage you to keep a sense of balance about the positives and negatives of therapy as we go on to discuss the myths and potential drawbacks of some therapy and therapists. You can think of it like this: if you've ever had surgery, you know that beforehand the doctor warns you about the things that *could* go wrong—every last one of them. *Do* these things go wrong for most people most of the time? No. If they can or do happen at all, though, professional ethics insist that the dangers be shared with the patient, a practice that should relate to traditional therapy as well. After all, both surgeons and therapists are digging into some pretty vulnerable, tender areas!

I wish I could say that the negative occurrences and outcomes in traditional therapy are as rare as the deaths that result from surgery for an ingrown nail, or as uncommon as losing the use of your legs after having a hair implant. Unfortunately, I can't. The fact is, while traditional therapy has tremendous potential, it's a potential that can go in either direction. When therapy works, it has the power to help you make important discoveries about yourself and to affect positive changes in your life. When it doesn't work, for whatever reasons, the harm can be negligible—or it can be incalculable.

SELF-THERAPY AS ADJUNCT OR ALTERNATIVE

I developed self-therapy and advocate it so strongly because I believe that people should have the option of an adjunct or alternative to traditional therapy. If you choose to use self-therapy as an *alternative* to traditional therapy, you will have the tools you need. If you choose to use self-therapy as an *adjunct* to traditional therapy, you will be an informed and active participant, guiding your own growth and learning and helping to move the process along more efficiently, so you create faster, more powerful change in your life. Either way, *you're ahead of the game.*

I passionately believe in your right to be informed and in your right to have alternatives in a field that has such deep potential to affect your life. Equally powerful is my sense of responsibility toward you. I want you to feel an equal sense of responsibility toward yourself, a commitment to receiving the best of what life has to offer: in therapy, in your treatment of yourself, in your relationships, and in every other way. The best of what therapy has to offer is warm, powerful, and equal person-to-person help, but I've come to believe that in order to get what you deserve, sometimes you have to be *both* of the people: the *helper* and the *helpee*. In order to get what you want and deserve, you must take charge of the process, whether it takes place in or out of a therapy office.

MOVING FORWARD

I've never been fond of wasting time, and never is this truer than in my work. That a field which offers so much potential for change and growth can also move at a snail's pace has always been a source of frustration for me. This is yet another factor that contributed to my development of self-therapy as a positive, effective alternative to professional intervention. So, if you're ready to leap in and start your self-therapy program, let's begin.

The first thing we need to tackle is an issue that temporarily may appear to slow your progress—but remember, I don't like to waste time, and I'll bet you don't either. What we're going to do first is essential, and it's going to set the stage for the challenging work you're going to do on the pages and in the days ahead.

We'll begin by discussing some of the myths about therapy: who seeks help, who provides it, what you can and can't get out of therapy—whether you're the therapist or someone else is—and more. We're going to demystify the process of therapy so that you can't help but realize it's not rocket science, quantum physics, or any other scary, complex subject. We're going to ditch the jargon, dump the fancy double-talk, and abandon any ideas you might have had that you need a doctoral degree, a goatee, or a black leather couch to turn your life into the one you want.

Once the myths are exploded, the result is inevitable: *you can develop absolute confidence in your ability to be your own therapist*, regardless of your education, training, or background. Even if you ultimately decide to see a professional—or are already seeing one—this step in the journey will be of immense help, because it will allow you to be informed about, and in charge of, your therapy. Primarily, though, exploring and exploding the myths about therapy will jump-start the process of self-therapy. It will put you in the driver's seat and hand you the map so you can start to be familiar with the territory—even if you don't yet know quite where you're going.

So let's get moving; time's a-wasting!

The 10 Biggest Myths
of Modern Psychotherapy

... MAN WILL OCCASIONALLY STUMBLE OVER THE TRUTH,
BUT USUALLY MANAGES TO PICK HIMSELF UP,
WALK OVER OR AROUND IT, AND CARRY ON.[1]

Winston Churchill

You've got the idea by now. There are different kinds of therapy and different kinds of therapists. You can take on your challenges by yourself, with a friend, with a qualified professional helper—or not at all, though I don't recommend the last approach if you want to have the best life possible. If you reach out for help, you can work with a gifted therapist who has your best interests at heart or with one who is lacking in skill or commitment or motivation. Don't kid yourself: It's just not true that "those who can't do, teach." Those who can't "do" are all over the place—*doing*, much to their client's detriment. In fact, there's the first myth. The real story is that the most gifted teachers in the field are those who are also the most skilled at practicing therapy. Imagine learning to play baseball from a certified couch potato, or learning to drive from the guy who has caused 30 collisions. I don't think so.

It's ironic that a field whose concern is with uncovering what's hidden and accessing reality often seems to be built on a foundation of secrets and myths like the one above. Does this mean that the foundation doesn't offer you sturdy, reliable places to walk, or walls that won't come tumbling down at the first strong wind? No. But it does mean you'd better watch where you step, and that's one thing we'll discuss in the course of this book. You'd think that the people and processes that are meant to help you shore up your own foundation would have foundations of stone: durable, unassailable, perhaps

13

complex, but certainly not chaotic. Unfortunately, that is the *big* myth, the one from which all the other myths seem to spring; and at the same time, it's the myth that leaves all the others in the dust. The therapist who charges $100 an hour to dispense words of wisdom might well be on his or her fourth marriage and popping Xanax just to get through the day. The "complicated" therapeutic intervention only a professional can perform, the intervention that will "cure" you, is just something another mortal like you or I thought up— and he or she may well have thought it up between calls from a neurotic husband or wife while binge-eating in the office.

I don't want to tell you that therapy is good or bad, because it's not that simple. When you decide to seek change, you need to be sure you're setting off down a safe, sound, and sensible therapeutic road with someone helping you— even when that someone is *you*—for as many of the right reasons as possible. *You* can go about it for the wrong reasons as easily as another person can. Motivations like trying to please your parents, wanting to win back an ex-lover, or looking for a way to avoid facing the concrete realities of life by escaping into psychobabble will take you nowhere fast. A therapist, of course, can get involved with you for the wrong reasons too. At the top of the list I'd include financing that new BMW, creating feelings of superiority or control, or engendering that less-than-admirable little shiver of power that comes from being in a one-up position around someone who is temporarily feeling vulnerable.

In order to send you off on your journey well-informed, I've laid out a number of the most prevalent myths or misguided beliefs about therapy and change. I think you will find that some, many, or even all of these myths have influenced how you view therapy, and are also influences on how you view your own potential for change. As light is shed on the myths, they will lose their power to intimidate, control, or influence you. And as the myths become ever less powerful, you will discover that *you* become ever more so.

COMMON MYTHS ABOUT THERAPY AND CHANGE

Myth #1

If you don't pay for therapy, it's not worth as much (also known as: "The more you pay, the more something is worth" and "Therapy isn't about the exchange of money").

Would *you* rather make $150 than $75 dollars for a 50-minute hour? Yes, well, so would I. The question shouldn't be about what you or I prefer, though; it should be about whether it is absolutely necessary to pay for help in order for that help to be of worth to you. Is it? Two words: *best friend*.

Have you ever talked to a close friend about a problem and found that the talk was helpful to you? Was there a fee attached? Of course you have, and of course there wasn't. Case closed.

The myths about the relationship between therapy and money run deeper, though. For instance, many people believe that there is a direct connection between what you pay and what you get. This is the justification you'll hear from therapists who insist on full payment, often before even beginning a session. While paying for therapy *is* a good thing—we'll talk about why in a moment—*more does not equal better*. The fact is, *more money paid for therapy simply equals less money in your pocket*. What really assures you of quality is the training, experience, caring, and commitment of the therapist. This just makes plain sense.

It's reasonable to want to see a quality therapist if you are going to see one at all, but don't let the money-quality debate muck up your decision. And know that when you're done with this book, you're going to have access to many of the same tools that a therapist employs, and then some—but as an added bonus, you (presumably) won't be charging yourself, so treat yourself to a vacation instead!

What about the issue of the exchange of money? It's an awkward issue, for sure. On the one hand, the therapist is demanding money before talking to you, even while trumpeting the authenticity and genuineness of the relationship between the two of you. On the other hand, therapists are professionals just like people in other fields, and they certainly deserve to be paid for the work they do, the training they've received, and the effort they put into helping you. In fact, this is why payment for therapy is a good thing. However, the reality that an authentic relationship is essential if therapy is to be helpful brings you right back to the money issue: how many other "authentic relationships" do you have that require that one partner pay the other in order to spend time together? Many therapists—perhaps because of their own unresolved feelings about this somewhat awkward issue—develop strict practices and rules regarding the exchange of money. If you choose to enter therapy with a professional, keep in mind this general rule: the more rigid the practices about money, the less the therapist has resolved his or her own role in relationship to you. Frankly, I'd prefer if a therapist didn't work out his own "issues" on my dime—what about you?

Myth #2

Therapy has to hurt to work, and tears are necessary for growth.

Different types of therapists have different types of beliefs about the blood, sweat, and tears approach to therapy. For some, the process should be gentle and encouraging; for others it's more like an emotional boot camp. The *real* issue, though, should be *you*: what you need, what you want, and—most important—what best serves your growth and learning.

I can guarantee you that almost any therapist will begin to believe that you are resistant to facing your demons if you make light of the process, want to attend less frequently than the therapist recommends, or miss appointments often. To some extent, this is right and reasonable; you may well be resistant if you're doing all those things. Give it a fair look, at the very least. However, too often therapists can make snap judgments about resistance based on a bias that says that therapy has to be hard work. If you're not in pain, you're not in progress—so goes the myth. You've heard it said any number of ways: no guts, no glory; no pain, no gain. This approach would tell you've found a therapist—and remember, this therapist may be you—who expects major suffering and will assume you're not trying hard if it seems that you're having fun. Heaven forbid that you might be enjoying the challenge of therapy, looking forward to appointments, and trying to make great strides efficiently!

Take this seriously: *therapy doesn't always have to be serious*. You can learn to laugh in therapy even as you learn to cry. You can lovingly poke fun at your thoughts even as you explore your "heaviest" feelings. If I stumbled upon a therapist who needed the whole process to be a drag, I'd drag myself right out of that therapy—and I suggest you consider it too, and try being your own joyful therapist instead, for a change.

Myth #3

Everything a therapist says is correct and/or therapeutic; everything the patient says is a symptom of problems: usually resistance, deception, and avoidance.

This myth is based on the misguided notion that the people who seek therapy are resistant to the truth and to change. Meanwhile, the belief goes, therapists not only have some sort of special access to the truth (or the "right" answers), but are always psychologically helpful as they attempt to educate you about what is true and right.

This is one of the most potentially damaging myths you can encounter. Unfortunately, it is also one of the most common. You're likely to find traces of this myth inside of your own belief system. Do you feel discomfort challenging authority figures? Do you feel frustration because you don't challenge a therapist, a doctor, or another professional about fees, for instance, or about being made to wait? Even these two examples suggest that the myth is alive and well and intent on convincing you that the authority figure knows more than you do, has rights you don't have, or is otherwise in a position superior to your own. You don't have to like it—in fact, I hope you don't—but if it's true, you do have to recognize and admit it so you can create change.

You must not allow a therapist to convince you that your instinctive sense of what is right for you is wrong. *You* know you—and this is one of the primary reasons that you can often be your own best therapist. When another person brings preconceived notions and self-serving beliefs into your personal process of change, it is impossible to avoid being influenced. Just imagine how difficult it is to avoid feeling as if you're resistant or defensive if you respond negatively to a therapist's beliefs—and are then accused of being resistant or defensive! That's an argument you can never win.

The greatest danger of this myth is that it typecasts you in a role that is wholly inaccurate—and wholly unfair. You're not resistant, defensive, deceptive, or avoiding making changes to your life; just the opposite! The guy over in the corner of the coffee bar reading a comic book and the woman at the counter getting into it with someone because she didn't wait her turn, maybe. But you? Forget it—you're ready for change or you wouldn't be holding the tools to create it. So if a therapist tells you otherwise, he or she is not right, and they're not holding *the* truth like a gift from the heavens. They're buying into this myth, and it's time to move on with your journey, leaving them and the myth in the dust as you accelerate toward change.

A friend says: I was uncomfortable in group therapy from the first day, but it wasn't until a few months into it that I understood why. I did know that the two leaders, a psychiatrist and social worker, picked apart everything I said. I was sure that they were looking for lies or ways we were deluding ourselves, and I didn't like it—it was like being called a liar for no reason—but I sort of figured it was just me. Maybe I *was* deluding myself and lying; they were the experts, after all—so I kept quiet about it. One night at the group's break people were talking outside. "You'd think you were crazy," this guy, Dan, was saying, "if you were only in individual therapy with them. You'd never realize that they don't believe anything *anyone* says until you start group and realize they think we're all making this stuff up." At that point I realized that the leaders were suspicious of all of us; I hadn't noticed until then, but they were questioning us *all* like we were natural-born liars. I quit the group the next day; I needed support and truth, not suspicion and lies.

Myth #4

Only therapists are qualified to help you change your life—and all therapists are qualified to help all people.

When the flu hits with its vague fever, scratchy throat, and aches and pains, you head off to your internist. You should usually be able to safely assume that you'll be referred elsewhere if it turns out that you have some tropical virus that has only been seen twice before in modern times. The system is based on the common sense idea that *no one person can effectively or efficiently contain all knowledge.* The same should be true in therapy, but too often it's not. Instead there's a myth that all therapists are qualified to treat all types of people and problems at all times—while at the same time the myth makes it plain as day that not just anyone can treat . . . well, all types of people and problems. That's a have-the-cake-and-eat-it-too if I've ever heard one! Either anyone can do it or only a select few can; you can't have it both ways. You can see where this myth doesn't leave room for bringing in an "expert," right? Everyone is *already* an expert on you—except you, of course.

The problem is similar to that of an ex-lover who doesn't quite measure up—you can't very well ask for a referral to *someone better . . . can you?* Many therapists are reluctant to refer you to someone else—unless they don't like you, of course, in which case they'll be happy to. If you go into therapy and find yourself uncomfortable with the therapist, the result too often is anger and a damaging attempt to convince you that you are resisting—since surely it can't be the therapist's personality! Only weeks ago, in fact, a trustworthy colleague told me about a therapist who actually started screaming at a client and accusing her of not working hard enough when the client decided to change therapists.

Here's the real rub, though: this myth can get you every time if you're wavering about whether you can handle self-therapy. It's a self-esteem buster that can easily convince you that you're not qualified to change your life on your own. But it can only do this if you let it—and you're not going to let it. You're going to read these myths and remember that therapists don't corner the market on brilliance, insights into who you are and how you function in the world, or what you should do to have a more satisfying life. There's really only one expert on those subjects, and it's the person who is living that life: *you.*

Myth #5

Only a very few therapists behave unethically, as, for example, by making sexual advances toward their clients.

Would that this were so. In fact, one survey indicated that 87 percent of psychologists and 81 percent of social workers who completed the poll reported being sexually attracted to one or more patients, and a great number of them fantasized about sex with clients. Now, I grant you that this is not the same as a sexual advance—far from it. It is natural and normal to have sexual attraction in certain situations and circumstances, even at inconvenient and inappropriate times. However, what is *not* appropriate, in any case and at any time with any client, is acting on these feelings. Unfortunately, the myth that says it doesn't happen is just plain wrong.

As an intern, I remember hearing stories of a former psychiatrist who routinely had sex with his patients in the hospital—he seriously referred to it as "therapy." In my training, I was taught something *very* different: one of my NYU supervisors told me that he had never heard of a "therapeutic erection," a phrase I've never forgotten, and one I repeat to my own students.

If a therapist does behave unethically toward you, whether the behavior is sexual or not, I strongly encourage you to report the practitioner to his or her regulating board. You can find a list of these boards organized by state, as well as information on how to file a report of this nature, on my website at www.drfarrell.net/self-help.htm.

However, I should note that while these breaches of ethics and professional behavior certainly do occur, they are not the norm. Are most therapists guilty of behaving unethically? No. I believe that most practitioners go about their business in an ethical and professional manner. However, if you do choose to go into therapy, you need to be alert to the possibility that a therapist may be more focused on meeting his or her own needs, sexual or otherwise, than yours. This issue applies to you even in self-therapy: it is not only an argument against traditional therapy, of course, but it can also serve as a reminder of the ways in which your vulnerabilities can be exploited. As you move on your journey of self-discovery in self-therapy, you may experience periods of vulnerability and learn tough lessons. Protect yourself emotionally. This doesn't mean closing up or shying away from intimacy with others, but it does mean being aware of what you want from others—and what *they* want from *you*.

Myth #6

Conflicts with your therapist always mirror something in your *life—it's* never *about the therapist.*

Many years ago I had a supervisor who was unreasonable. Everyone who worked for him agreed that a good many of his demands were capricious or downright impossible. It was common for him to scream names at the staff and to castigate us loudly and meanly for any faults we had—and for many we didn't have—as he went about finding ways to make life miserable for everyone. To this day, I believe that he was a bitter person who somehow took some pleasure out of the meager power of humiliation he held over others.

What I learned from my experience has served me well in general and as a psychologist specifically. It reminds me of the helplessness I felt when I was blamed for starting conflicts that I knew had nothing to do with me. In therapy, when a client tentatively and even fearfully brings up a concern about a conflict with the therapist, a common outcome is for the therapist to use psychobabble to convince the client that the conflict is of his or her own making. Surely it couldn't be about the therapist's "issues." The reasons therapists give for this are often quite creative: it's because you need to be angry at me, they might say. Or perhaps its because you want to distance yourself from me, or want to wound me since the therapy is bringing out old wounds for you. These all sound like respectable therapeutic discoveries—and they may well be accurate—but something far simpler might be taking place: you and I, as therapist and client, are having the inevitable conflict that occurs when two people with strong opinions are discussing something of essential importance. In other words, we're pissing each other off. *Big deal!* It doesn't require three sessions of discussion—especially not if you're paying for it. Watch for this within yourself, and with friends, family, and colleagues too, as you begin to make changes. It is common for others to react negatively if the changes you make inconvenience them, or engender fear, or if they feel that you're moving ahead—and leaving them behind.

Change is planted in the rough-and-tumble world where emotion and intellect collide. If it can't begin to flower there, it will never develop roots sturdy enough to withstand the questioning, the disagreement, and the assaults from inside and out as the changes you've made begin to have an impact on others around you. The therapist must be honest—both internally and externally—and acknowledge that you will both have authentic feelings—including anger, frustration, and irritation—and that these feelings may lead to conflict. Without this honesty, it is too easy to fall back on the "Blame the Client" game, where everything is the client's "issue."

Myth #7

Therapists maintain confidentiality.

Go to a cocktail party for therapists and you'll see everyone's cover being blown. Your secrets aren't safe; take my word for it. I've heard things I should never have heard about people who had every right to expect that their private lives would remain so—but their therapists apparently thought otherwise.

Where does this confidentiality get broken? In some cases it is sanctioned; for instance, many therapists seek supervision with a senior therapist, and your case will be discussed there. Your name may or may not be used, but don't assume that it won't be. Another blow to confidentiality can occur when you run into your therapist in public. He or she may show admirable restraint in not acknowledging you—a bow to stigma, not just confidentiality—but be assured that anyone with the therapist will recognize the nonverbal signals that indicate that they've run into one of Dad's clients or Mom's patients again.

Regardless of how the information is conveyed, your safest assumption when entering therapy is that somehow, someday, it will be public knowledge that you were in treatment. This is not necessarily a bad thing; it should not keep you from therapy if you can benefit from it. What it should do, however, is give you fair warning to address the subject with any therapist you do see, and to caution him or her about the extent to which confidentiality is important to you. If you decide to embark on self-therapy, remember that excitement about your new learning may create an urge within you to share what you're learning. This isn't necessarily a mistake, but do take a hard look at the source of your confidences; it's important to know when and how self-disclosure will best work for you.

Myth #8

Therapists are mentally and emotionally healthy.

I once had the misfortune of having a supervisor with an incredible panic disorder; he'd lock himself in his office every day, "reading files." This man, who made mental health his profession, refused to recognize his own need for help. There is also a reverse myth, by the way, which says that therapists are some of the *least* mentally healthy people out there, suggesting that they're drawn to the field to try to resolve their own issues. Unfortunately, this myth may be somewhat closer to reality than we'd care to believe, like the psychiatrist I knew who regularly talked to trees—and apparently often received answers. Yes, he had a serious problem—as did the other clinician who medicated himself into semi-unconsciousness in his office daily and mistook his wastepaper basket for the toilet. I don't believe in the absolute nature of either of these extreme myths—therapists are human, after all, people just like you, who struggle with their own issues. However, if your therapist is not relatively balanced and sane—and some won't be—you will not receive much, if anything, of use. Psychologists and others in the mental health field do not corner the market on mental health, so don't weigh a therapist's observations and insights more heavily than you do your own, or it will disempower you as your own therapist.

Myth #9

You will be shown your records if you request it.

This may not strike you as the most important of points, but let me assure you that it can be of great importance. Most "Patients' Bill of Rights" documents say that you have the right to see your records, a right you should have and may need. However, there is a loophole that allows records to be withheld from you if the therapist believes that seeing your case notes will cause you harm. I don't know about you, but I'd want to be able to see what was being written about me, since I know that these records, as confidential as they supposedly are, might well be seen by filing clerks, insurance company representatives, and who knows who else. I recall a colleague who had recorded notes about a client's infidelities, and when the client became involved in a divorce, a subpoena for the records caused all hell to break loose. We won't get into the moral implications of infidelity, truthfulness, or personal ethics here, since we could spend an entire book on that subject alone, but the fact is, the man went into therapy with a reasonable expectation of confidentiality. Writing down names, places, and dates—as the therapist did for some reason—provided the spouse with plenty of ammunition for her divorce and robbed the client of the confidentiality he'd been promised.

Myth #10

Regardless of what professional title a therapist chooses, all therapists are doctors, and all doctors can provide psychological testing and prescribe medications.

Sometimes it seems just about impossible to keep track of the many titles therapists give themselves: there are psychologists, psychiatrists, psychotherapists, counselors, life coaches, and more. Some therapists are nurses, some are social workers with master's degrees, and others are "doctors," in anything from psychology to education to physiology—all of which are not created equal when it comes to providing psychological help.

I'm loath to say it about my own field, but there are also "helpers" hanging out shingles who have no more than a high school diploma. And those who have completed a Ph.D.—and therefore have earned the right to use the term "Doctor"—are still not necessarily qualified to provide mental health services.

The issue of whether someone is equipped to provide quality psychological help is important, whether you seek therapy with a practitioner or choose self-therapy instead. First, there is the intimidation factor: if you buy into the myth that someone has to be able to get through medical school (or at least earn a master's) to be a good therapist, you're not as likely to trust in your own ability to help yourself. Second, if you're being advised to take medication or to submit to psychological testing, you need to be able to trust the person advising you. You may be prescribed medications under a physician's signature—many clinics operate this way—or administered testing by a therapist who does not have the training to do so. Can you be assured that the testing or medication is truly in your best interests, or is the "need" for it more about the therapist's belief in choosing a quick fix, perhaps, or about running up your fees with expensive tests? When either testing or medication is advised, it should be for a good reason—a reason openly shared with you. The bottom line is this: *only psychologists are qualified to administer and provide reports of psychological testing, and only medical doctors and, in some states, nurses are qualified to prescribe medications.*

Ask questions and check out the degrees on the wall. If you do seek medication or testing as a part of or adjunct to self-therapy, know that it's up to you to be well informed. Many therapists are well intentioned, but too many others don't see the problem, and so you simply can't count on all therapists to present the correct picture 100 percent of the time. Frankly, when complex test results and mind- or even life-altering medications are at issue, even 99 percent of the time just isn't good enough.

THE FINAL MYTH: LYING ON THE COUCH

I've often wondered how many people still expect to be shown to a one-sided black leather sofa when they arrive for therapy? Personally, although I've always enjoyed a couch for stealing a mid-afternoon nap, I fail to see how it is therapeutic. Freud, in fact, who experienced terrible anxiety when he had to interact personally with others, used the couch to avoid meeting his patients' eyes! Therapists caught up in the trappings of the power game still use it—after all, it does increase your vulnerability to be lying down while a therapist hovers above you in a chair, his or her expressions and responses unreadable as you share your thoughts and feelings.

The reality is that most therapy is conducted while you sit in a chair facing the therapist. No couch, no "*mmm-hmmm,*" and no constant references to your anger at your mother for not breast-feeding you. Therapy tends to be a lot more common sense today, and that can only be a good thing. Even so, the vestiges of the old days of therapy and analysis aren't gone; they rise up in the form of these myths, and plenty of others, that continue to influence therapists' views *and* your views about therapy and change.

Therapy can be whatever you want it to be: it can involve just you, you working with a trained professional, or you combing several methods for creating change and developing your own unique process of therapy. If it works for you, it's right—it's really as simple as that. When authentic and affirming communication flows, whether it's within your own mind or between you and another person, what you create is the magic of the unlimited potential for change and growth. There are no limits; there is no distance you can't travel and no road that is off-limits to you.

By becoming informed about, capable of and committed to proving that these myths are false, you've now got the keys to the car and no false leads. In the next chapter, you'll get the final map you need to set off on your explorations: the directions in Chapter Three will help you identify when therapy—self or otherwise—is appropriate, how your personality influences your choices and behaviors, and much more. With the myths dispelled and the learnings in Chapter Three firmly in your grasp, you'll be ready to acquire the tools that will give you everything else you need for your journey into the life you choose for yourself.

DISCOVERIES FROM THE TOOLBOX
TEN TOOLS FOR HEALING AND CHANGE

Challenge
and Change

WHAT DOES NOT CHANGE IS THE WILL TO CHANGE.

Charles Olson, from "The Kingfishers"

There is no overnight cure for changing your life or even one aspect of your life. You don't gain 20 pounds in an afternoon, and you won't take it off in a morning. Recognizing that reality, it was never my intention to create what amounts to no more than a *Cosmo* quiz, a three-quick-steps-to-a-new-you program. Instead, self-therapy begins with an intense, searching examination that will yield the answers to a number of questions, including:

- When you shouldn't use only self-therapy to face your challenges.

- How you can use self-therapy to assist in your own therapy and enrich your learning, even when professional intervention is recommended.

- Where you are right now in your emotional life, as you begin this journey.

- How your beliefs and behaviors affect both your mental health and your success at creating life change.

- What types of areas you need and want to address in order to create greater satisfaction in your life,

- How ready you are to take on the challenges ahead.

This chapter is going to help you identify the things that aren't working in your life, and to make sure you're ready to take on the challenges of making big and small changes in those areas. By the time you're done with this chapter, you'll be ready to open the toolbox that makes up the rest of the book, and to use the tools you find to change your life.

WHEN SELF-THERAPY ISN'T THE RIGHT ANSWER

Self-therapy provides a rigorous program that will take you where you want to go if you are energetic, positive, and committed to change. If you're feeling excited about the possibilities, it's a good sign, a clue that you're committed to achieving powerful results through self-therapy. If you're feeling a bit nervous or anxious, that's not a bad sign either—it often signals awareness, the recognition that making personal change is not always easy and not always a smooth ride. In fact I'd be surprised if, along with the exhilaration and excitement that accompany growth and learning, you didn't sometimes feel unsure, incompetent, a bit helpless, or frustrated. Knowing that these feelings and reactions are normal, you can also know not to quit if or when they arise. Contrary to what you might expect, these feelings are actually indications of the struggle that often accompanies growth and learning.

However you feel about the program of self-therapy, I want to emphasize that there are *certain situations where self-therapy is simply not appropriate.* To determine if self-therapy is a good choice for you at this time in your life, you must take a careful look at the important factors affecting you right now. For instance, some people might be facing issues that are potentially dangerous to themselves or others, while others might have mental illnesses that can best be managed with medication, which would obviously be unavailable in self-therapy. Take a moment to complete the checklist (see Figure 3-1). If you have experienced or are experiencing any of the situations noted, even if it occurred in the distant past, you should consult with a qualified professional. If the situation has long since been resolved, there may be no reason to continue with professional help, but it is still in your best interests to first "check in" with a professional to ensure your continued well-being. Think of it as the physical you should get before beginning a rigorous program of physical exercise; you and the physician talk together and make a joint decision about what is best for you.

That some people need to work with a trained professional doesn't change the potential drawbacks of traditional therapy. This might sound like a contradiction, since I've been saying that self-therapy is often a more helpful, efficient, and powerful way to create personal change than tradi-

YOU SHOULD SEEK QUALIFIED PROFESSIONAL HELP IF YOU HAVE OR ARE EXPERIENCING . . .

____ Repeated bouts of severe depression

____ Cyclical mood swings

____ Substance abuse or dependence

____ A history of psychiatric hospitalizations

____ A diagnosis of a psychotic disorder

____ Disorders of impulse control

____ Suicidal/homicidal thoughts

____ Self-destructive behavior

____ Dissociative disorders

____ Eating disorders such as anorexia or bulimia

____ Head trauma with resulting mood, cognition or personality changes

If you have checked any item on this list, you are *not a candidate at this time for self-therapy alone.* You should seek a comprehensive, one-on-one therapy plan to help you stabilize your condition, and you should continue in therapy with a qualified professional until you have achieved a significant period of stability.

tional therapy. But as I've also noted, not all therapists provide poor service, charge too much, or otherwise work against your best interests. And once you have an insider's view of the therapeutic process, even if you do choose to see a professional, you will be an informed consumer with a clearer idea of what makes up good, ethical, and effective therapy. Finally, you can use the tools in the coming chapters to enrich the process of professional therapy; you'll move faster, better, *and in the direction you want to go* with the assistance of the tools in this book.

If at this point you still have questions about whether you're ready to be your own therapist, I've included an interactive test in this chapter to help you decide. This test will help to crystallize your sense of whether self-therapy is right for you or whether you should seek assistance from a professional while also using the tools in this book to augment that process.

YOUR CURRENT EMOTIONAL LIFE

Only you can truly know how you feel. You can share your emotions with others, but they can never completely experience what you're experiencing, since your feelings are a product, in part, of your perception, your history, and your beliefs—and none of these are exactly the same for any two people. This is certainly an argument in favor of self-therapy, although it may make you question the worth of *any* traditional therapy; after all, if you can't expect to be completely understood, why bother? However, a gifted therapist can get close to understanding your experiences, just as you as your own therapist can explore how you feel, empathize with yourself, and accept yourself as you are. This is the first step in assessing your current emotional life, and what follows is a process that sets you on the path toward doing just that.

Exploration

Exploring your feelings means being open to *whatever* you feel, and learning to ask yourself the right questions. This will be an important process as you begin to use the tools in the following chapters, so it's also important that you begin to learn how to use this process now.

The first time you judge your feelings (saying "I shouldn't feel this way," for instance) or hide them (saying "I don't really feel this way") you've gone off track. Think of your feelings as *facts*—because they *are* your facts. *Your feelings are your truth.* As you try on this idea, also try out the following process to begin to familiarize yourself with the facts of your life:

On index cards, write down each of the major or "primary" feelings you've experienced in the past week (see Figure 3-1). Put each feeling on a separate card and then lay them out in front of you. Look at how they relate to each other and consider how they influence each other. For instance, you probably have an "Anger" card and a "Happiness" card. Think about their relationship: perhaps you were expecting to get together with a friend, which would have made you happy, but the friend canceled at the last minute, and so you felt angry. As you can see, your anger is inextricably connected to your happiness. You can mix and match the cards, shuffle them, and connect any two—each primary feeling you have is connected to a subset of other feelings.

Next, I want you to consider what I call the "secondary" or ""subfeelings" that relate to the primary feelings. A subfeeling is how your *feelings* make you *feel*. Subfeelings are the results of that first emotion you experienced. Using the example above of your friend canceling your plans, your first emotion—the primary feeling—was anger. What did you *then* feel as a *result*? Did you

---

PRIMARY FEELING
ANGER
Secondary or Sub-Feelings
Guilt
Sadness
Disappointment

FIGURE 3-1

suddenly find yourself feeling guilty because you were angry at your friend, who couldn't help canceling? Were you frustrated because you'd been counting on going out to distract you from your loneliness? Maybe you felt sad because you weren't feeling as important as you'd once been to your friend.

Write as many of these secondary subfeelings as you can think of on each card. Use these cards (tuck them in your purse, your datebook, or a desk drawer) to help you begin to get comfortable with exploring your emotional terrain. Each time you discover a new subfeeling that results from a primary feeling, add it to the card. Keep in mind too that there can be overlap: any emotion can be categorized as a primary feeling or as a secondary feeling. The only difference between the two is that the primary feeling is caused by *whatever happened*, while the primary feeling *causes* the secondary feeling.

Think of your emotional self as a research project. Don't jump to conclusions; don't even make hypotheses yet; simply identify all possible elements of who you are at this point in your life as an emotional being. Eventually you won't need the cards; you'll begin to recognize the presence of your most challenging primary and secondary emotions. Perhaps most important, in assessing your current emotional life you'll begin to see which cards are getting dog-eared—and that will tell you a great deal about the feelings that occupy a lot of your time.

Empathy

Once you begin to develop a clear picture of who you are emotionally at this time in your life, the next step is to learn to feel empathy for yourself. Look at your cards and imagine that they belong to someone else. Would you judge the other person for feeling angry, sad, or whatever other feelings you've listed for any given situation? If so, take an emotional step back; you're being too hard on the other person—and that means you're being too hard on yourself. Look at the subfeelings on the card and ask yourself why you're uncomfortable with the primary or major feeling and/or subfeelings. How is the primary emotion activating one or more of your subfeelings?

You'll find that it can often be easier to empathize with others than with yourself, which is why you should imagine empathizing with someone else first. Once you feel the skill begin to take hold, you can try it out in the more challenging area of your own emotions.

When you empathize, what you are trying to do—with genuineness and warmth—is look at the primary and subfeelings and say, "I can understand how you might feel that way." Empathy is not the equivalent of approval, and it does not mean you handled something the way you wish you had. It simply means that you can put yourself in someone else's shoes and understand why they walked in the direction they did. As you do this, try to identify several reasons that explain how you could feel the way you did and jot these down on the back of the card. It might look something like this:

- I've felt something similar.

- It seems like unfair behavior you've encountered.

- You lost so much when that event occurred.

Once you intentionally empathize with someone else, you begin to develop the skills and ability that you need in self-therapy in order to treat yourself with understanding, respect, and support.

Acceptance

There is only a fine line between empathy and acceptance, but the distinction is important. When you *empathize*, you let yourself or another person know that you can identify with or understand his or her feelings—but this doesn't mean that you necessarily agree with those feelings or approve of them. When you *accept*, however, you let yourself or the other person know that you believe those feelings are reasonable in some way.

For instance, you can empathize with someone's reasons for robbing a bank—after all, he is poor and perhaps trying to put food on the table for his children—but this doesn't mean you accept his behavior. Similarly, while you can empathize with the feelings of despair someone has that have led to suicidal thoughts, you probably do not accept that suicide is a good or workable solution to despair. Your job for yourself in this third stage is to accept how you feel. When you put together exploration, empathizing, and acceptance, you truly come to terms with the emotional life that serves as your current reality. Once you trust that your feelings *are* your facts—the truest reality you can experience, in a sense—it becomes far easier to identify what it is about that reality that needs to change.

THE IMPACT OF YOUR BELIEFS AND BEHAVIORS IN SELF-THERAPY

You are beginning to get to know yourself through your feelings, which may be new and different for you. Many people define themselves through their work, their relationship to others, their possessions, or some other external element of life. I'm asking you to get to know yourself through a set of facts that are more real and more lasting than any of the superficial things I've just mentioned. Your feelings, while they fluctuate from situation to situation and from moment to moment, are also constant because they represent who you truly are at your core: they reflect how you view yourself, how you view the world, and how you choose to live your life. Whether you are basically a happy person or a dissatisfied one, essentially a trusting person or more often a guarded one, your primary and secondary feelings reflect the true you.

In learning about who you are through your feelings, you are coming to terms with the foundation facts of your current emotional life. Now, after you've begun exploring and accepting the feelings that define your life—even as they present your greatest challenges—it's time to build upon that foundation. Doing so includes understanding how your beliefs and behaviors have an impact upon your emotional life even as you begin to make changes to it.

Like many of your feelings, a great number of your beliefs were established long ago—from your first moments of life, in fact. When you cried and your mother fed you, the belief began to form that the world would take care of you. When you staggered across a room for the first time and everyone applauded and whooped and smiled, you began to believe that you were clever and competent. These lessons continued—as they still do, through every action, reaction, and interaction that involves you—and they created and reinforced your view of yourself and the world around you. This in turn influenced your beliefs about the likelihood that you would be successful at making changes in your life.

If you believe that you're strong, flexible, and capable of change, you will be strong, flexible, and capable of change. If you believe that the people close to you are on your side, wanting what's best for you, supporting you and cheering you on, *others will typically behave in these ways*—not always, of course, but often enough. And if you instead believe that the world is a cruel and dangerous place, you will almost undoubtedly be guarded around others, withholding your trust—and in return, the world won't be likely to greet you with open arms. You can observe this in yourself and the world around you. I'm sure, for instance, that you've seen it plenty of times in the person who is rude getting the rudeness right back. The friendly person, in contrast, gets a warning instead of a speeding ticket, an occasional upgrade to first class for no reason, and great service even when the waiters are swamped.

You present yourself to the world—and that world includes you— through your behaviors. The behaviors you choose have everything to do with the response you receive in return. Similarly, as your beliefs guide your behaviors, it is only natural that the choices you make about self-therapy— and even the initial choice you made to begin the process at all—will influence both the quantity and the quality of what you receive in return.

This is another way of saying that *you are in charge of the outcomes of your therapy*, whether you go it alone or with a professional. If you're still not quite sure that you're in charge, take it on faith for the moment. As you begin to see the remarkable results, it will become easier to believe that you've created the change you set out to accomplish. Some people find it easy to believe they've created failures but difficult to believe they've created success; this is an issue of self-esteem, which we'll address throughout the tool chapters. For the moment, in order to move forward and take on the challenges of your life, you must agree that you are in charge, whether it's comfortable or not. Familiarity may sometimes breed contempt, as the saying goes, but in this case, as you become more familiar with your emotional life, the things you want to change, and my approach to self-therapy, I believe it will breed *confidence in your abilities*. Change begets change, but for change to occur, you must take responsibility for being in charge of that change. No pointing fingers, dodging blame, or denying that something needed a change anyway.

It's time to figure out what you want to change, and there's no point in idling: get out of the passenger seat and let's get moving!

CHOOSING YOUR CHALLENGES

You probably already have a sense of what you want to change in your life. Throughout these first three chapters, we've discussed your current emotional life, making the decision to begin self-therapy, and other issues. But you wouldn't have started reading, and you certainly wouldn't have made it this far, if there weren't things you wanted to change. That you already have a sense of your challenges is further evidence that you know yourself better than anyone else knows you. I can't tell you what challenges you face, for instance, and even if you provided me with a list of the things you wanted to change, I couldn't choose from that list, telling you which item should go first, second, and so on. Fortunately, you don't need anyone to do that for you; you already have an intuitive sense of what needs to change—you just need the tools to take on your journey.

As you read the tool chapters, you'll see that you can consider each tool as both an area to change and a method for creating that change. The specifics are up to you. With each tool, I've given you a road map to take along on the journey that will change what isn't working in your life. But the stops along the way, who you take along for the ride, and the final destination are yours to determine.

Before I present the tools, let's make absolutely sure you're ready for the hard work, determination, and success you will experience. Success? It might seem odd to lump that in with hard work and determination. I include it because some people, though ready to dive into the work, *are not accustomed to success*, and that's what throws them when they begin the process of self-therapy and start experiencing positive change.

It won't be good enough if you've got only what it takes to *try*. You have to be certain that you've got what it takes to *succeed*. Like the proverbial horse and carriage, you can't have one without the other—not the way I envision self-therapy, anyway. If you're not ready to succeed and succeed big-time, you're likely to set yourself up for failure, and then you may well blame *me* for having an ineffective program when things don't work out. Don't even try it! I've seen self-therapy work just fine when people have gone into it with motivations based on their own best interests and the courage of their convictions. If it doesn't work, it's time to take a step back to consider your motivation.

GETTING READY FOR SELF-THERAPY

We're almost there! You're packed and ready to go; you've got the map and you're looking forward to taking in the sights along the way. You know how it is with road trips, though—there's always one last thing, something you have to run back into the house to get, something that takes an extra moment before you depart. It's the same with beginning self-therapy.

This "something" is on the next page, where you'll find a simple quiz that will summarize where you stand when it comes to change. It's a review you can start off with that will serve as a reminder of where you're going and why. This simple yes/no paper-and-pencil assessment should only take you a few minutes to complete and score. Go ahead and take the test now, and we'll discuss it afterward. It will be your companion as you start out, an important gauge of your feelings about change in general and your feelings about *changing your life now* in specific.

S.T.A.R. ASSESSMENT
SELF-THERAPY ASSESSMENT OF READINESS

The going can get rough on any journey, so we've provided an initial assessment of how ready you are for the trip. It's important to know how well prepared you are for change, and what your beliefs are about making changes to your life. The timid suffer because of the paths they didn't take while the brave find renewed energy, excitement and learning when they pioneer new paths. Answer the questions, score yourself and see how ready you are to move forward at this time.

Select EITHER *"Y" for yes or "N" for no* for each statement below:

	YES	NO
1. I'm sick and tired of at least one major part of my life as things stand right now.	____	____
2. Me afraid to change? *Fuggedabout it*! I'm ready!	____	____
3. I'm no fool: I *know* I can screw up big time.	____	____
4. Others' disapproval doesn't scare *me*. I can take bumps and bruises if I'll be happier down the line.	____	____
5. *I* take charge of my life: right here, right now!	____	____
6. I'd rather be wildly interested but a little anxious than permanently bored and comfortable.	____	____
7. Stubborn? That's my middle name.	____	____
8. I'm person enough to handle *big* change!	____	____
9. My new motto is "I want the best life possible and I want it *now*!"	____	____
10. No one else is going to run my life anymore!	____	____
Total	YES	NO
	____	____

(continued)

8 to 10 Yes answers: You are ripe for *big-time* change: While your life may be agreeable in some ways, you are prime for growth and change in the significant areas of your life that are less than optimal.

5 to 7 Yes answers: You are moving toward being ready for big changes, but old beliefs continue to hold you back in some significant ways. Try making small changes now and your beliefs will change over time.

1 to 4 Yes answers: Even a 1 means there's hope! Something in you is curious about change and willing to consider it. Somewhere along the line you learned that change was scary, bad, and otherwise *unwise*. You'll need extra courage to move forward with changes—but you'll also regret it if you don't.

Now, look at your *No* answers and think about why these specific areas worry you, why you have the beliefs you do about change, and how you came to have those beliefs. Some memories of past changes—the ones that backfired or made you uncomfortable—may not be pleasant, but they're essential to consider because they'll tell you *where you've been, how you got there*, and, most important *where you don't ever want to be again!* There are no mistakes or failures, only places and things to avoid. Go for it.

As you go forward, your score will tell you where you are on the continuum that exists between a complete unwillingness to face your issues and a deep commitment to exploring these issues and creating change and healing in your life. No matter what you find in the results, I encourage you to begin this journey—and begin it now. Don't wait until it's more convenient or until you feel less resistant, which are just ways of avoiding what needs to be confronted. Part of self-therapy is about coming face-to-face with the parts of your life that you've avoided or denied until now, so it's not only okay to begin even if you're not of one heart and mind about the journey, it's essential. If there's even one thing about your life that you want to change, *you should make the trip.*

Self-therapy is all *about* change. It requires a willingness to acknowledge that change is a natural part of life and accepting that change will come, *like it or not.* One thing I can guarantee: the change will be more palatable if you're not dragged kicking and screaming toward its inevitable appearance! When you're ready for self-therapy, you're ready to be comfortable with yourself and your own power—*and* you're fed up with one or more aspects of your life. You're ready for self-therapy when you're prepared to move beyond deciding what to think, feel, or do based on the approval or disapproval of others; when you see how that affects your choices and goals, and you know that's not the way you want your life to work anymore. You want it to be about you—not selfishly so, but because you're ready for your needs, your wants, your beliefs, and your feelings to determine what happens in *your* life.

A FINAL REMINDER

One final reminder before you open the toolbox and involve yourself in the process of therapy, taking up the tools one by one, examining them, practicing with them, and meanwhile becoming more skilled with each step at dealing with your life: self-therapy is about getting what *you* want from *your* life. It's about you and your needs. Integrate the tools into your life, make them work in the situations you face, and be tough but compassionate with yourself when you make mistakes, run into a snag, or hit the occasional wall. Remember too that you will be expected to use some originality in handling these tools. They aren't so cut-and-dried as to prevent you from using creativity. See what works for you and use it!

This is big change we're talking about, and big change doesn't come without a proportionate commitment and effort. At the same time, don't forget that you're allowed to have fun along the way. Making change may be difficult, sometimes challenging and rigorous or even painful, but that's just a small part of the journey. Whatever direction you take, creating confidence and competence more often brings a sense of exhilaration, strength, and powerful pride. So celebrate along the way as you experience the success of taking your life where you want it to go.

Open Your Eyes and Face Reality

WHAT THE MIND DOES NOT KNOW,
THE EYE DOES NOT SEE.

Eastern Indian proverb

When you have feelings that seem a bit too much to handle, think about this: your feelings of anxiety, fear and anger, just as a beginning, are caused by the same physical response that occurs during great excitement or joy. Context is everything—context determines how you interpret the way you feel. A rapid heart rate and sweaty palms occur in fear and in sexual excitement, as an example. When a feeling is causing you intense distress, remove yourself temporarily—go into the restroom, your car, an empty office or, if your options are limited, close your eyes—and breathe slowly as you remind yourself that you've survived these feelings before, and even felt good about them! Then, work off the negative feelings: jog in place in the restroom or walk briskly through a hall at the office. You'll "fool" your mind into re-interpreting your physiological experience from something negative to something positive.

MISPERCEIVING REALITY

In today's world, it's become far too common for people to buy into the idea that reality is whatever you want it to be. If the market is packed but there's no one in the 15-item express lane, how many people will get in that lane with their 20 items, as if 20 is the same as 15? If there's a near collision as you're backing out of a parking space and someone else is driving too fast through the lot, how often have you seen another driver stop to apologize, mouth "I'm sorry" through the window, or otherwise accept responsibility? It happens, but it doesn't happen much. There used to be a time when reality was reality: an objective collection of facts that brooked no argument. Now it's just whatever you make it, whatever works for you or someone else—which is not only a pity, but also a way to avoid making changes in your life. If you deny the reality that exists, you don't have to change: you're not selfish for getting in the express lane with 20 items, and you're definitely not a careless driver. How convenient!

When it comes to facing reality, we as a society seem to generally accept the idea that if you don't like what you see, you're also welcome to turn away or withdraw in disgust, claiming some other reality that doesn't exist.

One psychologist, George Kelly,[1] hit the nail on the head when he said that we actually *construct our own view of the world that we find most acceptable*. What we don't like, we don't "see," and what we like we "see more of." In other words, we ignore the reality that doesn't suit our notions of what we want from the world and from the people around us. That "strong, silent type" turns out to be repressed, shy, or afraid of intimacy. That "optimist" turns out to be hopelessly out of touch with the reality that sometimes things just don't work out. We rename, reframe, and realign reality to fit what will work best in our lives. What Kelly said and what I'm saying is just another way of phrasing the truth in an old East Indian proverb: "What the mind does not know, the eye does not see."

The following situation a client shared with me provides an excellent example of just how we deny reality at times.

Terry believed that one of the young executives where she worked was secretly attracted to her. In sessions, she would tell me how he looked at her and how she knew "that look" and what it meant. Wishing to get closer to him and encourage him to verbalize his feelings for her, Terry would slip into the company gym while the man was working out. One day, just as she arrived, she noted that he smiled. Terry was convinced that the smile meant something more. For several weeks she went to the gym and talked to him, asking about his work and his home life. He never seemed to say more than a few words, but she "knew" his reticence was because he was shy.

One morning she was called into her supervisor's office to discuss "problems" in the gym area. She arrived at the meeting having no idea that her supervisor was referring to her interactions with the man.

"The gym area is for the use of executive management personnel," Terry was told. "It has been brought to our attention that you are using this facility, and I've been advised to speak to you. You are to stop using it, and furthermore, you are not to engage in any further inappropriate behavior with regard to our executives."

Terry was shocked. She knew there was a rule about the use of the gym, but she was an employee too, and felt that she should be provided with access like everyone else.

"Failure to follow this rule will result in your being written up," her supervisor concluded.

Since Terry continued to "read" the executive's facial expression and clipped remarks when she passed him in the hall or saw him at a meeting, despite what her supervisor said, she found it impossible to believe that the executive wasn't attracted to her. I know he likes me, she'd stubbornly tell herself. She would turn the slightest look, gesture, or verbalization into something that signified a relationship with the executive.

Stop for just a moment and ask yourself how many times you have "read into" a relationship—particularly in its early, uncertain days—and interpreted vague or ambiguous messages. Sometimes your readings have been on target; and at other times they've been far off base. Whether what you saw— and what Terry interpreted—was really flirting was in the eye of the beholder. The point is: often, we see what we want to see. There is a "real" reality that exists apart from the one created by your wishes and needs, and if you're going to be successful at making changes to your life, you have to be able to see and distinguish between *both* of those realities.

Depending on your self-esteem, your interpretations may be negative or positive in any given situation. Far too often, though, your perception of reality can be heavily influenced by your fantasies and your wishes instead of the *actual reality that exists*. This makes change virtually impossible: if you don't know what's real and what's fantasy, how can you even begin to know what needs changing and where to begin?

WHERE YOU'VE BEEN

Opening your eyes requires that you develop the ability to look frankly at what is happening in your life at any given time. It involves accepting that the reality of your life is largely *your* creation, but that your reality must be combined with whatever objective "truths" exist about a situation at any given point in time. There is no single, constant truth—instead, there is whatever is *objectively real* at any given time combined *with your perceptions about what is real* based on variations in what you've experienced and what you believe from day to day. These beliefs and experiences are largely based on your past: your upbringing, the beliefs you encountered in childhood and beyond, the family system in which you were raised, and other similar influences.

Psychologists know that the reality you've created for your life is heavily influenced by what you believe *best serves you.* Someone smiles at you, and perhaps you interpret the smile as liking or approval—so you learn to continue doing whatever it was that prompted the smile. You find a penny on the ground and decide you're going to have a lucky day—so your perceptions and behaviors during that day shift, and you tend to view the day's events in a more positive, "lucky" light. A teacher praises a picture you've drawn—so you incorporate "artistic" into your view of yourself. All of these reactions and responses from the world around you shade and color your view of the world and your place in it—sometimes subtly, sometimes overtly. No matter how large or small the occurrence, all of the incidents and interactions that take place in your life provide the backdrop to your view of reality.

As your reality forms, your *outlook* on life determines the out*come* of your life. For instance, if you've ever met a pessimist, you've seen how outlook affects outcomes. When you interact with others with a chip on your shoulder, others will respond accordingly; to the pessimist, the unexpected smile is suspicious and the found penny is useless. When you're upbeat and encouraging toward yourself and others, you see the success that results; the smile is a confirmation that life brings rewards, and the penny is an investment in good luck.

If you catastrophize, you look at life—and particularly at life's challenges—through a zoom lens. The negativity and insurmountability of change is magnified. When you accept reality and roll with its ups and downs, you look at life through the same zoom lens—yet see possibility, potential. Whether you are catastrophizing or minimizing—the terms used by psychologists—you are distorting the reality of your life. Obviously it is generally more helpful—or, at the very least, more palatable—to distort reality in a positive way, but in either case the result is often a view of the world that is out of sync with the reality seen by others. This is natural, since we all view the world from different vantage points and from different bases of experience, but it is also important to be aware of this viewpoint, since it influences the choices you make.

Depending on where you exist on the continuum between minimizing and catastrophizing reality, there are times when you will make the choice, unconscious or not, to avoid facing reality. Failing to face reality means living inside of a fantasy world of your own making—often one to which those around you contribute. Living in fantasies means missed opportunities, bypassed growth and learning, and a flourishing network of deception. Unfortunately, a failure to face reality also means a whole host of other troubles too, including these facts:

- You cannot deny reality without lying to yourself and others.

- You cannot deny reality without damaging your chances for success.

- You cannot deny reality without limiting your life potential.

- You cannot deny reality without creating potential harm to relationships.

- You cannot deny reality without short-circuiting your chances for change.

HOW YOU GOT HERE

Why deny reality? What possible benefit could be in it for you—or for anyone, for that matter? If denying reality means closing your eyes and keeping your life on hold as you cut off the opportunity for positive change, *why do it*? The answer is actually pretty simple: you do it in a misguided attempt to protect yourself. By denying reality, you're trying to create what *isn't* in order to rewrite what *is*, and you're usually telling yourself that your reason is to avoid hurting others in some way. Look at the list of troubles that are brought about by a failure to face reality. It's easy to make the argument that you're protecting the other in each case. I can make the argument, though, that you're always actually protecting yourself—but even if you disagree, hear me out.

In this chapter, the rewriting of reality is exactly what we're going to explore and exactly what you're going to learn to do differently: I want you to examine how you arrived at your perception of your current emotional life. Some of your perceptions are undoubtedly based on an avoidance of reality, even as the "real" reality remains constant, mixing with the sum of the workable and unworkable elements of your life: your beliefs, behaviors, choices, and goals. You're also going to learn how—and, most important, *why*—you must stop telling yourself that rewriting reality is about helping or protecting others when it's really about you.

Learning How to Deny Reality

As a first step, let's look at how you got to this point—and, if necessary, let me convince you that you are at this point to begin with. You may be thinking that in fact you don't deny reality, but I'm willing to bet that's not the case; in fact, I'd venture a guess that if you believe you don't rewrite reality, you're rewriting reality!

Assume for a moment, *whatever* you believe, that you actually do have this tendency to deny reality. You probably came to it as most of us adopt our maladaptive behaviors: you developed a taste for fantasy in your innocent youth. You saw others denying reality in one way or another, and you became convinced that there was something to this denial game. In order to see how denying reality might apply to you, consider the examples below—or similar incidents—and see if they ring a bell.

- You heard your father say he wasn't feeling well in order to get out of going to a party. *The reality*: he just didn't want to go.

- You heard your mother say a friend had given her something as a gift, but you'd been with your mother when she bought it for herself. *The reality*: she didn't want your father to know that she spent the money.

- Your health teacher constantly lectured your junior high class about the dangers of smoking. *The reality*: you saw your health teacher driving downtown one day, smoking a cigarette.

- You told someone you were busy Friday night. *The reality*: you weren't interested in going out with the person.

- You pretended your parents would only let you have five children at your birthday party. *The reality*: you didn't want to invite the remaining kid in your neighborhood gang of friends because you'd recently had a falling out.

Reading these examples, you might be thinking that they just sound like lies to you—so what's this "denying reality" business? Is it just a fancy term for lying? In a sense, yes . . . it is. When you lied and told your parents you hadn't had a beer at the party in high school, or when you lied and told your partner that nothing was "going on" between you and the attractive person at the office, the one you were frequently sharing lunch with, you were also denying reality. You did have a beer—or a six-pack—and you felt the zing from across the table with that person at lunch; so did everyone else in the restaurant, for that matter. I call your choice to lie "denying reality" because that's ultimately what it is: a way of saying that what is real, isn't. Looking upon lying as a failure to face reality has the benefit of giving you something you can do about it: it allows you to understand why you've chosen to lie, how it serves you, and, most important, why you should stop. Because you learned it early too, it is probably unconscious and ingrained in many cases, and so I call it "denying reality," rather than "lying," to give you the opportunity to view it through a different lens.

You heard the "white lies" your parents and other adults told, and you learned to imitate the ways in which they ducked reality as you saw them getting let off the hook again and again. In some cases, it seemed better than the alternative of facing the consequences of reality, and in other cases, you learned that it was just the polite thing to do. After all, when you hear that dreaded question ("Honey, do I look fat in this dress?"), surely you're not going to answer yes. You can't tell someone you wouldn't be caught dead at his party, or that you would no more go on a date with her than commit hara-kiri—right? Well—maybe, maybe not. As with most of the choices in life, it depends on your motivation and intentions. This is where you're most likely to fool yourself, however. Even as you argue that your motivation is to save someone discomfort, or you insist that your intention is to be kind, the underlying reality is more often that you're trying to save yourself the hassle of dealing with hurt feelings, anger or the other consequences of facing reality head-on.

How does this relate to your current life situation—in other words, to your reality? It's actually quite simple: those white lies and denials you heard as you were growing up were like attending an intensive training camp in avoiding reality. The problem is, you may have absorbed the lessons far too well from your coaches. Instead of using white lies judiciously, only bringing them out for their intended purpose—which is to truly protect another person's dignity or feelings—the training you received probably made little distinction between protecting others and yourself.

Think about this, and be truthful with yourself as I repeat a radical reality *about* reality—and about avoiding it: every lie you tell, no matter how "innocent" or "white" or "well-intentioned," isn't really about protecting someone else. *Every lie you tell is about protecting yourself.* I challenge you to think of a situation in which this isn't true; in fact, you can call me when I'm on a radio show, or e-mail me through my website, if you think you've come up with such a situation. I guarantee you there is no lie you can tell me that will convince me otherwise. You may be protecting yourself from wrath, from annoyance, from losing money or face or an opportunity, but when you fool around with the truth, what you're really protecting yourself from is reality. *You're avoiding the reality that there are consequences to each and every action, and that those consequences may not always be ones you like.*

Although they're subtler (and therefore harder to pin down), you didn't just learn how to dodge reality with white lies. You also observed plain old bald-faced lies. For instance, have you ever seen an adult hit an unoccupied car in a parking lot? I've seen this more than once, and I know there is the honest response, and then there are the three kinds of dishonest responses that avoid reality. You can simply drive away: this is a lie of *omission*, when you fail to tell the truth by not saying anything at all. You can stop and leave a note that says you hit the car, people are watching, and so you're leaving a note so others will think you're doing the right thing—but you leave your name, address, or other identifying information off the note. This is a lie of *commission*: you're replacing the truth with deception. Or you can use a lie of collusion, acting in concert with someone else to obscure the truth—perhaps by leaving a friend standing near the damaged vehicle as you drive off (and then having the friend walk away when no one is watching anymore). What seeing such incidents taught you about the price of reality and honesty may have taught you that facing reality had far too high a price; after all, if adults went to all that trouble to avoid reality, surely reality must be pretty awful.

Learning Why to Deny Reality

There's something about reality that can make everyone flee fast and hard when it rears its ugly head. How else can you explain the silence around the dinner table when a younger sibling asked how babies are born? Why the pained look in your father's eyes when your mother said, "We need to talk," and why the change of subjects when you kept trying to tell your first love that maybe you'd be better suited as friends? What's the denial all about? It's about a number of things, but among the most important are:

YOU WANT TO AVOID BEING HURT.   Let's be frank: life is painful sometimes. *Pain is relative*: the closer you are to others, the more openings there are for pain. If you don't care about anyone—so the illogic goes—you won't experience pain. So, you may isolate yourself, if not from others, then certainly from reality

YOU WANT TO AVOID THE FEELINGS THAT RESULT FROM FAILURE.   You may place unusually high demands on yourself, or your family may have pushed you toward something such as a career, educational efforts, or other achievements. If you aren't confident that you can succeed, you may opt out, or avoid reality. If you don't try, you can't fail.

YOU'RE IN THE HABIT OF BELIEVING THAT YOU ARE RIGHT AND THE WORLD IS WRONG.   This will resonate powerfully if your parents or other primary care givers were particularly dogmatic. When dogmatic people are faced with truths that don't seem palatable, they often simply deny the truth. *That just can't be*, they tell themselves. *That's absurd.* If you were raised around dogmatism, it's only natural that you picked up this counterproductive coping strategy early in life.

Many elements of reality do not match the myth that you have created around your life—yet without the myth, the reality would crumble. This is often the primary reason behind choosing to deny reality. If the reality crumbled, where would that leave you? What would you have left? The immediate example that comes to mind, though distant from my reality and yours in many ways, is the marriage of Great Britain's Prince Charles and Lady Diana Spencer. Whether you have read a dozen books or only the headlines about their "Fairy Tale Marriage," you undoubtedly heard gossip through the years. Among the stories I remember hearing were that Diana threw herself down a flight of stairs, despondent over her marriage, when she was pregnant; Charles admitted to having an affair with a long-time lover; Diana made hundreds of obscene, obsessive phone calls to a married lover; Charles disappeared to play polo while his eldest son lay in a hospital bed, his head injured after being hurt playing sports. Even as these stories played out, the need of both the public and the principal players to maintain a belief in fairy tales grew in strength. This need was so powerful that conflicting stories of the disaster status *and* the fairy tale nature of the marriage regularly appeared in the press, often even on the same day!

That the facts didn't square up with reality doesn't just happen in the strange world of royalty, of course. It's something you have to struggle with every day. You want to believe that your partner is your own Prince (or Princess) Charming . . . and yet he belches in front of company. She drools when she's asleep. He's defensive when you try to discuss issues, no matter how small. She badmouths you to her friends when she's angry. And so the bell tolls on your fantasy, but the question remains. *What do you rewrite, the facts or the fantasy?* I've got good news and bad. The good news: you *can* rewrite the facts, changing lovers, jobs, or anything else whenever reality settles in. The bad news, though, is that you'll never escape the real problem, and the real challenge. There's a gap between fantasy and reality, and there always will be. What you can do is change your view of the fantasy and see it as an ideal, an often unrealistic goal, but a goal nonetheless, toward which you can work even as you open your eyes and face reality. After all, this is your life; wishing it away is only going to get you one thing: less time for living your real life.

Sarah grew up in poverty, but she came to know two girls, very competitive twin sisters who were always trying to have and do and be better than the other. Their father employed Sarah's own father for odd jobs now and then. While her father worked Sarah would amuse the two girls who looked at her as something exotic. The twins had everything they desired, and so they would pepper Sarah with questions about how it was to live in a tenement house in Brooklyn. They were aghast that she had to eat a potato for lunch everyday for twelve years of school, the same potato she carried hot in her pocket in the mornings to warm her hands. The one thing Sarah remembered from these days was the sisters telling her that their father had taught them to always order the most expensive item on the menu when they went to a restaurant. Perplexed, Sarah asked why—she believed she would order what she liked best someday. The sisters explained that their father wanted them to learn to accept "only the best," so that in the future, they could avoid any man who couldn't—or wouldn't—give them the absolute best, since such a man didn't deserve them. Sarah heard from each sister separately every Christmas—she thought of herself, even now that she was successful, as their Charity Christmas Card—and got bits of news of the other. By the time they were all in their late twenties, both sisters had married brilliantly. One wore large dark glasses that everyone pretended hid the bruises—but she still had her Mercedes. The other went to see a therapist three times a week in the poor part of town—close to the old tenements, in fact, where Sarah had been raised. That way no one would guess that she needed help, or that she always stopped after the appointments for the bottles of liquor that helped her make it through the week.

WHY THE OLD WAYS DON'T WORK

If there's only one thing you take away from this chapter—and I hope there are many—it's the knowledge that *denying reality doesn't work*. It trips you up, it results in deception and a lack of intimacy with others and a growing feeling of distance from yourself. It also doesn't work because it is based on behaviors learned in the past—yet you are in the present, and, if you are psychologically intact and healthy, you should always be moving toward the future. Take just a quick look at the behaviors you used as a child and see how well they worked then, yet how "childish" they appear now. Your temper tantrums may have gotten you that Gumby-and-Pokey set when you were three or four—but only because your exhausted mother couldn't take one more minute of your screams in a public place. Try it *today*, though—go ahead, lie down on your back in the aisle of a supermarket and kick your legs up and down, scream that you *WANT* (and want for free, no less!) the Italian white truffles—and just see what happens. By the way, be sure to take bail money along—and don't mention my name.

What is behind you is not in front of you.

Remember that you are not the same person you were when you first developed your coping mechanisms, so the old ways no longer work. The events that you deal with are more complex than in the past, and so they require more complex coping mechanisms. You are older and wiser and need a greater arsenal at your fingertips. If you still question why you need to develop additional methods for facing reality in order to get on with your life, I've got a whole list of the ways in which avoiding reality just doesn't work. See if you don't recognize some or all of these results from times when you have avoided reality.

First, you may discover that avoiding reality doesn't work because it makes you *rigid in your approach and response* to what happens in your life. If you have used a specific coping mechanism over the years, and particularly if you have tended to get similar or predictable results each time, it is typical to develop a strong attachment to that approach. As you mature and face new challenges, however, you may find that the old coping method doesn't work anymore, and so you repeat it in its entirety or in part, perhaps growing increasingly frantic as you discover that it no longer serves you. A classic example of this relates to death. Many people do not experience their first significant loss until adulthood, when a parent dies. Perhaps you have previously lost a pet—a crisis in itself, certainly—or perhaps you have lost a relationship, although not to death. You are likely to use your responses to either of those two situations, if they are closest in character to your current situation—and it's likely you'll discover that the various elements you applied to the previous loss do not work effectively in this instance. When you lost that lover, for instance, you may have first grieved temporarily, and then rapidly switched into anger. That might have worked for your no-account, disloyal ex-love, but it won't fit the bill with a parent whose loss you're grieving, of course.

A second reason that avoiding reality doesn't work is that the very rigidity that comes from using the same approach again and again *doesn't allow you to form meaningful, fluid relationships that involve give and take.* Your relationships can take on the air of semi-intimate transactions, conducted "by the book." It is as if there is a set of rules, and in any given situation, you simply flip to a certain page and apply the four or six or eight steps in response to the situation without regard to its individual nature.

Third, you're likely to find that avoiding reality doesn't serve you because you are *wasting energy and increasing your negativity since you're at war with a world that refuses to come around to your way of thinking.* You view the world in a rigid way, insisting upon applying your methods to situations that do not yield to your interpretation of reality despite your pushing and pulling. Only one outlook tends to result: you set up an expectancy of disappointment. Eventually, though, despite your failure to face reality, you will recognize that you rarely if ever, meet with success—and therefore you create an angry outlook for yourself. How could you *not*? When everything you do is destined to fail, it is difficult, and probably impossible, to maintain a positive, energetic, and peaceful outlook.

Finally, by applying the same rigid approach time and again as you deny or avoid reality, you are bound *to create a destructive self-fulfilling prophecy.* Such prophecies are the result of believing that an outcome will occur, and therefore—consciously or unconsciously—you behave in ways that create that outcome. The student who says "I always fail tests" creates a self-fulfilling prophecy and always fails tests. The lover who says "I'm a loser at love" guarantees that it's so.

On a conscious level, you may insist that you long for good things to happen to you. Who doesn't, after all? But by approaching your life with a negative, rigid, stereotyped, and/or hopeless orientation, you imbue your outcomes with the same qualities, unfortunately. The reality is that life is full of a mix of good and bad, positive and negative, success and failure. Anytime you allow your thinking to shift you to one extreme in this mix, you create a situation in which the results will also be extreme. This merely serves to reinforce your original belief—that you're a failure, a loser, or some other extreme—and thus a vicious cycle is created.

It is time to make a change, to dredge the murky river bottom of your unconscious and bring your self-fulfilling prophecies to the surface, where you can examine them and turn them into *positive* self-fulfilling prophecies, the kind that say "I will succeed" and "I will grow"—*no matter what!* Each time you hear yourself making a statement about who or what you are, stop. Listen to the statement and determine whether it is positive or negative. If it's negative, you need to replace it with a positive message and belief, even if you don't yet believe in the replacement. Over time, as you repeat the positive message to yourself, you will actually come to believe in it—and in yourself.

ROOTS: SELF-ESTEEM AND FACING REALITY

One more thought about the tendency to deny, deny, deny. It's helpful to know as much as possible about how this tendency arises. Reaching a deep level of insight about the roots of your beliefs and behaviors allows you to perform a rapid assessment of how to remove yourself, with surgical precision, from the webs that bind you to an unworkable past.

Denial is about self-esteem. When you remain stuck in denial and in the unworkable patterns and rigid fixes of the past, you are dealing a blow to your self-esteem that keeps it on its knees. You refuse to change (you may believe that you don't know what else to do), and yet your habit of avoiding reality keeps bringing you more negative feedback from the world around you—and from you, yourself. You spend energy on "self-talk" that's negative: either you tell yourself that you're right and the world's wrong, or—in some subterranean tunnel of your mind—you whisper that you're wrong and the world's right, but you're too messed up to fix it. In fact, you may well do both, and ultimately this kind of negative self-talk will result in frustration and self-loathing.

This is where I draw the line. *There is never a reason for you to feel self-loathing, and if you do, there's something you need to change about your beliefs and behaviors.* The first step in creating this kind of change involves knowing where you stand—in this case, where you stand when it comes to facing reality. On the following pages you'll find an assessment tool and discussion about the results that will help you to determine what you've learned and what you practice when it comes to facing—or denying—reality.

KEEPING IT REAL: AN ASSESSMENT TOOL

Whether or not you're practiced and successful at avoiding reality, the assessment tool below will help you to do three things. First, you will *identify your lifelong tendencies toward facing reality.* Second, you will *identify the specific ways in which these tendencies are exhibited when confronted with challenges and choices.* Finally, as you answer questions based on the ratings you give yourself, you will *establish a foundation for creating new, powerful methods for accepting and facing reality head-on.*

The following 32-item assessment tool consists of several sections. In Section I you will identify your "Preferential Personality Type" (the PPT score), which assesses how you approach problems and their solutions. Next, Section II will clarify your "Preferential Activities" (your PA score), or the activities that you have generally preferred. With the data you generate through these assessments, you will receive helpful and pointed information about your tendencies. Then, having completed these first two sections of the assessment, you will have the opportunity in Section III, "Applications for PPT/PA," to apply these approaches to your own highly individualized tendencies.

As you consider the questions below, try to answer them from the standpoint of your "inner child"—in other words, think of the choice you would have made as a child, and try to avoid layering on your adult perceptions. Give yourself one point (1) for either the A answer or the B answer in each of the eight pairs of statements that follow.

SECTION I:
PREFERENTIAL PERSONALITY TYPE (PPT)

As a child, I preferred. . .

____ A.   Wearing clothes that adults chose and or had previously liked me in.

____ B.   Wearing what I liked or what I chose when I dressed for the day.

____ A.   Games that I already know how to play and could win.

____ B.   Games that offered new challenges and/or were unfamiliar.

____ A.   Playing sports that were team-oriented.

____ B.   Playing sports that relied more heavily on individual skills.

____ A.   Being with friends who didn't show negative or needy feelings.

____ B.   Being with friends who were open and honest about their feelings.

____ A.   When adults would explain rules before setting them.

____ B..   Figuring out the rules myself and making sure they made sense.

(continued)

___ A. Not to be noticed by teachers or other adults too often.

___ B. To be the center of attention at school or in other settings.

___ A. Seeking advice/directions from adults/others to solve problems.

___ B. Solving problems without input from adults or others.

___ A. To avoid my parents when they were upset about something.

___ B. To try to comfort my parents when they were upset about something.

___ Total A Points   *Sum of A and B total*

___ Total B Points   *points should be 8*

In a moment we will interpret your scores, but for now, continue on to the following section, in which you will assess your Preferential Activities score. Complete the following assessment as you did the previous assessment: give yourself one point (1) for either the A answer or the B answer in each pairing.

SECTION II:
PREFERENTIAL ACTIVITIES (PA)

As a child, I preferred. . .

___ A. Playing with many other children.

___ B. Being by myself.

___ A. Activities with clearly defined rules.

___ B. Games that required making up rules as we went along.

___ A. Eating what I was served without much complaint.

___ B. Requesting certain meals or refusing foods frequently.

___ A. Activities that required less physical energy, like watching TV.

___ B. Activities that required lots of physical energy.

___ A. Quiet activities such as reading or solving puzzles.

___ B. Louder activities, such as playing tag or hide-and-go-seek.

___ A. Activities that are orderly and neat.

___ B. Activities that make a mess.

(continued)

___ A.   Paint by numbers.
___ B.   Finger painting.

___ A.   Playing indoors regardless of the weather.
___ B.   Playing outdoors in all but the worst weather.

___   Total A Points   *Sum of A and B total*
___   Total B Points   *points should be 8*

SCORING THE PPT/PA RESULTS
KEEPING IT REAL ASSESSMENT SUMMARY OF TOTALS

Add up the "1's" in the PPT (1st) Test: A Answers ____   B Answers ____

Add up the "1's" in the PA (2nd) Test: A Answers ____   B Answers ____

*Each list should total "8" as you are choosing *either* the best A *or* the best B answer in each of the 8 pairs in the two lists.

*Analysis of results can be found on the following page.

SECTION III: APPLICATIONS FOR PPT/PA

As you continue reading the remainder of this chapter, in the "Present Tense" section you will examine and refer to your results from the "Keeping It Real" assessment. These results will help you to apply the issues of obstacles, benefits, and expectations as you learn new methods for facing reality head-on.

You'll find it helpful to keep a journal throughout the self-therapy process. You can use it to record your discoveries, make note of your progress, talk yourself through your obstacles, and share with yourself other observations that arise along the way.

In particular, you may find it helpful to make notes of some of the PPT and PA characteristics that seem to ring true for you—particularly if you experienced discomfort as you read about these characteristics. Spend a few moments focusing on these characteristics as you answer the following "wondering" questions in a journal.

Wondering

- Which characteristic (in the PPT/PA) made me feel most uncomfortable?

- Have I been "accused" of this characteristic before? In what context? Why does it bother me?

- When is the last time I avoided or "rewrote" reality? What resulted? Why?

- What would I most like to change about my PPT/PA scores and about how I face or avoid reality? What will it take to change it?

- What's stopping me from making the changes I want or need to make?

PRESENT TENSE

Now that you have completed the "Keeping It Real" assessment, you should have a better sense of your tendencies toward facing and avoiding reality. In addition, you should also have a better idea about the personality characteristics—some of which were "nature" (part of your genetic makeup) and part of which were "nurture" (learned early in life)—that intersect with and influence how you handle reality.

Armed with this knowledge, you can more realistically gauge the current obstacles to reality that exist, both independent of you and of your own making. Use this knowledge to examine the benefits that will result when you decide to face reality honestly and openly. And keep what you've learned in mind so that you'll know what to expect within yourself and from others in your life when you *do* make these positive, life-affirming changes.

THE OBSTACLES TO FACING REALITY

THE DIFFERENCE BETWEEN FICTION AND REALITY? FICTION HAS TO MAKE SENSE.

Tom Clancy

Tom Clancy, one of the most famous and prolific writers of our time, may have made the observation in jest, but truer words have rarely been spoken. We give up on books that don't make sense, saying, "That could never happen in real life!" Unfortunately, we often say something similar in real life too, and it gets in the way of dealing with life as it comes. Instead of saying that something could never happen, we insist that it should never happen. I'm sure you can think of plenty of examples of things that shouldn't happen but do.

The fact is, reality often does not conform to our expectations. Despite that, I'm asking you to face it. Here's the key: facing reality *doesn't* mean understanding or predicting it. Facing reality means *rolling with reality*, accepting that what is, *is*—rather than allowing it to stop you from making the changes you want to make in your life.

It doesn't seem like rolling with reality should be so difficult, and yet often it is. Why is that? What are the obstacles that stop you from making the changes that will improve your life, the excuses that arise and keep you treading water? What are the obstacles that get in the way time after time on your journey toward change?

Reality Rule and Obstacle #1

Sometimes Reality Makes No Sense

Have you ever heard yourself say that something's unfair, doesn't make sense, or just doesn't fit with the way you see the world? I'm sure you have. Sudden tragic events, unexpected kindnesses, and bizarre behavior all fit into this category. As you go forth on your journey toward facing reality, it's important to remember that sometimes reality won't conform to logic or to your way of viewing the world. In fact, that's a big part of why it's difficult to accept reality at times. Think of the tragic attacks of 9/11: many of us stared at our television sets, unable to comprehend the idea of a passenger jet—and then another—flying into the World Trade Center. Moments later our idea of reality was further shaken when the buildings began to crumble before our very eyes.

Reality is absurd at times. Things happen that bear no logic or reason, and this is one of the obstacles you may face when it comes to tackling reality. Even as you make the commitment to face reality head-on, things will happen that seem so bizarre, so scary, so overwhelming, or so illogical that you'll back away. You can't do this. If you're going to face reality, you have to face its good, its bad, and its very ugly. Don't allow the unpredictability of reality—the fact that sometimes reality makes no sense—keep you from facing it in your own life.

Reality Rule and Obstacle #2

Facing Reality Means Admitting You Were Wrong

You may also find that you have difficulty recognizing or facing reality because it can involve admitting that you're wrong. This is not easy for many people to do. It's hard enough to admit that you're wrong when the issue is whether you remembered to bring in the garbage cans or walk the dog. It gets even harder when the issue is more complex.

Think of a time, for instance, when you've been out of line in a relationship; you've said something unfair to a partner. Maybe you even regretted it instantly, knowing that your words had been mean-spirited and that your intentions had gone awry—yet you didn't apologize or admit to your regret. Why not? For most people in this situation, admitting to being wrong also means admitting something you'd prefer not to acknowledge about yourself. Maybe you'd have to acknowledge that you can be mean at times; maybe you'd have to admit that you're finally being truthful about how you feel toward your partner. It could be you're only forced to acknowledge that you lost your temper, of course, but even this might be hard to admit because it says you don't have the control you'd like to think you have. The reality is, there could be dozens of truths beneath your words, but *what* those truths are isn't the issue. The issue is, your words contained an unpleasant truth, one you'd prefer not to face.

Facing reality can mean giving up being right, and giving up the moral high ground is a tough thing to do. What you must remember, though, is that you *are* wrong sometimes—whether you like it or not. Admitting that won't kill you or cause permanent damage to your reputation, and it probably won't even cause you suffering much beyond the next few minutes. Instead, when you admit you're wrong, you open up the space for change, the space to learn new ways to handle challenges, and that's what this tool—and this entire book, in fact—is all about: learning, change, and growth. Admitting to wrong doesn't mean *being* wrong; you are *already* wrong—some of the time. It just means acknowledging reality. This can be tough, but the results are worth it—so give it a fair shot before you shoot it down.

Reality Rule and Obstacle #3

Others Continue to Enable You to Avoid Reality

Unfortunately, if you've gotten this far avoiding reality, you probably continue to have people in your life who encourage you to avoid reality, which can be a powerful incentive to give up the chase for sanity. If it also means disturbing their distorted view of the world, others can often be unpleasant, pushy, disconfirming, and manipulative when you insist on viewing reality realistically. Let me give you an example.

Let's suppose that you've always had a tendency to be dependent on your partners, yet, as you get older, you've begun to realize that your dependency doesn't work for you. You know that this dependency relates to your self-esteem, which is problematic in your current relationship. Your partner is better educated, comes from a wealthy background, and is more informed than you about world events, the arts, history, and many other areas. You feel particularly inferior with this partner because of all of these things. In addition, at times intentionally, when he's angry—and at times without even realizing it, simply because of the educational and other differences between you—he makes comments or observations that leave you feeling hurt and embarrassed.

You decide to go back to school to complete your college degree. You begin reading the newspaper and biographies of historical figures and other books about a range of topics, a real commitment, since reading doesn't come naturally to you. And you feel better and better about both the commitment and yourself as you learn more about the world. You also decide to confront your partner when he says things that embarrass or hurt you, and you practice ways to kindly but firmly tell him how you feel. As he begins to observe and experience these changes, he "teases" you, calling you "Sally Student" and "the Bookworm" and correcting you constantly if you make a mistake. At the same time, he starts paying more attention to you, wanting to snuggle, to watch movies with you and go for walks. Before, he always seemed too busy for these activities. You can't help but notice that it often seems that he wants to do these things when you've just started to watch an educational television show or movie, or when you need to study for an exam, or when you're involved in a newspaper article.

Others don't want you to face reality for any number of reasons. In the above situation, among many possible reasons, the partner may have self-esteem problems, a desire to maintain control, or a fear that if his insecure partner develops better self-esteem, she'll leave him. The bottom line is that if she continues to face the reality that her life in general and her relationship in particular has become dissatisfying, it will continue to have an impact on her partner.

If you make the decision to change how you see the world and become more realistic about your view as a result, it will be difficult, if not impossible, for the other person to continue to keep his or her reality intact. When one part of a system changes or shifts, the rest of the system cannot avoid changing and shifting in response. However, it is not your responsibility to keep everyone else's life—or even anyone else's life—in perfect balance, unchanged and unchanging. If the continuation of a relationship you're in (and this holds true for jobs, activities, and other major parts of your life) depends upon you remaining deeply dissatisfied with some aspect of your life, it's the wrong relationship for you.

Reality Rule and Obstacle #4

Facing Reality Requires Recognizing Reality First

If you can't recognize reality, you will have a far more difficult time embracing a more correct version. In other words, if you don't know how to recognize the "real" reality, you won't be able to *face* reality.

Imagine working for an Internet start-up company run by early-20-somethings. The atmosphere is intense and chaotic, and in many ways it's more like working in a dormitory than a business. You wear your favorite jeans with the ripped knees, T-shirts with slogans that no one over 30 would understand, and a baseball cap . . . and so does everyone else. When the high-tech market tanks, though, you find yourself out of work and going on interviews, hoping you'll get a job offer before you lose your apartment. With your skills, you can't understand why the offers aren't rolling in—until a former colleague tells you about her new job where she had to wear business suits before anyone began to take her seriously. You realize then that the odd looks you've gotten on interviews weren't because of any of the dozens of reasons you'd dreamed up; they were because you stuck out like the proverbial sore thumb. If you're going to create the change you need—in this case, getting a job, and fast—you're going to have to face reality. Those T-shirts will have to be relegated to the weekends.

A Final Note on Obstacles to Reality

Your personality is like a suit of clothes you wear, and people learn to recognize you by it. They identify you by what you do (your preferential activities) and by the choices you make and personality characteristics you exhibit (your preferential personality). When you begin making sweeping changes—which I encourage you to do, in all areas of your life that cause you dissatisfaction—those around you may well be baffled, angry, frustrated, or resistant as you become less predictable. As with each of the obstacles, this is not your responsibility. Others may well try to make it your problem, but you've got to understand that *it's their problem*. It's likely that at times you'll find yourself beginning to tailor your choices, opinions, and behaviors to what others seem to want from you, and to what others seem to find acceptable. However, when you do this, it keeps the "true you" under wraps and afraid to make the changes that are natural as you learn, experience, and grow. Your job, your goal, and your responsibility is to yourself, to creating the most satisfying life you can create. Though it can be hard to admit and even harder to accept, anyone who isn't cheering you on from the sidelines wasn't on your team in the first place.

These obstacles will present themselves as pressure from others, and you may find that at times this pressure will make you want to give up your experiment in growth. *Don't do it!* Do not allow any of these obstacles—or others—to slow down your search for reality. You are the only person who can "write your reality," and if you allow others to do so because of your fear of uncertainty or your fear of disapproval, you have given up on the magic and potential that fills you.

What are the benefits, though, of creating your own definition of reality, and facing it head-on? We've talked about many of the drawbacks: the pressure you will be exposed to by others, the uncertainty that will result when you make changes, and the ways in which others may deny your version of reality. While it's true that these obstacles exist, the payoffs are so powerful and so long-lasting that I can personally guarantee that if you develop a sense of trust in yourself and use that trust to form an unshakable view of what is true, the obstacles will fade from view like shooting stars. They won't last a second longer than those bits of backlit dust and debris in the night sky, and they'll leave no mark—perhaps just a distant memory—unless you allow them to.

Reality Reward #1

Facing Reality Is Easy

> O WHAT A TANGLED WEB WE WEAVE
> WHEN FIRST WE PRACTICE TO DECEIVE . . .
>
> ---
>
> *J. R. Pope*

While you may be among the few, the proud, the rare who have never told a lie, you've probably stretched the truth, at the very least, on occasion. If you're like most people, however, you have found yourself engaged in a full-scale whopper at some point, a complicated, tangled mess of details that started with a "simple" lie, perhaps even a lie you believed was intended to protect someone. I'll repeat what I've said before: The only person you're trying to protect when you lie is yourself. You may not want to deal with the other person's feelings, or you may want to cover up a mistake you made, but whatever the reason, you are the one being enrolled in the witness protection program. You know you did it, whatever "it" is, and you know you're not ready or willing to take the heat yet. The problem is, once you've told that first lie, you have a choice to make: either you admit it or you go along with it, creating yet more of a tangle. Many people make the second choice, unfortunately, and spend much of their lives bogged down in keeping their lies hidden.

However, *when you choose the truth, you choose simplicity, ease, and an end to that web of deceit, confusion, and negative feeling.* Facing reality is facing the truth about yourself, about your life, and about the way in which the universe operates.

Reality Reward #2

Facing Reality Removes Your Psychic Handcuffs

If you are committed to avoiding reality, you're also committed to avoiding a great many other things: people, events, interpretations, and feelings, as a start. Anything that does not correspond with your distorted view of reality is something you must assiduously avoid, and that makes for a complicated, difficult psychological existence.

On the other hand, if you accept the reality of not existing in a state of resistance, you're free to take whatever you encounter and, without wasting your energy on fighting what *is*, integrate it into that reality. This is far more productive, far more functional, and far more psychologically and emotionally gratifying than its reverse—resisting reality.

Reality Reward #3

Facing Reality Engenders Success

I know I'm about to make a sweeping claim here, but I can back it up with example after example from patients, friends, family members, colleagues, and my own life: *when you face reality, your life works better.* You become more successful professionally. Your relationships progress in intimacy, truthfulness, warmth, and satisfaction. Your creativity soars to new, unimagined heights. In fact, every area of your life, hidden and "out there," benefits from your commitment to existing in reality!

The reason this is true is that when you quit wasting time resisting *what is*, and when you give up the fight against the truth, you suddenly have untold energy left over, and it's available for devoting to all areas of your life. Your attitude improves, your sense of hopefulness increases, and your choices and behavior—essential to creating follow-through on that attitude change—fall in line with what *works*. The alternative—staying stuck in what doesn't work—may have been your unconscious choice over the years. Give this some thought. You may not want to acknowledge it, but I'm sure you've had your share of "stuck" moments through the years, just like the rest of us. Now, however, you're getting unstuck; you're freeing yourself from all of that wasted, clinging energy that went to denying reality, and you're jumping in—with both feet—to experience reality as it is. My promise is that although the water may seem cold at first, in no time at all you'll not only grow accustomed to it, but find it refreshing, energizing, and exciting.

Make Lots
of Mistakes

A STUMBLE MAY PREVENT A FALL.

English Proverb

Did you know that chocolate and potato chips are soothing brain food? Potato chips are believed to help alleviate depression because of their inter-action with the speed of your brain's processor.[1] Similarly, chocolate has a mild mellowing effect, among other benefits.[2] In a recent study some sub-jects were treated with Naltrexone, a drug that blocks any narcotic effects in the user.[3] Those taking Naltrexone soon stopped selecting chocolate from a range of food choices offered. The study suggested that without the psycho-logical boost provided by chocolate, there was minimal attraction remaining, even for confirmed chocolate lovers! If you're feeling low or in need of a rapid brain or mood boost, pop a piece of chocolate or crunch on a few chips—unless you have a condition that precludes it. It's a delicious way to feel better, as long as you don't overuse it!

BEING WRONG WON'T KILL YOU–
AND IT MAY MAKE YOU SMARTER

Let me venture a guess about how you and mistakes get along. If you're like most people, it's a rocky relationship. Mistakes are like friends with bad table manners: you're embarrassed when they come along, you feel guilty by association, and they seem to show up at the most inopportune times—often just as you're trying to appear at your smartest or look your smoothest. The similarities don't stop there, unfortunately. No one is immune, and yet you certainly *feel* alone when you're the one left cleaning up the mess left behind. It would seem logical that others could empathize, lessening your embarrassment, but instead you often see others scattering to the four winds as you try to explain or defend your mistakes: *Hey, that wasn't my fault!*

Let's face it: you have been socialized to view making a mistake as unseemly. In fact, it's even safe to say that there is a stigma attached. Make enough mistakes—or make just *one,* if it's a doozy—and you'll feel tremendous pressure from others, and from yourself, to either set things right rapidly or to sweep the mistake under the rug. This is because it is a human tendency—and foible—to view mistakes as inherently negative, harmful, and even shameful. For many people, unfortunately, setting things right doesn't necessarily mean resolving the situation while learning from it; instead, it means picking up the broken pieces, gluing them together as inconspicuously as possible, and hoping that no one notices the fragile results. Sweeping mistakes under the rug is ineffective, though, since nothing changes: not the situation that led to the mistake in the first place, and not the fallout that came about as the result of the mistake.

With the word *mistake* packing such heavy emotional artillery, the big surprise isn't that you try to avoid making mistakes, or that you sometimes avoid owning up to them if you can get away with it. What *is* remarkable is that you—or me, or the guy standing on the corner—ever try anything new, take the tiniest risk, or venture out onto the shortest limb in the first place, because it can feel so risky and scary. However, *avoiding mistakes is actually destructive to your well-being*—emotionally, intellectually, spiritually, and even physically. Once you start to go out on that limb and make mistakes, though, you can actually begin to experience your mistakes as positive, necessary, healing, functional . . . and, at times even fun!

I'm not alone in my beliefs about the positive role mistakes play in our lives. In fact, one of the preeminent psychologists in the world, Donald Super, conducted research for many years that supports this very contention. The information yielded by the study over the years offers valuable lessons in how we use mistakes to learn.[4]

Super found that in order for something to meet the true definition of being a mistake, *a negative outcome is necessary.* The research suggested that people who used their "mistakes"—outcomes that had traditionally been seen as negative—as part of their learning and decision-making process, tended to make better choices as a result. From this it followed that the choices you make and the outcomes that occur that allow you to discover *what you don't like* or *what you aren't good at* are *not* failures or mistakes—they are stepping-stones to eventual success. These *choices*—previously called *mistakes*—provide invaluable information upon which to base future decisions about your life. Super's findings remind me of the lament I heard from a 40-something dentist who, referring to himself, told me that "I should never have let an 18-year-old kid make a decision about my future career." That kid hadn't made enough "mistakes" to know what he really wanted.

Super could be seen as an advocate of "make lots of mistakes," though he may not have put it in those words. There are many other researchers and practitioners whose work reinforces the profound effect that our beliefs and emotions have on our willingness to make mistakes—and, consequently, on the outcomes of any number of life events. For instance, research conducted by Robert A. Josephs et al.[5] indicates that our decision making is influenced by the risk of experiencing regret; in other words, our fear of making a mistake influences the choices we make—including whether to take the risk at all. Because mistakes offer a surefire and rapid route toward learning and growth, when you avoid mistakes, you influence outcomes. One of the most significant ways in which you influence outcomes is by limiting your potential.

Underlying everything I say in this book, beneath each tool and each process, I am sending you the same message: The only way to learn and grow—the only way to realize your potential—is to take emotional and intellectual risks by making mistakes, and lots of them.

What you will ultimately discover as you explore your mistakes and examine your beliefs and behaviors related to mistake-making, is that mistakes are indeed stepping-stones to your full potential. This is a powerful incentive for *embracing* your mistakes—and even for making as many mistakes as possible!

Why, then, do so many people so assiduously try to *avoid* making mistakes? The answer is both simple and complex.

OBSTACLES

People avoid making mistakes for one or more of the reasons noted below. Understanding what is behind your avoidance will help you begin to embrace mistake making, which is the first step in benefiting from the tremendous learning—and experiencing the incredible growth—that can come from making mistakes.

OBSTACLES OF FEELING. You may feel fearful (of ridicule, embarrassment, and a host of other unpleasant, difficult emotions) about making mistakes. You also may feel angry at the lessons provided by the mistakes, frustrated if the lessons seem to require hard work on your part, or depressed if the lessons suggest that you haven't been successful at something you'd believed yourself successful. Regardless of the specific feelings brought up by mistakes, emotions can be obstacles. When you have a decision to make and suddenly find yourself resisting making the decision, dig beneath your resistance. You'll find emotions there, and until you address them, your resistance will continue and you won't be able to embrace the process of making mistakes—or benefit from their lessons.

OBSTACLES TO THINKING/PERCEPTION. We discussed myths and mistaken beliefs earlier in the chapter, and you undoubtedly have been exposed to—and possess—both. The way you think and the way you perceive mistakes can present an obstacle to learning from them. As with emotions, when you experience resistance to making a decision or solving a problem, dig deep: somewhere down there are the beliefs, sometimes faulty and often the root of resistance, that keep you from learning.

OBSTACLES OF ACTION. It may be that you don't have the skills, time, energy, or some other resource to make a decision or solve a problem. There are times when tangible obstacles present themselves, and, just like feelings and thoughts that interfere, these obstacles can stop you in your tracks. You may resist making mistakes because you know you will suffer as a result—for example, the boss will deny you a promotion or your spouse will get angry at you. Rather than allowing these real, worrisome obstacles to stop you, however, dismantle them piece by piece, breaking them down into their smallest parts until they are manageable—and scalable.

WHERE YOU'VE BEEN

Avoiding mistakes, while related to obstacles of emotion, intellect, and action, also has a deep connection to who you are and how you feel about yourself. The more fragile your positive feelings about yourself, the less likely you are to wholeheartedly welcome the immediate lessons—and long-term benefits—that come from making mistakes. Tafarodi and Swann conducted significant research that supports the idea of this connection.[6] They found a connection between feelings of self-liking/self-esteem and perceived (self-) competence. What they discovered was that the greater the sense of competence a person had, the better their sense of self-worth. Since mistakes are perhaps the primary way in which we gauge our competence, if you make lots of mistakes, you will begin to see yourself as incompetent, at least in the specific area in which the mistakes were made.

Your self-concept—the view you hold of yourself—is made up of your *own* perceptions of yourself, certainly, but it is also made up of the perceptions *others* have of you. When others communicate that they view you as lacking in some area, that view becomes a part of your view of yourself—and that affects *how you feel about yourself*. This is particularly true when it comes to making mistakes: you risk being seen as incompetent, unskilled, or lacking in confidence, for instance, when you try something new or difficult. This naturally opens the door to judgment from others (and from yourself), and it can therefore lead to an unfair and unfortunate downturn in self-esteem. It's a cycle. In its destructive aspect, experiencing this downturn, you buy into a negative belief that connects your competence to your self-worth. Or, in its positive aspect, the greater your competence, the better your sense of self-worth . . . and the greater your sense of self-worth, the greater your competencies.

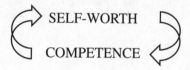

FIGURE 5-1

This cycle (see Figure 5-1) seems logical . . . and yet it's not. It can't be logical because of the results it creates: unless you are one of the rare few who succeed all of the time, you'll be caught in a cycle of ever-decreasing self-esteem. In order to reach the point where you embrace making mistakes, however, *you must first let go of the unconscious belief that this pattern and cycle is necessary and inevitable.* You must also abandon this related and self-limiting formula:

If you make mistakes you must be incompetent.
  If you are incompetent, you should feel badly about yourself.
    If you feel badly about yourself, you must *be* bad in some way.

Listen carefully: this logic is *faulty*. Mistakes don't make you a bad person anymore than successes make you a good one!

HOW YOU GOT HERE

It stands to reason that you view yourself more positively when you have the skills, knowledge, and other elements of competence that allow you to succeed at what you attempt. However, to *get to* that competence, few people move directly to success without first experiencing failures and mistakes. If you're afraid to take the scenic route through attempts and mistakes, you're going to miss a lot on your journey—and you may never arrive at your full potential. How did you come to believe in this cycle, when in practical terms it is so illogical and unworkable? And why do you hang on to it?

Myths and the Magic of Change

You have been socialized to believe certain things about mistakes and the results that come about when you make mistakes. We've discussed these fallacious beliefs or myths, and I've noted that they are unconscious. They can have a potent influence on your choices and behaviors—in fact, they perhaps have more of an influence *because* they are often unconscious. Let's look at a few of the most powerful myths about mistake-making and see if they don't feel familiar to you.

You're Stupid If You Make Lots of Mistakes

> MISTAKES ARE THE USUAL BRIDGE
> BETWEEN INEXPERIENCE AND WISDOM.
>
> ———————
>
> *Phyllis Theroux, "Night Lights," in Quotable Quotes*

I've said it already, so I'll make this brief: Competence—and its sidekick, intelligence—have an integral connection with mistake making. The more open you are to making mistakes—assuming you are equally open to learning from them and not making them repeatedly—the smarter you are. And the more open you are to learning from your mistakes, the more you will have an opportunity to grow. Eliminating this myth is really no more complicated than knowing this—and accepting it.

You promise to meet a friend for lunch but get busy and completely forget; when your friend calls halfway through the lunch hour, she's furious since this is not the first time you've done this. In the past when you've made a mistake, you've tended to beat yourself up about it, telling yourself—and anyone else who will listen—how stupid you are. It never seems to resolve the situation, but you've always figured that it at least showed your regret. Now you apologize, but you don't berate yourself privately or to your friend. Instead, you empathize with how she must feel—unimportant? foolish?—and you promise her that you will figure out why you allow this to happen so it doesn't happen again. Then, you *keep* your promise. Shooting yourself in the foot repeatedly isn't a good thing—and making promises without delivering is shooting yourself in the foot.

It's a Bad Move to Admit to Your Mistakes

This myth is tied up with self-concept. We discussed that self-concept comes about through a merging of your own perceptions of who you are with the perceptions others hold of you. It's natural, then, to experience a desire to hide what you perceive as your lesser self from others. Natural, yes, but helpful? Decidedly not! The only way to be truly known by another is to share who you are in totality, rather than sharing an edited version of the authentic you. In order to learn from mistakes, you have to let go of the embarrassment and the sense that mistakes—and their fallout—must be kept hidden from view. As long as you allow yourself to experience shame when you make a mistake, you will avoid making mistakes . . . and this will limit your potential for learning.

You send work to a client, knowing that it contained confidential background information, but forgetting to delete it. In the past you might have simply stayed silent. Now you inform your supervisor so that she knows she needs to plan a response. And instead of wasting energy hiding the truth, you use that energy to figure out how and why you made this mistake and how to make sure it doesn't happen in the future.

Mistakes Are Embarrassing

Sure, mistakes *can* be embarrassing. We've all said something foolish, whether by accident or from a Freudian slip or for some other reason, and everyone has had that first week on the new job where everything you do seems like a mistake. The fallacy here is that mistakes *must* be embarrassing, which is simply not true. Embarrassment is a question of mind-set, and you can choose to *reframe* anything, including a mistake, in order to see it in a positive, productive light. Reframing, in fact, is something we psychologists teach people to do all the time.

You're introduced to a woman who has a slightly rounded belly, and in an attempt to make conversation, you congratulate her on her pregnancy. Her expression changes to one of irritation as she says she isn't pregnant. Now, rather than berating yourself for saying too much, you apologize and say that you noticed the glow on her face from across the room and just assumed she was expecting. Suddenly she is beaming.

Mistakes Always Cost You Something

Exchange theory is a psychological principle that comes from economic theory and concerns interpersonal relationships. In essence it says that in every relationship there are rewards and costs, and we will continue in the relationship as long as the rewards outweigh the costs.[7] How you define "costs" and "rewards" is highly individual. For one person, being alone is the highest imaginable cost; for another, the costs associated with being in a dissatisfying relationship far outweigh the costs of being alone. When it comes to making mistakes, the same balancing act is true. The short-term costs of making a mistake can often obscure the longer-term value of the mistake: the learning, the growth, and the increase in self-esteem, for instance, that ultimately may result from having made—and learned from—the mistake.

After a particularly rough time in your relationship, you and your partner are at each other's throats about even small issues. You find yourself in a conflict about something small and silly, but the argument escalates until it is about every major issue that exists between you: responsibility, honesty, and fidelity are all on the table, even if not consciously so. Your partner triggers deep hurt, a sense of betrayal, and outraged anger in you by confessing to an affair. You lose your temper and slap your partner's face. You've never hit anyone and never even imagined that you could do such a thing. As soon as it occurs, you feel regret, embarrassment, and a deep sense of shame. Now, with your heart racing from the extreme emotion, you take several deep breaths to try to regain your equilibrium. You instantly apologize—and continue to do so repeatedly—as you tune in to how you feel. Your regret tells you that you wish you hadn't slapped your partner—and so you share this out loud, to very little response. Your embarrassment tells you that you are aware of how out of line your behavior was—and so you not only share this with your partner, but also spend time focusing on how to be more constructive with your anger in the future, regardless of what provoked it. Your shame tells you that you do not approve of your behavior or your lack of control. You ask your partner what you can do to try to show your regret and shame. For now, your partner has no answer for you, and perhaps the best thing you can do is to live with the feelings for a time, as a reminder of the depth of the mistake you've made and its fallout. At some point you and your partner may decide to agree on a "signal" that indicates that things are getting too hot and that you need to cool down. Two brains are many times better than one when it comes to learning new behaviors.

The most productive step you can take when you make a mistake is to choose to interpret the mistake as a neutral experience, even if at first it more closely resembles an experience layered with feelings of foolishness, frustration, or disappointment. When you make a mistake, you open up space for learning and you tend to withdraw, simultaneously. Instead of using this space as an opportunity to berate or criticize yourself, you can use it as a time to reevaluate the choices you made and examine other possible solutions, choices, and feelings. *Use the withdrawal as a chance to focus on what you can learn from the mistake.* Awareness of any tendency to criticize yourself can be reframed as an opportunity to replace self-criticism with self-supporting messages.

ROOTS

As you were growing up, you formed beliefs about what defined mistakes and why you should avoid making them. You formed these beliefs in large part because of two types of messages you heard when you made mistakes— messages from within and messages from others—and because of the modeling you observed as others made mistakes. Your beliefs about mistakes were further instilled in you by beliefs you developed that became part of your psychological makeup, defining features of who you are and how you choose to behave.

Messages and Modeling

Whether the messages come from within or are delivered by an outside source, they can be a potent force in influencing our behavior. As a child, you heard feedback almost constantly, and it was probably both positive and negative, but it's likely that most of what you heard when you made mistakes was negative, regardless of how kind or understanding your parents were. Whether you heard that you were embarrassing yourself or your parents, annoying them, or simply costing them time or energy—even if it was energy they were glad to expend—you received messages that influenced your view of mistakes. As you read the case study following, imagine hearing the messages given to this man, a client I worked with for several months in therapy:

Jim was seeking a solution to his long-term lack of a relationship. He was attractive and had a good job, so there had to be another reason. Rapidly, the picture became clear. Jim's terrible self-esteem kept others from admiring him; he criticized himself so often and so soundly that it was hard for new acquaintances to develop a liking for Jim. Though I rarely encourage spending much time discussing childhood—I'd rather focus on now and the future and improvements to both—we talked a bit about Jim's upbringing. His mother and father were perfectionists, and they were generous with criticism when Jim made mistakes. Whether he missed the bus or a basket on the basketball court, they always told him how incompetent he was. Once, Jim's mother was driving him somewhere and backed into a light pole; he listened later as she told his father an elaborate tale about another driver hitting her and then rushing away. On another occasion, Jim's father, a lawyer, forgot a filing deadline and almost lost his job over it; things were tense until he had successfully convinced a senior partner that it was the fault of a now-unemployed paralegal.

Jim's beliefs were formed early and powerfully, first by the messages he received from his mother and father, and then by the modeling his parents provided when they made their own mistakes and attempted to hide and deny them. Jim learned to accept the myth that connects making mistakes with incompetence and even worthlessness, and he learned that mistakes are a source of shame and should be hidden and never owned up to. These lessons soon taught Jim to send similar messages to himself: he would tell himself, *I'm no good, no woman will ever want me,* and so on. It's no wonder that Jim had difficult finding or maintaining a long-term relationship—and it's also no wonder that Jim, as I soon discovered, avoided trying new approaches and taking risks.

Think about the messages you received when you made mistakes as a child. Your training in how to perceive mistakes would have started early, as early as you can recall. Whether you were criticized for bed wetting or ostracized for incorrectly using a big new word you'd just heard, you listened and learned, and those lessons are still with you today, influencing the freedom you feel to make choices. Did they call you "stupid" when you made a mistake?

Examine too how the people around you handled mistakes. If your mother hid her mistakes or your father routinely denied his, these will be clues to your own tendencies today. Such early lessons are powerful ones, but are often buried in the subconscious mind. However, by identifying them, you can extract them, examine them, and rid yourself of their limiting and even destructive effects.

Messages and modeling are not the sole influences on the freedom you feel to make choices and take risks. You can also be influenced by your own psychological makeup, the beliefs, values, attitudes, emotions, and the like that make you who you are, different from anyone else.

In the seventeenth century the philosopher John Locke wrote an essay on the kinds of people who have mistaken opinions.[8] Locke said that there are three basic factors that contribute to these faulty opinions. Although I have modified them over the years as I applied them to mistake making, Locke's ideas provide an excellent jumping-off point for our discussion.

Locke's theories help us to look at how certain elements in your psychological makeup influence the likelihood that you will make mistakes; that these personality features say something about the risks you're willing to take; and that they say something about the mistakes you're willing to make.

You Don't Think for Yourself

When you don't think for yourself, you allow others to influence you; you model your behaviors, thoughts and choices after others' rather than coming up with your own solutions and decisions; and you don't intellectually work through the potential consequences and outcomes of your decisions. As a result, you are far more likely to make mistakes than is someone with a mind of his or her own. You will use others' solutions for your problems, a surefire way to ensure failure much of the time. You will also apply others' thinking to your own situations, with the same result: a failure in originality and individualization that can't help but result in mistakes.

At the same time, however, because you're afraid of or uncomfortable with thinking for yourself, you are less likely to embrace mistake making as the opportunity that it is. Far better to rely on the *tried-and-false solutions* you've always used, even though they are miserably ineffective, than to risk your own mistakes. At least if it's someone else's solution you can blame the failure on them. Does the phrase "But we've *always* done it that way" sound familiar?

Without the willingness to risk mistakes, you close yourself off to learning, and although no one has purely positive feelings about learning things the hard way through mistakes, sometimes it's the best—or only—way to absorb your lessons.

*You Allow Emotion and Need to Dominate Thinking and Logic . . .
or the Reverse*

People sometimes say that a person is "unbalanced" when they mean that he or she is exhibiting symptoms of a mental illness. I use the term differently. To me, to be unbalanced is to overdevelop and overuse one significant aspect of the personality. For instance, if you are rational, stoic, and committed to keeping your feelings under lock and key—all hallmarks of the traditional socialization of men in our society—regardless of the demands of the situation, I would consider you unbalanced. Or if you are emotional, relationship-oriented, and feeling-excessive in every context—again, hallmarks of traditional socialization, but for women—regardless of the requirements of that context, I would also say you are unbalanced. In other words, your personality is out of balance; there is too much of one thing and not enough of another.

Life is full of a richness of experiences and challenges, and each one requires subtle shifts in how you respond. If you have no subtlety in your range of response—being unable to be soft when softness is required, or unable to be tough when toughness should rule the day—you're bound to make more mistakes than you otherwise would. By being unable to adapt to the special demands of each situation, you guarantee maladaptive responses—otherwise known as mistakes. What you *do* with these mistakes is the essential issue: if you use them to learn and adapt your behavior, you're doing exactly what you need to do. If you avoid facing your mistakes, don't take responsibility for them, or refuse to learn from them, you create a repetitive, ineffective, and maladaptive pattern of behavior, one to which you will return time and again.

You Expose Yourself to Only One Viewpoint

Similar to—and certainly including—the difficulties created by not thinking for yourself, exposing yourself to just one viewpoint limits you, as well. Imagine that it's ten P.M. and a stranger is knocking at your door. Your typical viewpoint is that the world is a friendly, kind, and safe place, one in which you can be assured that others will treat you well. If you don't consider other views before you open the door—for instance, that perhaps suspicion or care are in order—you may well be in for trouble. Or let's suppose that you see yourself as the golden child at the office, the one who will always succeed. You probably hold this view because you were always the favored child at home; in your mother's eyes, you could do no wrong—no matter how much wrong you actually did. You're going to run into major difficulty in the workplace if you ignore the signs that say your hold on perfection is slipping. When the boss no longer gives you the plum assignments, your colleagues don't seem as friendly toward you anymore, and your last performance appraisal was markedly poorer than previous ones, it's time to consider an alternate view.

One reason to avoid limiting yourself to a single viewpoint is that it often comes from someone else and is inadequate and inappropriate for your life. Perhaps you've chosen to subscribe to this viewpoint because it is held by someone you admire, someone who seems to have everything under control. We all know a person like this, and it's understandable to want to borrow their coping mechanisms, their attitudes and beliefs, even their ways of interacting with others—in order to achieve the same results they're getting. There are flaws to this approach, however, as I'm sure you can imagine. What you're seeing is at least partly illusion. Sure, some people have a better handle on their lives than others, and some people have developed ways that leave the appearance that they don't make mistakes, but *appearance* is the key word here. Mistakes are part of the human experience, and either you're making mistakes or you're lying about not making mistakes. Mr. Perfect and Ms. Got-It-All-Handled are no more immune than you and I to the vagaries of life. Another possibility is that they've learned how to embrace making mistakes. If that's the case, you can learn how they handle their mistakes: how to gracefully take the lessons out of mistakes and move forward.

Another reason to avoid approaching life from a single viewpoint is that, although it may be an amalgam of others' views and your own perceptions, the drawbacks are no less significant than if you drew your views solely from another person. If you subscribe to just one viewpoint, regardless of its genesis, you are still more likely to make a greater number of mistakes, since no single, rigid, and limited point of view—regardless of how all-encompassing you may believe it to be—can possibly cover the vast number and variety of experiences you encounter. Going into every situation with a standard M.O.—modus operandi, or method of operation—and a standard mind-set means going into every situation with a handicap. Then, as with the previous two personality features, a single viewpoint creates the mistake-risk-resistance paradox I discussed above.

A third drawback to the single viewpoint is that it inhibits creativity. In part because you simply won't see the vast options available to you since your perception is limited, and in part because you will rule out many of the options that *do* appear when they don't fit with your mind-set, you will approach situations from a narrow perspective. What gives mistake-making much of its richness and potential for learning, though, comes about during the discovery process that results from mistakes. If you approach them from a stance of narrow, limited thinking, you will solve them in the same way. In contrast, if you come at mistakes and their solutions from an open stance in which you're willing to take risks and see things you haven't seen before, the opportunities are correspondingly huge. When you make mistakes, you can learn things you didn't know, try things you've never experienced, and become someone larger than you were—but only if you embrace mistakes with openness to change and risk.

The bottom line is this: a single viewpoint limits your perceptual field, while a larger perceptual field increases the range and number of choices available to you.

WHY THE OLD WAYS DON'T WORK

By now I hope you believe, as I strongly do, that it is not beneficial to constantly focus on not making mistakes. To do so limits the options open to you and blocks the learning process. We've now talked at some length about the inhibiting effects of running from mistake-making and the fact that avoiding mistakes limits your creativity in problem-solving. To summarize, however, and to emphasize the importance of this point, I want to throw in a few more reasons for embracing mistakes. I suspect you'll recognize some of them.

Without Mistakes ...

Life Is Bland, Predictable, and Boring

In this post–terrorist-attack world, safety has become central to many people, an issue discussed over the water cooler and dinner table alike. We worry about whether we can protect our loved ones and ourselves, and we talk about the emotional fallout from the events of September 11, 2001. You may view your thinking before that day as a mistake, just as you may view your thinking before any traumatic event or crisis as mistaken, as if your inability to predict difficulty somehow caused it. Maybe you've heard someone say something along those very lines. For instance, perhaps you've heard something like, "We let our guard down, and now we're paying for it," or, "We weren't prepared and it cost us thousands of lives and our sense of security." I have, and I know that what's really being said is that, collectively as a country, we made mistakes. Perhaps we did, but the real issue is that the *perception* that we made mistakes is being used by some to retreat into a stance of fear and guarded self-protection.

The fact is, you can live *too* safe a life. Whether the danger lies in terrorism or love, you can protect yourself right *out* of a life. Surely someone living in an underground shelter to avoid biological warfare doesn't have much of a life. Nor does someone who won't fall in love because it might hurt too much if the relationship ends. In effect, you've put yourself into an emotional deep freeze. Is there only *one someone* for everyone? I don't think so— but there will be no opportunity to learn from your mistakes in the earlier relationship and find a new, more compatible partner if you won't venture out from behind the screen of fear.

We all know people who live with this kind of fear, and it's a sad sight to behold. At its worst, this kind of fear of making a mistake freezes you into inaction; it results in a boring, bland life.

Relationships, Experience, Distancing, and Disconnection

It is simply not possible to develop true, deep intimacy with another if you're crouched in a position of self-protection. Guarded against the dangers of feeling hurt or loss ensures that you can't experience love or connection; we're not given the option of straining experiences for only the positive feelings and outcomes, as if we had a colander and were holding back the painful experiences. Kahlil Gibran said this beautifully in *The Prophet* as he talked about the inseparable nature of joy and sorrow.

Your joy is your sorrow unmasked.
And the selfsame well from which your laughter rises
was oftentimes filled with your tears.
And how else can it be?
The deeper that sorrow carves into your being, the more joy you can contain.
Is not the cup that holds your wine the very cup that was burned
in the potter's oven?[9]

In order to connect and feel love deeply, you must be willing to risk disconnection and sorrow, and this means being open to making the mistakes that are an inevitable part of life in general and relationships specifically. That you must take risks may not seem fair, but that's life—and so is this.

There Are No New Answers or Creative Solutions to Anything

Although I've already discussed this in some detail, I want to emphasize again that resistance to making mistakes inhibits creativity and new solutions and, in fact, actually brings the process of discovery and learning to a screeching halt. Mistakes offer a doctoral degree in living and on-the-job-training for life—but you cannot learn if you won't do the course work.

There Is an Unnecessary Ceiling on Success

You've heard the saying "The sky's the limit." Well, the sky is far closer to earth for those who are unwilling to make mistakes. Just as the greatest winners on the stock market are those who sometimes take tremendous risks, the biggest winners in life—whether you're talking about your employment, your love life, or some other aspect of living—are those who embrace risk. So, give the Chicken Little philosophy a rest. The sky is not falling.

MOVING FORWARD

Your fears, your wish not to appear foolish, your desire to seem on top of things—*whatever* inspires you to avoid making mistakes—is sometimes complex, sometimes simple, sometimes a bit of both. Now that you understand what's holding you back, though, it's "crunch" time—time to let go of the obstacles and embrace the process of change. You don't have time for excuses, for tentative steps, for maybes or "I don't wannas": If you're going to succeed at learning and growing, it's time to move forward, and it's time to do it now. How to proceed? Now that you know where you are with *not* making mistakes, let's figure out where you stand on *making* them.

ASSESSMENT TOOL

Select the choice in each scenario that sounds most like you. Then record the score in the parenthesis on the right of the scenario in the space at the left of the scenario.

MISTAKES AND MIX-UPS: AND SO . . .

You attend a black-tie awards banquet for people in your field, and you are seated with seven strangers at a small round table. Among other utensils there are six forks at each place setting, and although you know each one has a special use, you don't know which one is for which course. When the first course, a salad, is served, you pick up your fork and begin to eat. A colleague across the table comments that you've got the wrong fork, and so you:

____ Feel stupid and embarrassed and rapidly switch to the fork others are using, hiding the used fork in a napkin so it won't be a reminder to you or the others of your mistake. (1)

____ Deny that you have the wrong fork, insisting that you're right, and perhaps even coming up with justification (i.e., "This is how it's done in Europe"). (3)

____ Casually switch forks but make a note to observe which forks go with which courses so you will know this etiquette in the future. (2)

____ Continue to use the same fork you started with and tell yourself and others at the table that it doesn't matter. (4)

Your mother is visiting over the holidays and confides in you that she has been unhappy in the marriage to your father for some time. You share this information with your sibling, who promptly calls your mother, distraught to hear this. Your mother comes to you feeling betrayed and angry at the breach of confidentiality, and so you:

____ Apologize and promise not to share confidential information again, after discussing what troubled your mother about you sharing this with your sibling, so you can understand when to share things and when not to do so. (2)

____ Swear that you weren't the one who told your sibling, and, if necessary, come up with alternative theories for how your sibling found out (i.e., "Maybe she sensed it"). (3)

____ Berate yourself for hurting your mother and promise you won't ever share another word she tells you, although you don't really understand why this upset her. (1)

____ Continue to share whatever information you want to with your siblings and others since your mother is overreacting. (4)

(continued)

You are taking an adult education course, and one night in class the instructor asks everyone to get out an assignment. One by one the students begin reading the assignments aloud at the teacher's request. You soon realize that you've done the wrong assignment, and so you:

_____ Continue to operate in the same way in the class, telling yourself that it's not that important anyway and that many instructors won't even notice. **(4)**

_____ Approach the instructor after class to show her your essay, explaining that you misunderstood the assignment and are requesting time to do it correctly, and then figure out how you made this mistake so that you don't repeat it. **(2)**

_____ Mentally kick yourself for being so stupid and quickly throw together a short essay like the ones others are reading. **(1)**

_____ Say you forgot the assignment, or read your essay when it's your turn and then deny that it's not right if the subject is raised, explaining that you simply had a different interpretation. **(3)**

Your partner asks you to bring home carryout for dinner, but it's rainy and cold by the time you leave work and you don't stop for food. When you arrive home, your partner is angry about having to deal with making dinner, and so you:

_____ Go out to pick up carryout or order food to be delivered, and give some serious thought as to why you didn't keep your agreement in the first place so you won't continue having similar conflicts. **(2)**

_____ Admit to your partner that you're insensitive and thoughtless, and go out to get the carryout, all the while muttering to yourself that it wouldn't have killed your partner to have ordered delivery or to have cooked something for a change. **(1)**

_____ Refuse to get the food or solve the problem and tell yourself your partner is being unreasonable. **(4)**

_____ Say you misunderstood and thought your partner was picking up carryout, or deny that you made the promise that you'd handle the meal. **(3)**

Your supervisor asks you to relay a message to a colleague, which you forget to do. When the supervisor realizes this, she approaches you and asks if you failed to deliver the information as she requested, and so you:

_____ Tell yourself what an idiot you are and how likely it is that you're going to be fired any day, and try to identify things your supervisor needs done to make it up to her. **(1)**

(continued)

___ Tell your supervisor that you did relay the message, and even offer fabricated "proof" if necessary to convince her. **(3)**

___ Apologize, taking responsibility for the mistake, and let your supervisor know that you will do what's necessary to avoid a repeat of the mistake. **(2)**

___ Pretend to acknowledge the mistake in order to get out of the situation but don't give it further thought since your supervisor probably won't notice if you do, anyway. **(4)**

You are at a shop and get in a line to check out with your purchases. Another shopper approaches you, irritated, and says that there is only one line serving all of the registers and you've cut in front of several people, and so you:

___ Defiantly stay in the line, telling yourself that you don't know the other shoppers anyway and it was a genuine mistake and since you've spent time waiting too, you shouldn't have to move. **(4)**

___ Insist that you've been waiting as long as anyone else and refuse to move. **(3)**

___ Apologize and explain that you simply didn't understand, and move to the back of the other line. **(2)**

___ Feel ashamed and embarrassed, knowing you look rude—even though it was a genuine mistake. You go to the back of the single line, avoiding eye contact with any of the other shoppers. **(1)**

You are standing around the coffee machine with several colleagues, listening to gossip about another coworker, when you realize that the coworker being gossiped about has come into the room unobserved and heard some of the gossip, and so you:

___ Step away from the group, apologize privately, and promise yourself that you won't participate in gossip again, even as a passive participant. **(2)**

___ Feel embarrassed, guilty, and stupid, emotions you will recall and experience again throughout the day. You quit gossiping, not really seeing any harm in it but not wanting to feel as bad again. **(1)**

___ Insist that your coworker misinterpreted what he or she heard and/or deny that you were participating even passively, perhaps by saying you were defending them. **(3)**

___ Stay with the crowd and resume gossiping once the coworker has left, telling yourself that it's harmless. **(4)**

(continued)

You're in a huge hurry one afternoon when you run to the market, and you park in the loading lane directly in front of the store. Another shopper knocks on your window as you prepare to leave after returning to your car, and begins to berate you for your rude and thoughtless behavior, and so you:

____ Deny that people aren't supposed to park where you are parked, insisting that it's fine—everyone does it—if you're just running in for a quick purchase. **(3)**

____ Apologize, acknowledging that you made a mistake in choosing to park in the loading zone. Then you think about why you did it, and you figure out a better plan for the future. **(2)**

____ Refuse to acknowledge the other shopper's complaint and continue to park in front of the store when you're in a hurry. **(4)**

____ Feel like an insensitive jerk, just as the other shopper suggested, and move your car quickly, wanting to get away from the situation and the other shopper. **(1)**

SCORING AND INTERPRETING THE MISTAKES AND MIX-UPS SCALE

Instructions: You should have a check mark next to one of the responses to each of the eight scenarios. A number from 1 to 4 follows each response. To find your score, add up these numbers. Then, find the range below into which your score fits.

8 to 13:   The Ashamed Conformist
You tend to berate yourself to others and to yourself because you subscribe to the belief that making mistakes means you are bad, stupid, incompetent, or a collection of these negative and destructive terms. You also tend to change your behaviors and thinking rapidly in order to match the behavior others are exhibiting. You do this in order to avoid feeling the destructive emotions just mentioned, and to avoid being seen as a lesser person than those around you. You need to put serious energy into rewriting your belief system about mistakes, eliminating your near total buy-in with the myths surrounding making mistakes.

14 to 19: The Student
While you often change your behaviors to match those others are exhibiting, you do so out of politeness, a desire to observe simple rules of etiquette, or a wish to practice new behaviors you have

(continued)

learned from others. You recognize that there will always be others who have more skill or knowledge than you do in certain areas, and you're comfortable with the idea that you aren't perfect. Likewise, you're comfortable making mistakes—as a result, you tend to make mental notes when you realize you've made a mistake, so you can learn why you made the choices you did in the first place and how to handle the situation more effectively in the future.

20 to 25: The Rebel Without a Cause

You've learned that mistakes are critical errors of judgment or events that cast you in a highly unfavorable light, and so you're quick to make attempts at hiding the mistakes—or the fallout from the mistakes—that you make. You also have a tendency to deny your mistakes, even when it's clear that you've been discovered. One form these denials take is an insistence that you're right and the other is wrong, even when your insistence flies in the face of logic or proof. The unfortunate result of these tendencies, of course, is that you don't allow yourself the opportunity to learn from your misjudgments. You can also damage trust, since others often know when your denials are false, and you can waste precious energy hiding the results of your mistakes rather than learning and moving on.

26 to 32: The Defendant

You are uncomfortable with making mistakes, but your tendency is to strike a stance of resistance and defensiveness. You tend to continue to exhibit the mistaken behavior as a way of denying its truth and insisting on your rights to behave as you wish. As a Defendant, you differ from the Rebel in that you won't openly argue that you're right, nor will you hide the behavior, as the Rebel often does. Instead, you proudly continue to exhibit the mistakes (even as you experience embarrassment and shame inwardly, knowing that you're wrong). You get around these feelings of discomfort by telling yourself and others that either the mistake or the correct behavior or attitude doesn't matter to begin with. The Defendant and Rebel do share one significant similarity, however: both experience the harmful psychological and interpersonal effects that result from resisting mistakes and denying their existence.

WHERE YOU ARE NOW

Now that you have identified your individual tendency when it comes to embracing or resisting mistakes and making mistakes, let's look briefly at what happens to the lessons that offer themselves to you when you make mistakes. There are just four basic ways in which you respond to the information mistakes provide to you. Remember, a mistake occurs in a context—some situation comes along requiring a choice on your part, and then you are in a position to make mistakes. Whether you make the "right" choice or a mistake is largely immaterial, because either way, you are being handed valuable information about how to handle this situation—and others, almost undoubtedly—in the future. With that in mind, consider taking the information you receive from a "right" choice or a mistake and you:

Ignore It

If you choose to ignore the lessons being offered to you, you will continue on the path you've been on, eventually creating a larger problem in time, with the situation unresolved or the problem unabated. In a sense, you ultimately become smaller than the situation or problem; like a wound allowed to go untreated, the problem festers and infects you systemically. A situation of just this sort with a former client comes to mind.

Moira was a good student in high school, a fair student in college, and now she wanted to earn an MBA. A university near her home had given her conditional acceptance, meaning she had to maintain a certain average or she would not be fully accepted. Her problem began with the first paper she wrote for a class she was taking as an elective. The professor had given her an F, and Moira was more than distraught. She went to the instructor after class, crying that she didn't deserve that grade, saying she'd worked hard and spent hours in the library, giving up her weekends to finish it in time. The professor, who used a special software package that uncovered plagiarism, told her the paper was "nothing more than a cut-and-paste job" and refused to change the grade. Moira found him cold, insensitive, and rigid.

We discussed the problems; was it the paper or the professor or Moira's work habits? She admitted that she hadn't given herself enough time to do the research, although she had spent hours in the library—only those hours took place the day before the paper was due. She also acknowledged that she had selectively included sections from papers she'd found in an on-line website. "But," she said, "I've always worked this way and I've never had this problem before." I asked her if she'd always relied on the work of others for her papers, and she said, "Sometimes I have more than other times." Moira came to realize that this wasn't the way to an MBA, and an F grade had to be the turning point toward better planning and more individual effort. This wasn't the professor's problem—he was doing his job; Moira had ignored hers, and she needed to admit that and learn from her own history. The professor, the software package, and the new technology all forced Moira to see and to learn from her past mistakes. It was a matter of either learning from them or withdrawing from the university and forfeiting her plans for a better future. For too long she had ignored her sloppy school habits and just concentrated on getting by.

Downplay It

If, instead of ignoring the lessons being offered, you choose to downplay their benefit or significance after taking them in, you'll find yourself in a worse position, eventually, than if you took in and embraced the information offered by your mistakes. Downplaying lessons means straining out parts and taking what is most comfortable, perhaps even changing because of it, but only in ways that are not threatening—and that require little effort—and ignoring anything else the mistakes have to offer. In this case you will "survive" your situation or problem, but you certainly won't thrive; in fact, you will lose ground as a result of the mistake. Because you're picking and choosing your learning, rather than accepting the lessons as they are presented, you will not fully absorb the learning offered to you through your mistakes. I've worked with any number of people who chose this route—one in particular, Jason, comes to mind.

 Jason had a problem with what I called "fiscal responsibility," meaning he was always late paying his bills or found himself looking down the throats of bill collectors on a regular basis. Things were manageable, in his mind, as long as he could keep himself afloat. Don't worry, it's nothing, he would say to himself time and time again. He was able to do this until he landed a bank job where he was responsible for moving funds at specific times of the day or night. The bank earned significant sums from these "sweeps," and it depended on timely moves on the part of the employee in charge of this area. A new girlfriend, a night out with friends, and a new apartment had all kept Jason's mind elsewhere on the night the money was to move. Fortunately, the next day a supervisor was looking over the records from the night before and caught the error. The supervisor quickly moved the funds. Jason found his job in jeopardy and knew he had to find a way to resolve his problem. "I was lucky I didn't lose my job," he told me. "I can't afford to do the same things now."

Alter It

A third possibility is you choose to take in the information, just as you would before downplaying it, but instead of straining out the lessons for what's most palatable, you actually change the messages your mistake is sending to you. The result of doing so is that you will, at best, maintain your functioning or skills at their previous level, neither backsliding nor growing as a result of the challenge, problem, or situation you faced. Often the mistakes we make provide us with information about ourselves that is less than palatable. It's hard to hear that we're lacking in any way, and so it's a natural human tendency to want to change the messages we receive so they're more in line with our ideal view of ourselves. Unfortunately, doing so erases any possibility of growth or learning. You must take your lessons, just like your lumps, as they come. You've heard the phrase, coined by Friedrich Nietzsche, "What doesn't kill us makes us stronger," and surely learning about our foibles and flaws provides proof of this. Read what happened with Sierra, who chose to "rewrite" the messages her mistakes were trying to give her.

Sierra was on her way up the corporate ladder, or so she thought. She was young, very attractive, had a quick wit, and was sharp when it came to seeing ways to ingratiate herself with her bosses. The only problem, which she didn't see, was that when new projects were being distributed, she wasn't getting any. New projects meant chances for advancement, but Sierra told herself that they knew she was too busy with her current projects and couldn't take on new ones. "I'm never getting the really good, new ones," she lamented to me. "My projects are all almost done and I'm helping everyone else, so I guess they know I'm good and think the others really need my experience on their stuff." The problem was, Sierra wasn't getting new projects not because she was overworked, but because there was a feeling that she was an All About Eve type of woman who was looking to take someone else's corporate slot. The executives were giving her repeated signals that the door to the executive suite was closed for her, but she wasn't seeing the signals. Instead, she turned them into affirmations of her abilities. When a woman several years younger than Sierra got a promotion that Sierra thought should be hers, she finally knew she had a problem.

Embrace It

Finally, you may decide—as I've been urging—to embrace the lessons your mistakes offer to you. No other approach makes sense to me, although I understand, psychologically, why people choose not to embrace the sometimes painful, sometimes unpleasant, sometimes embarrassing truths about themselves. However, taking in, examining, and accepting the lessons offered by our mistakes is the surest, fastest route to becoming our best selves. Nothing else compares in speed or efficiency. Doing so requires open eyes, willing ears, and a strong heart. One client I worked with, Marion, learned how to embrace both her mistakes and the learning they offered; it was exciting to watch her as she made one new discovery after another about herself.

Marion was a young intern who always seemed to be efficiently running from one case to another in the hospital. Her efficiency, however, seemed to be based on her selection of cases, which included procedures she had done before. The chief of service knew that interns needed to have experience in many things, and it seemed that Marion was limiting herself. "My evaluations are suffering," she said. "I do everything right, but I'm having problems with the rest of the staff and the other interns." The breakthrough came for Marion when one of the head nurses took her aside and explained, as only head nurses can, that "you're hiding from your work and you're not learning." The nurse went down the litany of procedures Marion had avoided and the ones where she excelled. "Now, what kind of doctor are you going to make if you can't do all of the different procedures?" she was asked in the kindest yet sternest way possible. "I was upset that a nurse would have to tell me," she told me. "Why didn't my resident tell me, or someone else?" It rocked Marion sufficiently, however, for her to see that she was fooling no one and getting nowhere fast by avoiding the cases where she most needed experience. The next rotation saw a different Marion, one who was looking for challenges and willing to risk experiencing the feeling of not being perfect, which would ultimately make her the best doctor she could be.

MAKE LOTS OF R.E.A.L. MISTAKES

I want to offer one final set of ideas for "how to make lots of mistakes"—and how to make each one count. The process below is based on a foundation called "Paradoxical Intention,"[10] an approach used by psychologists to help people rid themselves of bad habits, whether those habits concern how they think, feel, or behave. In this context, the R.E.A.L. process can be used to help you quit avoiding mistakes out of fear, faulty thinking, or any other obstacle, so that you instead embrace mistakes as the rich opportunity for learning that they are.

Reframe the Experience

If you find yourself facing a problem, challenge, or decision, and also find yourself resisting its resolution because you might make a mistake, *Reframe the Experience* can help you overcome this resistance. Rather than seeing failure as a disaster, allow yourself to see it as a learning experience. Rather than viewing something difficult as impossible, see it as a challenge. And rather than accepting that mistakes are tragedies or disasters, let yourself see them as rich opportunities for experience. Identify what you fear. In this case, let's say you're a perfectionist and therefore fear making mistakes. Then allow yourself to experience that fear of making mistakes as a chance to let up on yourself, a chance to be imperfect. By doing so, you take a small step toward defusing the power of mistake-making. You will learn that simply *experiencing* the feelings and thoughts that result from making mistakes will not kill you. If you're neat, see neatness as a curse and sloppiness as a relief. While you're at it, let yourself be around people and places that are messy. If you're a slob, see sloppiness as a burden and neatness as a point of pride—and try hanging around other neat people and places to reinforce the experience. Again, the result will be reassuring; you will rapidly discover that the change is not so overwhelming, after all, which will open up new vistas for you in multiple areas. You will soon be able to try new things in not only the area you addressed, but in other arenas of your life. Remember too that *in this step, no one is asking you to change—at all*. I am simply asking you to explore the other side of the equation, and to change your perspective on the side you occupy presently.

Eliminate with Opposites

A second approach that I recommend is to *choose* behavior that is opposite the behavior you want to eliminate. This is similar to the Reversal technique but takes you a step further into *action*. In this step you will actually experience the opposite stance as a result of your choices and behaviors. If it seems essential to you to win, for instance, try coming in second—or last! I'm not suggesting that you purposefully lose, merely that you not put everything you are and everything you have into winning. It may help to first do a run-through of what will happen when you make this change (the world won't end, I assure you). How will you feel? What will the consequences be? The perfectionist can consciously choose to make more mistakes—as many as possible, in fact. The messy person can choose to keep a neat house, and the obsessively neat person can let things go a bit on his or her desk. The eventual familiarity with a range of experiences through these "practice sessions" at (or approaching) the opposite end of the behavior spectrum will make you far more likely to open up to change—and this includes changes in your openness to mistakes. This method also *attacks the fear* associated with the previous orientations.

Abandon the Goal

When you give up struggling for a goal that has become a central focus, an amazing thing often occurs: you reach that goal. This is frequently true when insomniacs stop trying to force themselves to fall asleep, and it is often true when couples having trouble conceiving a child quit making it their one focus. Allow yourself to deemphasize the importance of avoiding mistakes. Once your mind is off this goal, you're likely to find that mistakes don't hold the same power to intimidate.

Let Go and Learn

Some dreams are impossible, and I include in this the dream of being perfect. The fact is, you cannot *not* make mistakes. We all do, and the only difference that exists between you and the next guy is what you do with your mistakes. Why not be the one who turns his or her mistakes into gold? When you quit holding yourself to an unreachable standard, you can apply your energy to reasonable, realistic goals and plans. And when your energy is focused in a productive direction, you'll discover that the mistakes you do make yield far more—and far more useful—lessons for you.

CONCLUSION

Make lots of mistakes. It probably sounded like a strange title when you first saw it, and perhaps you wondered how anyone could possibly urge mistakes on someone else. Mistakes are possibility, opportunity, *a pathway to potential*. Make lots of mistakes: make them soon, make them often, and when you make them, *take* from them. When you do, you'll be amazed at the newfound opportunities.

Quit Whining

I HAVE ALWAYS DEPENDED ON THE
KINDNESS OF STRANGERS.

Tennessee Williams, A Streetcar Named Desire

At the supermarket, approach one person and ask where an item—rye, mayo, grapes, or anything else—is located. You may believe that the person will turn away or otherwise "diss" you, but the odds are you're wrong. You're far more likely to get a positive response—after all, most people like to be helpful, and you're limiting the request to something a person can easily assist with. As a result, you can almost guarantee that you'll walk away reaffirmed from having had a positive interaction with another person. This Quick Fix may sound overly simple—and it probably also sounds a bit dopey—but it is surprisingly powerful! Humans are motivated by three basic needs: the need for affection, the need for inclusion (or being connected to others), and the need for control, or creating the outcomes you want in your life. As simple as this Quick Fix sounds, and as easy as it is to execute, it meets all three basic needs. It feeds your hunger for basic human kindness, reinforces your connection with those around you, and affirms your ability to "manage" the world, even if it's just by getting someone to give you a kind answer. Rarely do you meet any of these needs often enough, let alone all three at once!

THERE'S MORE TO LIFE THAN SUFFERING— OR COMPLAINING

If you are like many people seeking personal growth and changes to their internal and external life, suffering and seriousness probably occupy some significant portion of each day. In Chapter Three we discussed the myth that therapy—and the learning and positive psychological shifts that ideally result from therapy—must be hard work and even painful. This chapter presents a set of skills that will allow you to permanently rid yourself of this faulty belief, and it also provides you with surefire methods for approaching the process of change with open arms and excitement. At the same time, the tools in this chapter will help you identify and eliminate the inhibiting, destructive, and downright annoying behavior of whining, which often accompanies challenges and change.

For a moment, think about how a three-year-old behaves. I'm sure you'll recognize this common scenario:

> It's six p.m. and the market is crowded with after-work shoppers, everyone hungry and hurrying to pick up something for dinner on the way home from the office. You're doing the same. The lines seem interminable, particularly because you've found yourself behind a mother with several young children; one is an infant, the other looks to be around three or four. The infant is fussing and trying to climb out of his carrier. The older child is asking for—and being denied—candy from the display that sits so conveniently next to the checkout counter, the perfect location for impulse purchases spurred by the exasperation of parents who can't take another moment's whining. When the mother persists in saying no, the child's expression turns to one of pure frustration. "Aw, *c'mon*, Mommy" she wheedles. When that doesn't work, she raises her voice and her pitch becomes higher as she whines, "Mommmy . . . pleassse." You see the mother rubbing her head as if an ache is beginning, and when the whining continues for another moment, you feel the start of a headache too. The greater the intensity of the child's whining, the stronger your urge to throw yourself on the floor and have a pity party for having to listen to this after you've worked hard all day. Some parents just don't have any sense— or thoughtfulness about others—bringing their kids to the market at this time of day. This is so unfair to you!

Was I right—did it sound familiar? Who among us hasn't witnessed or been an unhappy part of this unpleasant scene? If you read it again, however, and look closely at the feelings it evokes for you, you might notice a belief running through your feelings: the belief that *life is supposed to go the way you want it to go*. That fallacy is at the core of whining. When we allow our-

selves to believe that life should be fair, that things should work out well—
and a whole host of other "shoulds"—we create an atmosphere that supports
whining when the shoulds turn into "didn'ts" and "don'ts" and "cannots."

The child who cannot (or may not) have that candy is upset, and indicating it because she believes she should be given what she wants. It's a typical
delusion of three-year-olds. The 13-year-old who wants to stay out until two
A.M. with friends and is denied that privilege is angry because he believes he
should be allowed to make his own choices. The 23-year-old who wants to
move back in with Mom and Dad and not pay rent is frustrated because she
believes that the world should grant her wishes and meet her every expectation—and yet the world is not doing so. On and on it goes for some people
into each subsequent decade, with a narcissistic view of the world—a "me-
centered" view—determining their response to every situation. And beneath
that narcissistic belief system is the fallacy that life is always supposed to
cooperate with you fully.

In your logical moments, you know that whatever has overriding gover-
nance over life, it isn't you (or me, or any other individual), much as we
might believe that at times. I don't pretend to know who or what *does* play
that role—some people say God, others say fate, while still others say they
don't know. I *do* know that while we have tremendous power over the individual choices we make and many of the specific outcomes that occur in our
lives, we're not in charge of the big picture. A dump truck runs a red light
and broadsides your Volkswagen Beetle, even when you don't want it to do
so. It rains on your wedding day. The worst stomach flu you've ever had
appears on the afternoon of the biggest date you've ever planned. You get the
picture—and you know it's true. Some things are beyond our control, and
when you resist accepting that fundamental truth, you create the ideal climate for whining to take root and flower. This climate is built on a foundation of self-pity.

PITYING OTHERS AND BEING PITIED

Pity is ugly, whether it comes from you or you're the recipient. When someone pities you, there is a one-up/one-down dynamic involved, and the same
is true, of course, when you pity someone else. You *cannot* pity someone, in
fact, without feeling sorry for them. Feeling sorry for someone then evokes
feelings of *superiority* in the person doing the pitying and feelings of *inferi-
ority* in the person being pitied. This is hardly the way to create or sustain a
positive relationship, which can't truly exist without equality.

Think for a moment about which people or groups of people you pity. The homeless? The poor? Those who are suffering a chronic, debilitating illness? In each case, the person *has* less—or is even seen as *being* less—in the eyes of the person doing the pitying. In other words, pity says: "That couldn't be me . . . nor would I want it to be."

Pity, then, carries with it a rider saying that you could not possibly be in the same situation. Some of that belief stems from the very human and understandable desire to distance yourself from what frightens you. The stark, hopeless sight of homelessness is scary, and the misery of abject poverty and serious illness is no less so.

Rather than coming from a stance of empathy and saying, "There but for the grace of God go I," when you feel pity, you say, "That couldn't possibly be me, *because . . .* " and then you fill in the remainder of the sentence with whatever line of reasoning works. *That couldn't be me because I'm stronger. That couldn't be me because I'm smarter. That couldn't be me because . . . I'm more responsible.* It's a far leap from pity to empathy, in which you identify with another's feelings, putting yourself in their shoes; the distance between the two contains a whole host of requirements that feed into a cycle of whining.

When you consciously or unconsciously request pity, in effect you're saying, "Oh, poor me." By feeling sorry for yourself, you try to enlist others in the proverbial "pity party" that you're hosting.

Why would someone do this? Actually, there are plenty of powerful reasons for throwing such a party—ones you'll need to recognize within yourself and then vanquish if you're going to quit whining. These reasons make up what I've come to call the Eeyore Syndrome.

The Eeyore Syndrome

Unless you were raised by wolves in a forest, separated since birth from other people—and possibly even then—you're familiar with Winnie-the-Pooh and his woodland cronies. I've always loved Eeyore the donkey; he's such a caricature of a purely miserable being, a character who seems to revel in his misery with the same dedication that he brings to reveling in mud. His tone of voice—that sorrowful, "Poooor me" inflection—and the way he walks with his head hung low are pure, unadulterated self-pity. I'll bet you can think of times when you've been prey to the Eeyore Syndrome, and in such moments, as you glory in whining, you're inviting pity from others for any number of reasons. Here are just a few:

You Want Others to Take Care of You

We all have times when we'd like to regress, diving back into childhood—even infancy—to experience the total dependency, and total safety and care, that childhood affords most of us. This is a natural desire, and if you act on it rarely, it can even be productive. After all, it doesn't hurt, every once in a while, to feel totally enveloped by another's care and caretaking. The problem, of course, is if you grow to rely on it *or* if you never outgrew relying on it in the first place. Adulthood demands a level of self-care that is sometimes unpleasant, sometimes burdensome, but always ultimately freeing, since it doesn't create dependency and the problems associated with dependency. It is in the intersection of those unpleasant, burdensome demands and the presence of someone who might remove or lessen those demands that whining is most likely to occur. Whining serves as a signal to the other person that you are willing to give up autonomy if the other is willing to provide total care for you.

You Want Others to Comfort You

Just as you may whine in order to secure caretaking for yourself, you also may find yourself whining in order to access the warmth and comfort that you recall from days long gone. Nurturing and comfort feel good, and if whining works for infants, why can't it work for adults? I'll tell you why: it's a short leap from nurturing and comfort to dependency and its ensuing feelings—frustration, helplessness, and rage, to name a few. Dependency can stem from comfort just as easily as it can from caretaking. And, similar to caretaking, there's nothing wrong with a little comfort; add it to your list of things you want and you can sometimes have, but things that also aren't good for you in great quantities. In bulk, comfort becomes rescuing, and the search for comfort becomes victimhood. Comfort is emotional sugar, psychological fat. You've probably heard the beer slogan, and it's just as perfect for the cloying strength of too much comfort: *tastes great, less filling*.

You Want Others to Solve Your Problems

Although there are many lines separating emotional maturity from immaturity, one of the most important, and obvious, differences is who you hold responsible for solving your problems. It's natural at times to want others to rush in and take over, particularly when a situation seems more complex or painful than challenges you've faced before. However, when you allow others to rescue you—whether they provide comfort that removes any emotional spur to meet the challenge you're facing or through solutions that have the same effect—you shut the door on the potential for learning and growth. Relying on others to solve your problems suggests a high degree of feelings of helplessness that must be overcome if you are to be independent and strong.

You Want Others to See How Hard Your Life Is

It may not be a particularly attractive trait, but at times each of us puts on the mantle of the martyr and plays it out for as long as it works. Does this sound familiar? You look at your life and sigh heavily, recounting the difficulties and challenges you face—burdens that are surely heavier than those borne by others. You may contain your "inner martyr" or you may let the martyr out to see the light of day, but either way, you're weighing and comparing your life against others and finding your life lacking—and this allows you to feel a degree of superiority. After all, if you were singled out to bear this much pain or difficulty, you must be special! I realize that this thinking might sound absurd, but it springs from a dynamic I've seen again and again. Illogical or not, people often explain suffering by telling themselves that it points out their greater strength or ability to withstand difficulty; thus, you are "the chosen" if you suffer. The truth is, however, that it's up to you to "choose" martyrdom. It's a rough path to tread, and when you're looking for kudos from others, I'd recommend a road less traveled—one that gets you where you want to go without all that suffering and whining along the way.

MOVING ON: VANQUISHING THE SUFFERER WITHIN

The first step in changing any behavior is understanding and recognizing it, and you're now well on your way to having the ability to do both. You recognize some of the main reasons that people invite pity from others and cultivate feelings of self-pity within themselves. As you read on and understand more about your own particular need to whine, as well as some of the disadvantages and advantages of doing so, you'll get ever more competent at changing your behavior once and for all.

HOW YOU GOT THERE

You know some of the reasons that you invite pity from yourself and others, but how did you learn that this was a worthwhile behavior, one that could get you what you wanted? As with most behaviors, you learned it early—and you probably learned it well—in your first and most potent learning environment: your family system.

It's normal for children to whine. Infants do, although we probably shouldn't call it whining, given the negative associations the word carries. There is a voluntary and intentional nature to whining, and in infancy, communication behavior is neither. At about 18 months to two years, children move beyond that reflexive communication that they were born with or developed early on. This initial communication behavior allows them to indicate physical discomfort such as hunger or pain, and, in a sense, the same needs are behind the whining in which older children and adults engage. However, the whining is manipulative for an older child, while it is reflexive and, again, involuntary for the very young.

When an adult whines, it indicates arrested development; you are stuck in a stage of childhood in which few means are available for securing what you want. It's harking back to that old "Carry me!" whine of your childhood. Remember when it was time that you wouldn't be carried anymore? When you whine as an adult, you regress back to the last thing that worked, and whining was it. Children have tunnel vision and tend to see things in black and white terms; adults, on the other hand—if they're emotionally and intellectually mature—see shades of gray, and can see that both positives and negatives exist in most situations. This "glass is half empty" thinking invariably leads to whining, and it's no surprise; how can you be positive and hopeful if you believe you have few options or that every situation has at most one solution? So when you whine, it's the adult version of "Carry me!"

While everyone would agree that whining is unpleasant, it's still a time-honored response to any number of situations. You've probably seen it work, which is the chief reason behind why it is used so often. I raise the idea that whining works because I've had more than one client ask me why it's so bad to whine when it creates the desired results. In practical terms, they argue, it does the trick.

I always explain that while whining may result in a temporary victory of some sort, it comes about at great cost down the line. Whining does not create the desired results, unless those results involve manipulative behavior, diving into martyrdom, and ducking from responsibility. It may appear to do so on the surface, but hovering beneath the appearance of success is an absolute mess consisting of the annoyance others feel, the helplessness that you create and increase in yourself, and the stale, ineffective lessons you learn when you whine. Contrary to shallow appearances, whining is not only an ineffective tool, but a damaging one as well.

WHY THE OLD WAY DOESN'T WORK

There are myriad reasons for why the old way—whining—doesn't work. Think about these reasons as you read through them. Then try to identify examples from your life of times when you've whined and others have responded to you in ways consistent with the reasons listed below. At the same time, identify examples from when you observed others whining and responded to them—whether directly or simply to yourself—in any of these ways:

Others Find the Behavior—and You—Annoying

No one likes to listen to a child whine, and the resulting annoyance is only multiplied when it's coming from an adult. The cost to you is a decrease in liking, respect, and admiration from those around you; when others see behavior in you that does not fit your age, your role, and/or your abilities, they tend to respond with annoyance. In addition, whining is a way of saying you're powerless, and others can see their own powerlessness mirrored in you then, which is a difficult thing to witness. I'm reminded of a situation that illustrates just this dynamic.

Tara's family learned early on that whining was her sole means of getting her way. If she didn't, there would be the devil to pay. "Just give her what she wants!" was a phrase she heard for most of her life, as she managed to make family and friends give in rather than face her wrath or the self-pity, need, and greed that was all rolled into her tone of voice. Friends grew few and far between, and her family tried to avoid her whenever possible. The turnaround came when Tara had a boss who managed to top even her whining, and then the shoe was on the other foot: her boss sat at staff meetings sucking on a silver pacifier to let everyone know that *she* was top kid in the group and only her whining would be tolerated.

Whining Strips Away Your Personal Power

Just as whining creates annoyance in others, it also diminishes your personal power. When you whine, you recreate yourself in a childish, irresponsible, and impotent form, which weakens your personal power and choices. In effect, you're presenting yourself to the world as a child, and when you exhibit this, you cannot be anything but powerless.

Media types such as Gina know the importance of a mature voice that has just a sufficient hint of authority, but Gina had been too busy for the better part of her 30-odd years raising her voice in anything but mature tones. The writing was on the wall for her as she saw herself sending résumé tapes out and receiving only form letters in return. The moment her audio came up on the monitor, the illusion of power and authority was gone. "It's that voice," one station manager said. "Who wants to listen to somebody reading the news with *that* voice?" Clearly, Gina had to break the whine barrier if she was to make a move into a bigger market.

Whining Is Built Upon the Fallacy that You Want to Be Rescued

While you may whine about how difficult your life is and how rough you have it, and think you want someone to make things better for you, this is rarely the dynamic involved. Much more typical is the situation in which the "whiner" wants pity, caring, and agreement—about how rough his or her life is, and therefore about how special they are to be handling it—but in fact the whiner does not want a solution. A solution would automatically eliminate his or her standing as put upon and long-suffering, and so it is in their best interests—if they intend to keep whining—to refuse to allow solutions to their problems.

Whining is a stereotype from the films of the 1930s and '40s, where damsels in distress wanted men in double-breasted, pin-striped suits and fedora hats to rescue them from the villains in the factories where they worked. Did those poor young things ever get what they wanted? Were they rescued? Remember what happened to Shelley Winters in *A Place in the Sun*? If not, watch the movie—it's instructional. Usually, the types like Joan Crawford, Bette Davis, and Ingrid Bergman were rescued—and they didn't whine. So whining, even as a rescue technique, doesn't always work. Whining is also something that many women fall into without realizing it. Listen to your friends: do you hear it?

Others Quickly Get Exasperated with You

This response from others may sound similar to annoyance—and in fact exasperation consists in part of annoyance. It goes a step further, however, and results in abandonment: others will not only be annoyed by you when you whine, but they will eventually quit trying to help you, even when your requests for help are genuine and legitimate.

Have you ever heard anyone make one of those awful sounds with chalk on a blackboard? It sends shivers down your spine, and that's what whining does both on a physical and an emotional basis. It grates on the nerves and strips away the tolerance that someone might ordinarily extend to you.

You Don't Solve Your Problems or Meet Your Challenges

The bottom line with whining, and the reason that it's ineffective and unproductive, is that you remain in the same bad position, running into the same problems and challenges that you faced initially. Whining is the superglue that keeps you stuck in an unconscious, irresponsible, and impotent position when it comes to taking on your life and its myriad challenges. If you never grow up, you can't function as an adult, and whining is a sure signal to everyone within whining distance that you're not up to adult jobs.

HOW DO YOU IDENTIFY WHINING?

How do you know if you're whining? Sure, you can wait for others to tell you—or you can wait for each new relationship to go sour, as sooner or later it surely will once you've started whining. Fortunately, there are ways to catch yourself before whining has done untold damage to your relationships, your family life, your career, and your self-esteem. Are you an Eeyore type, whining and negative, or are you more like Winnie-the-Pooh, relentlessly positive and optimistic? Check out the behaviors below to identify your own whining habit so you can start to rid yourself of it. In particular, look at the italicized words for cues and clues to whining. When you hear yourself using absolute language (such as *I always*, *you never*, *everyone*, or *no one*) or self-pitying language about life being unfair, others treating you poorly, or the world being out to get you, you can be sure you're entering a whining zone. Similarly, superlatives or powerfully negative language (*hate*, *worst*, *most awful*, etc.) and words that create superlatives (like *soooo*) suggest whining. So does language that is obviously out of sync with the reality of a situation:

when you describe yourself as poor or misunderstood, for instance, you're
often overstating—and that can mean you're whining.

THE STATEMENT	HOW A WHINER SAYS IT	WHAT IT REALLY MEANS
I'm tired . . .	I am *soooo* exhausted . . .	I'm more put-upon than anyone.
This is hard to do . . .	I *can't* do this . . .	I don't want to do this.
I'm afraid . . .	I *hate* this . . .	I don't like unfamiliar things.
This feels unfair . . .	*Nothing's ever* fair . . .	I want everything to go my way.
I messed up . . .	*Everything's* awful . . .	I don't like feeling embarrassed.
I feel alone . . .	*Poor* me . . .	Keep me from feeling this way.
I don't like this.	*Why me?*	Why not *you* instead?

Listen for these key words and language patterns in your own speech in
order to "catch yourself" whining. When you do, stop. Stop right then and there.
I'd even recommend that you tell the other person that you've caught yourself
whining and are working on ridding yourself of the behavior; keeping it conscious like this will help you immeasurably. You can also do what a colleague
of mine has done, a clever approach: whenever she hears a whine in her voice,
she stops and says, "Carry me!" to remind herself—and to let the other person
know—that she's whining. Since what we really want when we're whining is
for someone else to take on our load or sympathize or agree that we've got it
tougher than anyone else, it's helpful to lighten the atmosphere with something
humorous and to the point like this. You may find that it's useful to choose your
own statement, one that represents what you want when you begin to whine.

ROOTS

In each tool chapter, we've discussed the core or root dynamic associated
with the behavior you're attempting to change. These roots, consisting of

self-esteem issues, self-concept issues, and issues of helplessness and hope-lessness, tie what would otherwise be fragmented behaviors to every facet of who and what you are. No behavior you exhibit—whether it's choosing to deny reality or choosing to avoid making mistakes—operates in a vacuum; instead, each springs from one of these root areas: issues of self-esteem, self-concept, helplessness, and hopelessness.

The situation is no different when it involves whining, which grows out of issues you have surrounding helplessness and hopelessness. Whining creates a vicious cycle: you whine because you're experiencing a challenge or situation that feels difficult, and then—because of the whining and the pessimistic, defeatist attitude it represents—the situation becomes even more difficult to negotiate. You can go around and around in circles like this when you whine . . . and unfortunately, many people do just that. Whining creates a self-fulfilling prophecy; the moment you say that you'll never win, you guarantee that you will never win. Remember the cartoon character, Chief-Rain-in-the-Face, in *L'il Abner*? He walked around under a dark cloud that rained on him all the time. It's hell on your clothes and creates a terrible impression when you walk into a roomful of strangers. Maybe it's time to let the sunshine in.

Because you are acting from a child's position of weakness, you don't feel competent to handle the challenges that arise, and you receive feedback from others confirming that very feeling. This rapidly increases your feelings of helplessness, but you must remember that you're trapping yourself into these feelings: you were not—and are not—helpless to begin with.

Self-esteem and self-concept are also related to the choice to whine, of course. You'll recall that self-esteem is how you feel about yourself, while self-concept is how you perceive yourself, or who you believe yourself to be. You may have good self-esteem while having a distorted self-concept. For instance, you may see yourself as someone who needs to be taken care of: I've worked with clients, women particularly, who have come to see themselves as needing a "care mate" instead of a "soulmate." In other words, they deny their adult needs for intimacy, connection, intellectual and emotional stimulation, and the like, provided that a partner meets their need to be taken care of, whether this involves financial care, emotional care, or some other type of care. For the partner of this type of person, the "bargain" is that they are acquiring a child to take care of—although what kind of bargain that is, I couldn't tell you. One partner gets to be the always incompetent, but available one, and the other is the strong one who does the caring for the child-incompetent one. For the original partner, the one looking for a care mate, the benefits are obvious, if sad: it is unnecessary to step up and take responsibility. Men can certainly fit into this role too, but you'll be more likely to see it in personal situations where the wife or girlfriend steps forward to defend the man or to demand what he should be demanding for himself.

Responsibility and whining behaviors are so closely intertwined as to be inseparable. While they are not the same thing, they are like weights on a scale: increase the acceptance of responsibility, and you decrease the likelihood that you'll feel the need or desire to whine. Decrease the responsibility, and you immediately increase behaviors indicating powerlessness—such as whining.

Locus of Control

This connection between responsibility and whining can best be understood in the framework of the power outlook each of us possesses, or what is referred to as a "locus of control."[1] What this means is that you have certain beliefs about your own power—based on your upbringing, the experiences you've had so far in life, your personality, and other factors, perhaps even including genetics—that influence how you view the events and people around you.

If you have an *internal locus of control*, you believe that you have a significant amount of control over what happens to you. You believe that the choices you make, the perceptions you have, and the ways you choose to behave are all strong determinants of what will happen to you. On the other hand, if you have an *external locus of control*, you believe that the world happens *to* you; in other words, you are certain that you have little or no control over the events that occur and impact upon you, and you also believe that you have little significant power regarding how you choose to behave, or how those behaviors will impact on your life. Most people will be somewhere between the two extremes and will have certain areas of life where they are more "internal" than "external" on locus of control.

Essentially, an internal locus of control is one where a person believes that things happen to them *because of their own effort or ability*. External locus of control is where someone believes that things happen *because of luck, or the malevolent intentions of others* toward them. "I didn't get a good evaluation because I didn't work hard enough this past year," as opposed to: "I didn't get a good evaluation because I don't have any kind of luck," or, "My evaluation was poor because the boss doesn't like me." Chance operates here, not individual control—or so the thinking goes—and when chance is the operative word, where is the reason to try hard? This attitude assumes that the dice are *always* loaded against you or that people *just don't under-*

stand or like you. What would be the reason anyone would ask the mournful question, "Why doesn't anybody like me?" A person with an external locus of control can't imagine answering the question with practical solutions, because this type of person believes he or she cannot influence the liking one way or another.

Understanding the theory of locus of control—and, more important, identifying where you fall along the continuum between internal and external, since few people will be located precisely at one extreme or the other—can help you change your whining behavior. It's essential to get to the roots of a behavior, the reasons you choose the behavior, and the beliefs you hold about it, in order to uproot it, and understanding your own locus of control is an effective way to do so.

In the assessment tool, the "Personal Control Locator" that follows, you will rate the likelihood that you would make certain choices in given situations. These choices will provide you with a Locus of Control Score, which will tell you where you fit between an external and an internal locus of control. We'll then discuss some specific behaviors associated with each personality type, and ways to change these behaviors.

ASSESSMENT TOOL

Scale: 1 = Strongly Agree
         3 = Agree Sometimes/Somewhat
         5 = Strongly Disagree

Select the most appropriate choice (strongly agree, agree sometimes/somewhat, strongly disagree) for each of the 12 statements:

_____ 1.   Stores won't give me refunds, even when I have receipts.

_____ 2.   There's not much I can do about it if my food isn't right in a restaurant.

_____ 3.   I might as well park far from the building; I won't find a close space.

_____ 4.   It's just about impossible to avoid getting into bad traffic.

_____ 5.   Cavities cannot be avoided.

_____ 6.   I don't have much control over whether people laugh at my jokes.

_____ 7.   I don't have much influence over my salary.

(continued)

___ 8.   I don't have much influence over whether people like me.

___ 9.   Getting the flu is just one of those luck-of-the-draw things.

___ 10. Appearance is largely a matter of genetics and good fortune.

___ 11. Finding true love is part timing, part fate, and part luck.

___ 12. My weekends often get taken over with things I don't want to do.

To score your scale:

1. Total the scores you have filled in next to the statements.
2. Look for your score in the groupings below.

If you scored between . . .

48 and 60:   You have a strongly internal locus of control. This indicates that you believe you have tremendous influence over what happens to you, and that you're aware of the power in the choices you make. You should be aware of one cautionary note: it is possible to believe you're in control of everything, and therefore have an *inflated sense of your own impact and power*. This is probably the case if you find that you're often frustrated by the unwillingness of the world to bend to your will. Some things are out of your control, and resisting that reality will only create trouble for you.

25 and 47:   You are in the mid-range of scores, which indicates that there are some areas in which you believe you have significant impact in your life and other areas in which you believe yourself to be lacking in power. This may be the best position, but a word to the wise: be certain that you're allocating your power beliefs in the right direction. In other words, you need to be sure you're not extending futile energy in areas where you don't have control and believing yourself to be powerless in areas where you are, in fact, powerful.

12 and 24:   You believe you have very little, if any, control over what happens to you. This results in tremendous frustration and can lead to depression, given the lack of power you believe yourself to hold. The powerless are buffeted by the winds of chance—or so they believe—which is painful and frustrating. You need to take a careful look at your life and at the power you do in fact possess. Read on.

WHERE YOU ARE NOW

Having identified where you fit in the locus of control scheme, you are now in a good position to look at the specific ways in which you keep yourself feeling powerless—and therefore, the reasons that you choose whining over a more productive and potent form of protest. It can be difficult to face reality and the challenges of life head-on, and whining, for many people, is the antidote to that. Better to whine, they unconsciously reason, than to face the real feelings of fear or powerlessness or helplessness that this situation creates in them. Read on about just a few of the obstacles I've seen people put in their own paths when they've had the choice—as they always do—between being powerful and weak.

OBSTACLES

If I stop whining and face this difficulty in my life, I might have to admit that I've been willful and childish up until now.

If you are afraid of having to admit this, take a step back and look at the situation with logic: You already know you've been willful and childish at times. So what? In other words, who hasn't? Admitting that you have your strengths and weaknesses, your flaws and your strengths, is only difficult until you do it. Once you've faced yourself honestly, the relief is profound, and resolutions seem to flow almost magically.

If I stop whining and deal with this situation like an adult, I might have to face reality head-on, which frightens me.

It's a fallacy to think that reality is only real if you acknowledge it. This is one of the most destructive—and common—thought patterns I see with clients, and you would do well to consider whether you are engaging in this same pattern. This is a "See no evil, hear no evil, do no evil" type of scenario; if you just cover your eyes and ears, does the "evil" disappear? Of course not—and in fact it frequently worsens. It's all right to be afraid of reality; reality can be fearsome. What is not all right, since it freezes you in your tracks on the way to growth and learning, is to let that fear rule you.

If I stop whining and address this challenge powerfully, I might have to acknowledge that I don't have the skills or ability to deal with it.

The older you get, the harder it is to learn certain skills—perhaps any skill. We become established in our ways of thinking and learning, and taking on new knowledge can be a challenge to the inflexible mind. Just like with exercise, though, the only way to keep yourself limber is to do it; you can't make a promise to lose weight and expect the pounds to roll off. You have to work at it. The same is true with learning; no one expects you to lift 250 pounds the first time you venture into the weight room, and no one expects you to have every other skill or ability down at first glance either. If this obstacle sounds familiar to you, you are your own worst critic and enemy. Lighten up!

If I stop whining and confront this fear with maturity, I might have to accept things about others or life that I'd rather not know.

Admit it; just like the others obstacles of thought, this is built on a crumbling facade. You already do know those things you're so afraid of learning: that life can be difficult and painful; that others can betray you or be unreliable; that being an adult is damn hard work sometimes.

BENEFITS/METHODS

If you aren't convinced by now that whining is an unproductive and unpleasant approach to the challenges you face, I want you to do two things.

First, go back to the moment when you first picked up this book. You were probably in a bookstore, and something—the title, the cover art, the blurb on the back cover—drew you to the book. Something caused you to take the book home with you. Figure out what that was. I'm guessing that you were, and are, dissatisfied with some aspect or aspects of your life, and that's why you got the book. That's nothing to be ashamed of; all of us have things we'd like to change in our lives and in ourselves. Now, has that aspect of your life changed? Probably not—not yet, anyway. Hold the thought that this aspect of your life remains unresolved.

Second, look at the table of contents and review the chapter titles you've read so far in Section II. First you read "Challenge and Change." The reality is that something about your life isn't working, or isn't working as well as you'd want—that's why you bought the book. If you're going to change that aspect of your life, you must face it head-on. Next, you read "Make Lots of Mistakes," and you *must* be willing to make mistakes if there are to be changes in your life, as you undoubtedly hoped when you bought the book. And now you're reading "Quit Whining"—and if you aren't convinced that whining is futile and even destructive, you're neither living in reality nor willing to make mistakes. You're stuck in a rut, and it's time to get out of it. Make a commitment now—not tomorrow, not next week—to quit complaining and make change.

I often tell my patients that the most important step they can take is to realize they need help, and then to do everything they can to include that help in their everyday lives. You've taken one extremely important step in reading this book. Now put what you're learning into action. Procrastination won't do you any good; there's no better time than today to begin.

If you need further evidence that whining isn't in your best interests, here are additional reasons:

When you quit whining, you will . . .

- *Develop authentic relationships rather than false ones built on dependency.* Whining is symptomatic of dependency. It's a way of telling others that you have little or no power—or at least that you believe this to be true—and as a result, you will attract those who want to be caretakers, with all of the costs associated with such imbalance in a relationship. Being dependent means always waiting for the other shoe to drop; your partners and friends and family will eventually tire of taking care of you—I guarantee it. Do you really like walking on eggshells all the time?

- *Eliminate much of the isolation you feel as a result of others distancing themselves.* When you develop authentic relationships, you will immediately notice a profound change in the quality of those relationships and in your experience of loneliness and isolation. While no human can entirely eliminate loneliness—it's part of the human condition and experience—you will experience it far less when you break down the artificial walls and barriers that exist in relationships built upon rules and roles. An important distinction needs to be made here about the difference between loneliness and being alone. One is a feeling of emotional deprivation, while the other is a choice, in that you decide to be in your own company rather than with others. The second one isn't sorrowful, while the first one is.

- *Discover more opportunities to interact in satisfying ways with other adults.* As you increase your relationships and deepen their quality and connection, you will discover that myriad other opportunities open up for interaction. The satisfaction that comes from interacting at a more authentic level carries over to other relationships and situations.

- *Discover that you are far more competent than you thought.* When you quit whining, you replace the behavior with choices and moves that stem from your personal power. What you will discover is that your whining was simply a veneer coating a competent person; all the time you've been complaining, a competent you has been waiting beneath the complaints, wanting to come out and succeed. An end to whining means a beginning to you as a successful adult.

- *Learn new things, have exciting adventures, and explore unfamiliar vistas.* Last, but far from least—because the benefits of quitting whining are nearly endless—you'll have opportunities to learn new skills and new ways of interacting with the world. You'll also have adventures that were closed to you when you did not believe you had the power to control events in your life. "I can't" is the surest show-stopper in the world, but when you stop saying "I can't," you suddenly discover that you *can*—learn, grow, change, discover—and so you *do*. Replace "I can't" with "I'll try."

CONCLUSION

A change of this magnitude—if indeed this is a big change for you—will not happen overnight. You'll experiment with calling a halt to the whining, and then you may find yourself retreating, perhaps, into the old, familiar patterns for a time. This is natural when it concerns personal change, and should not be seen as a sign of failure. Do not let "relapses" discourage you from your path; you must learn to see them as opportunities to learn and fine-tune a new set of skills and beliefs. Life is a series of forward steps interspersed with a few ministeps backward. Expect a few slips and you'll be fine.

In addition to the challenges you're likely to face within, you will almost always encounter some resistance from others. Remember, if you are in a dependent role in a relationship, it means that the other person—whether partner, family member, or friend—is in a power position. They may not respond favorably to giving up that power over you. It's not uncommon to see distrust, surprise, and even shock from others when you make a change this significant.

In order to succeed at quitting whining, you need to develop a set of replacement skills, and these will be in the realm of communication. The most important skill you can develop is to ask yourself (and then answer) this brief series of questions when you feel a whine coming on:

- How did I create this situation?
- What is it about this situation that makes me feel powerless?
- How can I change my feelings of helplessness?
- How can I handle this situation without whining?

Once you've answered these questions, you will be in possession of everything you need to know about handling the situation from a position of power and strength. And once you have done so several times, I promise that you'll begin to see the fruits of your labor—and wonder how you could have ever chosen whining over the heady, intoxicating experience of being in charge of your own life.

Act Like the Person You Want to Be

BEING A FUNNY PERSON DOES AN AWFUL LOT OF THINGS TO YOU.
YOU FEEL THAT YOU MUSTN'T GET SERIOUS WITH PEOPLE.
THEY DON'T EXPECT IT FROM YOU, AND THEY DON'T WANT TO SEE IT.
YOU'RE NOT ENTITLED TO BE SERIOUS, YOU'RE A CLOWN,
AND THEY ONLY WANT YOU TO MAKE THEM LAUGH.

Fanny Brice

Try something completely out of character. Wear a wild hat, give someone else that close-to-the-entrance parking space, or tip the waiter at the pancake house 50 percent instead of 20 percent (it will only mean a few extra dollars for you, and the outcome will be worth it!). Then, be conscious of how you feel after each act. You'll begin to recognize that sometimes the most powerful way to change your beliefs is to behave as if you're already feeling the way you'd like to feel. So, if you want to experience how it feels to be generous, don't wait around indefinitely to *feel* it: go ahead and act on the concept: in other words, *be* generous! If you'd like to feel carefree and casual on a buttoned-down day, eat lunch outside—barefoot. If you'd like to feel like a kid again for a little while, throw water balloons with the neighborhood kids. They may roll their eyes, but so what? If you wait for the belief to arrive, allowing rules and roles to constrain you, you just may wait forever. Change the behavior instead!

From the moment you're born, you receive training in becoming a person. Your parents and the others who are closest to you sent you a multitude of messages, in a number of ways, signaling what was acceptable and what was not. You adapted your behavior to conform to these messages because, like all children, you aimed to please and be a part of things, and the messages contained an implicit warning that you could only be connected to others if you conformed. However, you're an adult now, and as long as you allow a desire for conformity or any other motivation—including bowing to the wishes of others (such as your parents)—to rule you and win out over individuality and being true to yourself, you will not be the person you want to be.

WHERE YOU'VE BEEN

You notice your mother frowning at you as you pick up a piece of broccoli with your fingers, and so you switch to the fork she has provided. In this way you not only rapidly develop the manners your parents value, but this same value also takes root in your own psyche, becoming part of who you are, regardless of who you might have otherwise been or wanted to be. Later in life, when it's appropriate to eat asparagus with your fingers, you will find yourself rebelling against this offense against your internal eating rules.

You see the joyful expression on your father's face as you make a goal on the soccer field—perhaps the same field where your father excelled—and so you unconsciously try even harder to succeed at sports, internalizing your father's values and probably giving little, if any, thought to your own wants or needs in the athletic arena. Parents, grandparents, siblings, more distant relations, and, as you grow older, your network of friends, colleagues, and even casual acquaintances all tell you how they expect you to behave; this in turn indicates both who they want you to be and who they think you already are. The more these two "you's" are out of sync, the more messages you're likely to receive about your behavior, and the more discomfort you will experience, because the underlying message is that you are not good enough just as you are.

The views others have of "who you are" or "who you should be" are not based on objective reality. Rather, they consist of what others see and what they *want* to see. And since each person you encounter has a unique way of looking at the world—and thus their own perception of who you are—you can be left with contrary and confusing images and expectations, in addition to the discomfort arising from the notion that you're not measuring up.

ROADBLOCKS TO BEING THE PERSON
YOU WANT TO BE

If all you had to do in order to "be the person you want to be" was to ignore the messages others send, it would be simple to reclaim your life. It would certainly be a relief to ignore those negative, controlling messages, after all, and it would seem simple and exciting to just step into being yourself. The problem, of course, is that it's *not* so simple; far from it, in fact. Suggesting that you ignore the sometimes subtle and sometimes blunt messages others deliver about who you are is like instructing a jury to ignore the confession just blurted out by the accused. In the legal field this is referred to with derision as "unringing the bell." The idea is that you can't *un*-ring a bell; once that ringing sound has been heard, expecting someone to erase reality and *not hear it* is impossible—and absurd.

Although many people are frustrated and dissatisfied because they are not who they want to be, they perceive a nearly endless collection of other roadblocks, on top of the "unringing the bell" obstacle, that stop them from becoming themselves. By far the most common obstacle is a myth, subscribed to by many people, that you must first change your beliefs—a complex, long-term, and sometimes tedious process—before your behavior can change. More than any other roadblock, this myth keeps you distant from being who you want to be. Another obstacle is the belief that you don't have the skills to make the changes necessary. And yet another is the belief that being in a constant state of internal struggle, which is how it feels when you're not truly yourself—is natural and inevitable.

In fact, while being out of sync with yourself is the farthest thing from natural, it is inevitable; everyone has at least an unconscious desire to merge the "ideal self" with the "real self," and everyone exists somewhere along a continuum that represents this merging. You can make rapid and major changes—or rapid and subtle ones, for that matter—by changing your behaviors and letting the beliefs follow, by trusting and fine-tuning your abilities, and by letting go of the need to be in a state of internal struggle.

Be Patient with Yourself

You can further increase your chances at success by letting go of the impatience that refuses to allow this kind of change to be gradual. The guy who got sand kicked in his face at the beach in that famous ad didn't become

Charles Atlas in a single afternoon, and you're not going to become the person you want to be in the space of a few hours either. Making changes to who you are is a gradual process with gradual results; it begins with laying the foundation of understanding, which you are doing now, and it builds upon itself until change naturally results. We'll discuss how to start this gradual process and how to build *upon* this foundation a bit later in the chapter, but for now your task is to actually build the foundation itself, which, like so many of the tools, first involves recognizing the faulty and self-defeating beliefs and thought patterns you hold that keep you from being the person you want to be.

In order to identify these faulty beliefs, it's useful to take a moment to consider how they developed, and why they're so deeply rooted at times.

FIRST THE BELIEFS, THEN THE BEHAVIORS?

Let's face it: One of the effects of traditional therapy, which we discussed in detail earlier, has sometimes been to brainwash patients into believing that they couldn't change or grow without the help of therapists. We can credit Freud with starting the whole belief system that even today lies beneath many of the beliefs and practices in therapy. As far back as the 1890s Freud was promoting the concept that you must understand all of your beliefs and the motivation behind your actions before you can make any behavioral changes, substantive or small. This idea became firmly entrenched in the American psyche, perhaps out of convenience—after all, this makes change a very difficult task, and therefore one that most people would have every excuse to abandon somewhere along the way.

The idea that your beliefs must change before your behaviors can change is nonsense. Does it mean, for instance, that we can't expect sociopathic murderers to stop killing until they believe that killing is morally wrong? Does it mean we must tolerate a young child's stealing until he or she fully believes that stealing is wrong not because of the risk of being caught, but because it is an offensive act regardless of the consequences? Tell any parent of a troubled adolescent that beliefs must change before behaviors will follow and he or she will throw their hands up in the air in despair, and for good reason. The temper, the mood swings, the rudeness that can accompany those massive hormonal changes of adolescence simply must be responsive to the cliché, "I don't care if you don't like it or understand it, you can't talk to your teachers that way!" This powerful myth of "First the beliefs, then the behaviors" is a major obstacle to being the person you want to be. In fact, you reached this point—of not being your authentic self—in part because this myth is so prevalent and accepted in our society. This makes for a vicious cycle of defeat.

SELLING YOURSELF SHORT

The second dynamic that keeps you from being your authentic self is "short-selling," a psychological process that I see in abundance. Far too many people don't believe in themselves in some significant ways, and I'll bet you have your own ways in which you sell yourself short. Perhaps you do so in terms of your skills, believing that you aren't capable of the thought or action that would be required to become the person you want to be. Or perhaps you sell yourself short by subscribing to the rules and roles that were prescribed for you early on in life by parents and others close to you. You accept that you're the black sheep of the family, or the pretty-but-dumb one, or the failure, or the bumbling, absentminded professor. Whatever role you accept, you can be sure that it isn't you, since roles are not authentic, but are made up of stereotypes of behaviors and thought patterns that allow you to know how to behave without going to the trouble of figuring out what you want and need.

Along with the dynamic that says you must change your beliefs before your behaviors can change, short-selling yourself in any number of ways has brought you to the place you now occupy, somewhere distant from your authentic self. Before we move on to bringing you closer to yourself, you must recognize how these dynamics influence your life, and you must begin to extract them from both your conscious and unconscious thinking and behavior. One of the best ways to do this is to examine just how such patterns of thought and behavior work against you.

WHY THE OLD WAYS DON'T WORK

Call it being "centered" or being "true to yourself," whatever the label, becoming the person you want to be is one of your lifelong challenges. Unless and until you face this challenge head-on, you will continue to feel frustration and dissatisfaction with your life. You will also continue to experience relationships that don't live up to their potential, creativity and productivity that can't fully blossom, and a nagging sense that something is missing from your life—and it *is*. Living your life as anything different from or less than who you truly want to be is not really living *your* life, it's living within a limiting role that has been randomly assigned to you based on *others'* needs rather than your own. If this is the kind of life you're living at present, then your feelings of anxiety, discomfort, frustration, and dissatisfaction will continue unabated until you make the changes you need to make.

These sensations are your warning signals. Just as a car has lights that come on to tell you that the oil or antifreeze is low or that your battery needs charging, your psyche sends you signals through feelings. You must learn to watch and listen for these signals, and to respond to them when they come.

Your body sends you the signal of a physical sensation like pain in order to warn you when you're injured or ill. Likewise, your mind sends signals to warn you when you are adrift from yourself. These signals—the anxiety or discomfort you experience as a result of not being who you want to be—are actually useful, up to a point. Countless research studies have shown that an appropriate level of anxiety is motivating, that it moves you forward and makes you more goal-oriented and focused than you might otherwise be. You wouldn't be likely to go to the emergency room if you felt one slight twinge in your chest, but once those twinges become a tightening, painful sensation shooting down your left arm and through your ribs and upper chest, you're going to do something about it—if you have any sense!

I'll wager that you can identify any number of times in your life when this dynamic has proven true in terms of your psychological makeup. For instance, I've often noticed that on an *unscheduled* day when there are plenty of things I could and even should do, I'm less productive than on a day when I have a more defined schedule with a greater number of obligations. Logic would suggest that I would get more done on the unscheduled day when there is more free time; reality shows me, as I'm guessing it has shown you, that we accomplish far more when there is at least a moderate level of pressure or anxiety motivating us. Too much anxiety backfires, of course, but a moderate amount can spur you toward action. Another example that comes to mind concerns interpersonal relationships. Are you more motivated to change yourself or certain dynamics in a relationship when you're content, and yet aware that there are areas where you and your partner can grow, or are you more motivated when you're dissatisfied? Your motivation is obviously stronger in the latter case, because you are uncomfortable and want to eliminate the discomfort.

There are many factors—in addition to anxiety and other unproductive feelings—that explain why it just doesn't work to wait for your beliefs to change in order to be the person you want to be. You will recognize some of these factors from your own life, and even those that you have not experienced consciously may well be dynamics that are affecting you on a subconscious level. Sometimes it's difficult to find the objectivity to identify these factors, but read over them and think about each example to see if it isn't familiar to you at some level of your experience.

DEAL WITH THE BEHAVIORS

"First the beliefs, then the behavior" means . . .

SLOW CHANGE, IF ANY. Beliefs don't change overnight; in fact, for many people they don't change at all. They are deeply embedded in your psyche, created through your experiences, learning, upbringing, and values. In fact, you might think of beliefs as deep psychic tire tracks in your mind, forcing you in a predetermined direction. If you wait around for your beliefs to change before your behavior changes, you're going to be waiting for a long time. Behavior change is the "equipment" that regrades that psychic road, making it possible to explore new territory.

Marybeth, an alcoholic, would not acknowledge her drinking problem, although she did freely admit that her life was unhappy. Still, she insisted to me that she was sure that if the problem were the drinking, she'd know it; she'd lose her job or her marriage or both. Surely others, besides me, —would confront her if the drinking were out of hand. She assured me that if she really believed she were an alcoholic, she'd make changes instantly. But because Mary did not believe that she was addicted to alcohol, she did nothing to change her behavior. Sadly—and true to her earlier predictions—she eventually lost both her job and her marriage.

NO GUARANTEES OF GROWTH. After all that time spent contemplating your navel, which is about all you can do while you're waiting for beliefs to change, there's no guarantee whatsoever that the change will even occur! People sit around passively waiting for something to happen—although I've never been able to figure out what that "something" is—to change their beliefs. Change doesn't occur without action, and action equals behavior. That automatically means "first the behavior, then the beliefs," rather than the opposite.

Penny came to therapy wanting to deal with her fear of trusting others. She said it was an issue she'd been "working on" for a long time. When I asked what this meant, she explained that she'd been in therapy for five years but still hadn't succeeded in eliminating her distrust of others. It turned out that she'd been *talking* about her fear for five years, not *working* on it! I convinced her that talking about something doesn't cause it to change, using dieting as an example. I asked Penny: If you talk about losing weight, how many pounds come off? We established an action plan, and Penny rapidly began to experience a lessening of the distrust she'd felt for others.

BEING DISENGAGED FROM OTHERS.   Not only are you wasting time while you're waiting for your beliefs to change, you're also not out there in the world, trying on and trying out new behaviors. Remaining in a state of introspection as you wait and watch for your beliefs to change means accepting disconnection with others and with the world around you, one of the surest ways I know of to guarantee *no* change.

Mark was nearly addicted to self-help; he went to therapy twice a week, read every new emotional wellness book that came on the market, attended lectures and participated in groups that explored self-help issues. When I asked him what he was looking for in his self-help quest, he said that he knew there had to be more to life than he was experiencing; he knew that life couldn't be as boring and predictable and unchallenging as it was for him. While he was busy searching for the answer, others who had the same questions were busy trying new behaviors—discarding those that didn't work and personalizing those that did. The result? Mark was one of the most introspective, unchanged men I've ever known—and he was one of the most bored and unchallenged men too.

WASTING A VALUABLE RESOURCE.   You only have so many days here on earth, and each one you spend as someone you don't want to be is a day you don't spend living the life you want and deserve to have. Your time is the valuable resource, and it can't be replaced once it's been squandered, so put it to good use!

In my initial intake appointment with Jody, she casually mentioned that she'd been in therapy since she was 17 years old—and she was now 45! She told me that she wanted to have a good relationship with a man but had come to accept that it wasn't in the cards for her. She hoped that she would someday find a therapist (perhaps it would be me) who could help her discover the root causes of her relationship troubles so she could then make the necessary changes. All those years she'd been in therapy, her life had been going on, one day after another, with Jody alone and unhappy and with no change occurring. I gave her a time limit—six sessions—to have a different life plan in place that she was beginning to work on, and that at the end of that period we'd quit, because I wasn't going to stand by as she squandered her life or money. Six weeks later, with a new set of behaviors tried out and beginning to show promise, Jody agreed that she had a different life. She still believed that she wasn't meant to have a satisfying relationship, but she had a date planned for the next weekend and had reestablished contact with a man in whom she'd once had a great deal of interest.

Each of the above results came about because of faulty thinking. If you cling to the notion that you cannot make changes until your beliefs have shifted, you might as well throw in the towel. Nothing is going to change. You can dig in your heels further as a result of yet more self-defeating beliefs about the nature of change and the expectations others have of you.

For instance, you may believe that the old behaviors are more comfortable—and you're probably right. An old, broken-in pair of shoes makes for a more comfortable walk than a new, stiff pair. Similarly, those behaviors you're familiar with, the ones that allow you to predict the outcome—even if the outcome is negative or damaging—are the ones most people cling to. Far better, you reason (perhaps unconsciously), to know what will happen, even if it's negative, than to risk an unknown. I say it's far better to risk a new, outrageously successful result rather than to stay stuck in time and place.

Another obstacle to changing your behaviors, and thus yourself, is that others often expect you to behave in predictable ways. This is the flip side of what I just mentioned. Friends, family members, colleagues, and anyone else you regularly deal with have expectations for your behavior. When you do not behave in accordance with these expectations, you're likely to face anger from others, disappointment, and general resistance to the *new* you.

Some people don't become the person they could be because being someone else hasn't caused enough problems yet. You will tend to stay in a relationship as long as the costs don't outweigh the rewards. It's anyone's guess, as you'll recall, what constitutes a cost. For our purposes, we can define it as something that you don't want, something you are averse to. Until you have a big enough pile of these costs, the cost of changing may simply seem too exorbitant.

Yet another obstacle to making the changes you need to make is that you learn, over time, to expect less of yourself if you're not living up to your full potential. As a result, you dream less, hope less, want less, settle and scale back on your vision of what your life can be. In effect you've clipped your wings—and all the while you insist on believing that someone else, often a therapist, has the magic to make you new feathers.

Trying to be the person you want to be by using traditional therapy and/or the old ways of approaching change simply doesn't work. The powerful oppositional force of your anxiety gets in the way, as well as your beliefs about how difficult it is to be the person you want to be, and your therapist's beliefs that you cannot make change rapidly or effectively since it requires uprooting deep-seated beliefs. If you keep telling yourself that change is difficult, and you do this for enough years, chances are you'll believe it so thoroughly that you'll be "presold" on not being able to make changes.

When it comes to becoming the person you want to be, there is one point on which Freud and I agree: The only time you'll be totally free of anxiety is when you've gone to your final reward. How you *interpret* anxiety is the important point here, and it is that *interpretation* that I want you to keep foremost in mind as you go about changing your behaviors, and allowing your beliefs to follow.

ROOTS

When you believe that you must fit into some predestined role and conform to some long-established set of rules, you give up your personal power and subscribe to one primary underlying belief: *that you are helpless.* You are not helpless, of course—no one is, except by choice—but if you buy into a role that isn't custom-shaped for you and you alone, you will soon discover that your self-concept is built around the designs others have made for you. Soon your self-esteem will plummet, if it hasn't done so already. It is impossible to spend any significant length of time in someone else's life, pretending it's yours, while still maintaining a host of good feelings toward yourself. You may feel ashamed, embarrassed, or even humiliated at being unable to come up with a clear picture of who you want to be, and at being unable to carry out an action plan for becoming that person. You may also feel frustration, or even rage, at how your life has unfolded. But beware: it's easy (and typical) to turn this anger into hostility directed at others, rather than taking responsibility for the fact that your life is not what you wish it to be—because you haven't done what you need to do to make it so. Sometimes, in addition to or instead of shame and outrage, people feel suffocated when they aren't being themselves: It's no easy task occupying the stultifying space of someone else's life. Think of it as being eternally crouched in someone's closet, trying to fit into his or her too tight clothes.

There is one other set of feelings I've observed that occur when you go through life living inside of a role that isn't you: fear. That may seem counterintuitive; often, my clients initially balk at the idea. Some will intellectualize, saying that they're safer inside of an artificial role, because they aren't exposing their vulnerability to others when their true self is hidden, or nonexistent. Others will object on more emotional grounds, arguing that they resonate with the other feelings I've mentioned—such as embarrassment, anger, and suffocation—but do not connect with fear. If they can't feel it, they argue, it must not be true. To the contrary, I would argue that fear is the feeling you are most likely to hide, even from yourself, because to show it seems to make you vulnerable. This is not true, of course; you're vulnerable by simple virtue of living life as a human being and engaging with others. If you can be hurt—and who can't be?—you're vulnerable. You hide your fear in a number of ways; you may cover it with a veneer of false bravado or confidence, or may try to disguise it beneath your anger, frustration, and other feelings. Fear is a common reaction to living life outside of yourself, and hiding it—though it often happens unconsciously—is just as common.

What can you do, then, to move yourself beyond these beliefs, expectations, and feelings, all of which act as obstacles to becoming your true self? The first step to move you closer to yourself is to synthesize the things you have already learned about being yourself. This includes understanding how your beliefs and behaviors brought you to the point where you are now, and recognizing why the "old way" doesn't work. It also involves recognizing and eliminating the many obstacles that block your path on the way to becoming yourself. The second step is to recognize, in concrete terms, the extent to which your functioning or actual self—the one you bring forth day after day—differs from your real self. An assessment tool follows that will help you do just that.

The Real, Ideal, and Imposed Selves

The Real Self: This is the person you believe you truly are, rather than a set of roles you occupy with more or less discomfort. Your beliefs and behaviors feel most authentic and comfortable when you are operating out of the "Real Self" paradigm.

The Ideal Self: The Ideal Self is the collection of beliefs and behaviors you would like to have and/or exhibit. You do not do so at all times—or even most of the time—but hold up the Ideal Self as the standard to which you subscribe.

The Imposed Self: The Imposed Self is the group of beliefs and behaviors that make up the "you" that others demand or expect. When you occupy the Imposed Self you are least comfortable as it is not authentic or natural for you, at times.

ASSESSMENT

What are your beliefs about who you are, who you would like to be, and who you can be, realistically? How far apart are these three selves? How much hope do you have that you will be able to bridge whatever distance exists between these selves? Two assessments follow. Combined, they will help you determine the answer to these questions, preparing you to then make the changes you need and want to make so you can become your authentic self. The first assessment, "Bridging the Distance," consists of three columns, each representing either the "Real Self," the "Ideal Self," or the "Imposed Self." Below, you'll find a brief description of each, to prepare you to identify which of the three selves you most often occupy in certain areas of life. The second assessment is a simple series of questions that require a yes or no response. This tool gauges the extent to which you believe change is likely and possible. Before you begin the first assessment, however, be sure to read through the sidebar "The Real, Ideal, and Imposed Selves." This will ensure that you have a clear understanding of the three selves that you occupy.

Bridging the Distance

As you read down the left-hand column of the first assessment tool (see below), you will identify which of the three selves, listed along the top, corresponds best to the item in the left-hand column. For instance, if the left-hand column says "I give in to others in conflict" and this is true, put a check mark on the corresponding line under "Real Self." If this item is not true for you at this time, yet you believe it would be best and you'd like to change in order to give in to others in conflict, put a check mark on the corresponding line under "Ideal Self." If this item is one that you believe others expect of you, rather than one that represents who you truly are or would like to be, put a check mark on the corresponding line under "Imposed Self." See the assessment tool directions for an additional example.

A 15-Point Assessment of Self-Alignment

Put a check mark under one of the three "selves" shown on the top line. The check mark should represent your behavior and should correspond to the quality shown in the left-hand column. In other words, for the quality "Brave," do not mark "Real Self" unless your *behavior* is in fact consistently brave, rather than because you prefer to *think* of yourself as brave. The check mark should accurately represent *who you are on a day-to-day basis*. Even if an item seems not to fit into any of the three selves, you should identify that item with the self with which it is *most consistent*.

Do not leave any item unmarked.

	REAL SELF	IDEAL SELF	IMPOSED SELF
Happy-go-lucky			
Brave			
Generous			
Optimistic			
Outgoing			
Positive			
Independent			
Graceful			
Witty			
Unafraid			
Proud			

(continued)

Responsible	_____	_____	_____
Competent	_____	_____	_____
Forgiving	_____	_____	_____
Hopeful	_____	_____	_____
TOTAL MARKS	_____	_____	_____

Assessing the Assessment

Examine the "Bridging the Distance" worksheet after you add up the number of check marks in each column. If you add the total of the columns left to right, you should have a total of 15 check marks. If you do not, go back and fill in any items you skipped. In order to gauge the results of this assessment, you need to look at how the columns are balanced. Do you have a high number of check marks in one of the three columns?

Ideally, you will have the highest number in the "Real Self" column, which, if you answered truthfully, indicates that you experience your beliefs and behavior as being aligned with your authentic self. As a "High Alignment" person (note this for use on the grid that follows these two assessment tools), you should continue to be on guard to maintain this beneficial situation, and continue to avoid the powerful temptation to behave as others or socialization norms expect that you will behave. If the highest number of check marks are in the "Ideal Self" column, you need to bring alignment to the real and ideal selves. You're spending too much time wishing and not enough time doing or being. Your job is to *be* your authentic self, not to *want* to be your authentic self! You tend toward the "Low Alignment" personality type at this time; note this for use on the grid that follows.

Finally, if the highest percentage of marks are located under the "Imposed Self" column, you need to focus your attention—soon and hard—on no longer acquiescing to whatever others seem to want of you. You are not here to be a puppet for others; you're here to identify and fulfill your own life plans and dreams, and you cannot do so if you're being someone else. You are a "Low Alignment" person right now; note this for use on the grid that follows.

The second assessment is intended for use in tandem with "Bridging the Distance"; it will provide you with an indication of the extent to which you believe change is likely and possible. Respond by selecting the number and corresponding statement on the scale below that most closely corresponds to your attitudes and beliefs about each of the 12 beliefs shown in the "Optimism Toward Change" assessment that follows. Try putting the "I believe" statement at the beginning of each belief as you read it to make it easier to see which one is most accurate for you.

Scoring the Scale

    1 = I never believe that...
    2 = I don't usually believe that...
    3 = Sometimes I do and sometimes I don't believe that...
    4 = I usually believe that...
    5 = I always believe that...

Optimism Toward Change

1. _____ I will advance in my chosen career.

2. _____ I will do well in future learning opportunities.

3. _____ If I enter a competition, I will have a good chance at winning.

4. _____ If I make something, it will turn out as I want it to.

5. _____ If I try hard at overcoming an obstacle, I will succeed.

6. _____ I will get much of what I want out of life.

7. _____ If I drop something, it probably won't break.

8. _____ My relationships are likely to be successful.

9. _____ If I do someone a favor, it is likely to work out well.

10. _____ If an illness is going around, I probably won't catch it.

11. _____ If I'm in a hurry, I probably won't run into a traffic jam.

12. _____ If I lose something, I am likely to find it.

_____ TOTAL POINTS (MUST BE BETWEEN 12 AND 60)

Assessing the Assessment: Optimism Toward Change

Once you have a total score from both the "Alignment" and "Optimism Toward Change" scales, locate yourself on the grid that follows.

	High Alignment	Low Alignment
Moderate to High Hope (38-60)	You are flexible with a good sense of self, open to change, and looking for ways to make positive changes in your life. High probability of success due to self-fulfilling prophecy. Work on maintaining your self-esteem, self-concept and hopefulness by continuing to use your effective behaviors while eliminating those that create negative feelings for you.	Often unrealistic about who you are and unyielding in seeing yourself accurately. Good probability for change if you focus on your needs vs. others' expectations. Work on improving self-concept as you reinforce self-esteem and hopefulness by increasing your effective behaviors and decreasing your ineffective ones.
Moderate to Low Hope (12 to 37)	You have generally low self-esteem; you are authentic yet have a limited view of your potential. There is a low probability of success in changing because of low hope and no motivation to change, since you already feel alignment within yourself. Work on expanding your self-concept and self-esteem by observing others who are clearly effective and who have high self-esteem and then by "borrowing" their behaviors.	Poor self-esteem and low hope limits you in many ways. Until you can work on all three areas, you are likely to remain stuck and to experience the negative and damaging effects associated: negative feelings, lack of achievement of goals, poor relationships, and the like. Work on your self-esteem. Learn new skills, model your behaviors on those with higher self-esteem and ask for positive feedback.

PRESENT TENSE

By now I hope that you agree that being *anyone* other than yourself—warts and all—is not the way to live your life. Even a moment spent off center or out of sync with the "you" that is most authentic slows you down in your pursuit of good things: happiness, success, closeness with others, and a host of other positives in life. Your emotions will serve as both rewards and warning signs. If you're veering off course, you will feel negative emotions: disappointment, frustration, anger, self-doubt, and more. If you're being true to yourself—if you are truly being you—you'll feel a sense of contentment, pride in yourself, happiness, and satisfaction. If you still aren't convinced, read on to see some of the benefits that come from being your true self. Even if you are convinced, read on—there's nothing like a little reinforcement early on, when the challenges are frequent and the road unfamiliar.

The Benefits of Change

I don't advocate change just for the sake of change, unless boredom is the primary issue facing you, in which case change is the antidote. However, the changes you're considering are about returning you to who you truly are, rather than creating a "new you," and you will rapidly discover any number of benefits as a result. The reality is, when you become aligned with yourself, many of the positive effects are sweeping, immediate, and even profound. What are some of these benefits associated with becoming more aligned with yourself?

Fast Systemic Change

Almost immediately, you will observe changes happening within yourself and throughout the systems in which you function: the networks of relationships, the family and workplace systems, and even the larger world. There's a domino effect: When you make one small change that heads you in the direction of yourself, a positive chain reaction is put into motion. Or think of it as throwing a small pebble into a pond. No matter how small the pebble, it ends up spreading ripples out over the pond, affecting all in its path.

Prevention of Backsliding

When you make even one small change, others around you must shift in reaction. One of the ways they will shift occurs in their expectations of and for you; others will begin to expect you to behave in a manner consistent with your new behavior—in other words, to continue to be true to yourself. Because of these expectations, your changes will be reinforced and you'll find it easier not to backslide into the old, ineffective, and inauthentic ways of functioning.

Increased Confidence

Every time you try out a new behavior and meet with success, not only is the behavior reinforced, but you are reinforced too. Your self-esteem gets a need-

ed boost. It may surprise you, but there are positive benefits even if you try
out that new behavior and *don't* meet with success. In gaining a greater base
of experience, you reinforce your courage to live your life as you see best,
and this never takes away from confidence. To the contrary, the more strate-
gies you have for coping, the better you'll feel when faced with obstacles. It's
like building up a charge in a battery; experimenting with change builds up
a psychic charge inside you, which enables you to use your energy in beneficial ways. I am a great believer in not wasting energy. Instead, I believe in
using energy in positive ways that are reenergizing.

The simple truth is that anytime you make changes that move you
toward greater authenticity, you improve your self-esteem, increase your
sense of self, and decrease the helplessness that can keep you stuck and
miserable.

Use the step-by-step flow chart (Figure 7-1) to see an example of how
making one change among the many possible changes available—or not
making any change at all—can create powerful results.

MAKING YOUR LIFE FLOW: THE POWER OF POSITIVE CHANGE

Keep in mind: In thinking about a change such as the one shown in the flow
chart, change doesn't have to mean ending, leaving, breaking, or abandoning
something. In the example, Liz left her relationship, but she could have also
chosen to make other changes: seeking couples counseling (with a skilled
and qualified therapist, of course!), working together with her partner to
overcome their distance, or any number of other options. It is easy to fall into
the belief that change must be radical or immediate, but it can also be gradual or subtle *if that's what will work best.*

DEALING WITH FAILURE OR RESISTANCE

As we discussed in earlier chapters, those around you may not be as pleased
as you are when you start changing—whether you're changing your behaviors, your beliefs, or both. Becoming more authentic is no different: some of
the people around you will applaud you and support you in any way possible, while others will resist even the tiniest change you make, fearing—and
rightfully so—that your changes will result in the necessity for them to make
changes as well. This is no reason to halt your own journey, of course. When

MAKING YOUR LIFE FLOW: THE POWER OF POSITIVE CHANGE

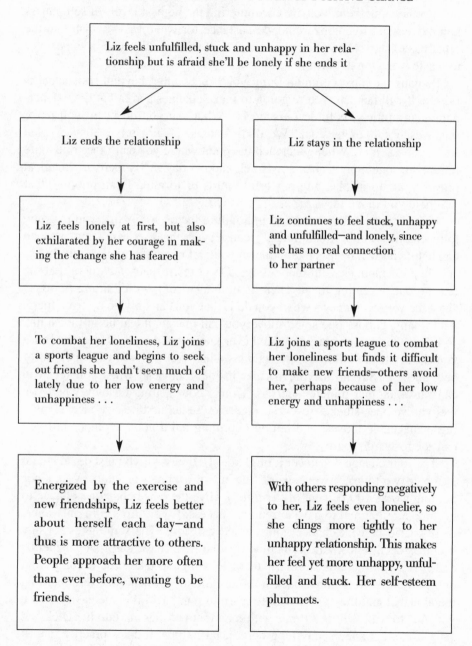

FIGURE 7-1. *Flowchart showing the power of positive change.*

you encounter people who would prefer that you stay stuck rather than inconveniencing them, you are encountering the highest levels of selfishness and narcissism. Recognize others' resistance for what it is—a wish that the other has to stay stuck—and move on. You don't have the time or the energy to waste worrying about it.

Perhaps the most common thing you'll encounter, beyond resistance, is failure. It will happen. You're going to make changes and fail at times—perhaps many times—before you succeed. What can you do when you make mistakes, or fail, or get stuck? We all do—and so it's not only realistic to plan for it, but essential. When you reach the point where you can't face one more failure, cry one more tear or stay stuck another day . . . is there any magical prayer you can invoke, any powerful words or formula I can provide, that will help you move forward?

First, I suggest that you build in a failure factor. *Know* that you're going to reach this point in life at times, because *everyone* does. Knowing as much can help; you will be less likely to beat yourself up on if you have this understanding. Second, sit with the feelings. Don't resist them, *feel* them. Let the fear go out of feeling them. There is nothing wrong with "hitting bottom," since the very worst news when you do is that you can only go up from there. And finally, choose one small move you can make—it can be infinitesimal, so minor that no one but you would ever know you'd made the move. Raise your head off the pillow for 10 seconds when you feel you can't get out of bed: success. Say no to your partner inside your head when you feel you can't take another minute: success. Think about getting unstuck when you feel you've been stuck forever: success. You're taking bite-size pieces, making manageable moves, and letting one thing build upon another until you can see forward progress.

Try your change, whatever it might be, 10 times—if you just decide to do it one or two times, it won't work (the law of averages is against you, since nothing works 100 percent of the time!). Give the new behavior a chance to become familiar and to have a trend of success. If you flip a coin only once, there's a 50 percent chance your choice will lose. The same goes for any event or occurrence. And remember: Failure can have surprising benefits, and it is also a natural, normal part of learning, so take it as it comes and don't sweat it! Remember back to your childhood when you were learning the alphabet and then you began to learn to read? Did it come easily? Were you able to read *War and Peace* within a month of digging into the Dick and Jane stories? It's the same thing here: it takes time, it takes practice, and it takes continuing motivation.

EXPECT THE UNEXPECTED

You should also be prepared to expect the unexpected. Since you've never acted this way before, you can't be sure how people will respond, but if you're acting in a positive manner, you'll generally get a positive response— not always, but most often.

It's also normal to experience feelings of surprise, so be ready for this. You have expectations of yourself and of others based on your *old* behavior, so you may be quite surprised at how people respond to you and how you perceive others. When you change one part of the system, the whole system shifts, and that means meeting up with a surprise around every corner.

Not only will you feel surprise, but you should expect to feel other emotions, some of which you may not have felt in a long time—if ever. This doesn't necessarily mean the emotions will be upsetting or negative, just unexpected and perhaps unfamiliar. A normal life containing a balanced selection of emotions is like a well-seasoned meal. The ingredients blend together beautifully when combined, but if taken individually they might be unpleasant—think of garlic, for example!

You will also do well to expect that others may comment on the "new you"—even if the new you is only new in terms of one small behavior you've changed. Others may make comments that will tell you something about how they used to see you: they may have seen you as unimaginative, boring, uninteresting, or cold, for instance, and they will comment on this because it shows up more plainly in relief against your new behaviors.

I'd advise you to spend some time giving thought to your new behavior and its potential consequences. This doesn't mean you shouldn't try out the behaviors you're considering changing—you should, absolutely, if they are positive and well-intentioned and not harmful. However, it may be that you should scale back the behaviors in one way or another the first few times, if others will be discomforted or shocked. Only you can really gauge this. My approach isn't like a suit or dress that you buy off the rack, expecting it to fit perfectly. The approach needs *your tailoring*, and *only you* know what you can handle and how fast or slow you need to go to feel comfortable.

CONCLUSION

Think of how many times in your life you've heard yourself say, "I wish I hadn't done that" or "I wish I was _____" (fill in the blank: stronger, smarter, more confident, a better speechmaker, etc.). If you're like most people, you've spent a lot of time wishing against reality. Now it's time to stop wasting your breath. Wishes are nice when you're a child with a penny beside a fountain. You can wish for the stars, wish that you'll fly to the moon in a rocket ship, wish that you could eat ice cream for your meals all week and never have to see another lima bean as long as you live. That child with the penny may have something you don't have—a penny, untested optimism, and unbridled faith, for starters. You, though, have something that child doesn't have, and you cannot let it go to waste. You have the ability to stop wishing and start doing. So? What are you waiting for?

Accept Yourself, Warts and All

SELF-REVERENCE, SELF-KNOWLEDGE, SELF-CONTROL—
THESE THREE ALONE LEAD LIFE TO SOVEREIGN POWER.

Alfred Tennyson

There will be times when you find yourself questioning your right to self-indulgence. Whether you do so over an indulgence that occurs as you are giving yourself the time to do something you want to do, as you are buying yourself a small luxury or as you are just sitting and doing nothing at all, recite a phrase written by Hillel, an ancient scholar and philosopher. "If I am not for myself, then who will be for me? If I am but for me, what am I, and if not now, when?" Write this on a piece of paper and keep it folded in your wallet or purse. Take it out and read it three times, whenever you need validation or support in being good to yourself. It is not a criminal act to be on your own side, but it is unconscionable to ignore who you are and what you truly need from your life.

NOBODY'S PERFECT

Knowing and accepting yourself as you are, rather than trying to achieve some unrealistic level of "perfection," is essential to achieving positive mental health and peaceful satisfaction in your life. It's time to face the cold, hard truth: Perfection does not exist in this world. In fact, this truth can be a relief, for without the need to achieve perfection, life is easier and more pleasant. Certainly, all the unrealistic expectations you place on yourself, which in fact cannot be achieved by mere mortals like you and me, will not be missed when they disappear into the ether, as they should.

The reality is, you will never be rid or "cured" of the unpleasant or imperfect aspects of life. And it's also time to acknowledge that you'll also never rid yourself of the imperfect aspects of your personality. This is nothing to be ashamed of or embarrassed by; it's nothing to hide. That you are not and cannot be perfect is a simple truth that the realistic among us face head-on. It is our very *imperfection* that makes us who we are and provides our sense of uniqueness.

When you face yourself with openness and acceptance, you'll find a paradox: Knowing yourself and accepting yourself, warts and all, will not make you *less* satisfied or *less* comfortable with who you are. To the contrary, this level of self-awareness will make you *happier*. In terms of self-therapy, it will enable you to recognize and transform those things that can and should be changed, even as you let go of those things that cannot or should not be altered. No doubt you've heard "The Serenity Prayer,"[1] which addresses this very point.

FIGURE 8-1. *The Serenity Prayer.*

Without an awareness and acceptance of your flaws, there is no hope for eliminating them or smoothing out their rough edges. After all, if you can't get a clear picture of what comprises your "good, bad, and ugly," you can hardly know where to start reinforcing the positives and eliminating the negatives.

YOUR STRENGTHS ARE NOT A WEAKNESS

If you think that focusing on the positives is too narcissistic or arrogant, you should stop thinking it—and stop *now*! Imposing this kind of self-defeating message is a trick played by your poor self-esteem. (Whether you believe it's there or not, telling yourself things of this nature proves that you have a self-conflict.) You're afraid to look at the positives because you can't believe they exist; your faith in them might be fragile, but it's not as if bringing them out into the light of day will cause them to disintegrate into thousands of unrecognizable pieces.

In this chapter, we'll discuss a powerful three-part alternative to the unhappy existence that results when you hide from yourself and refuse to accept who you truly are. Whether shaky self-esteem is the sole cause of your failure to accept yourself—as it so often is—or whether you simply don't believe that change is possible, the ideas in this chapter will help you move past the stuck state that occurs as the result of not facing yourself truthfully.

First, you will gain the *understanding* that you are a collection of the good, the bad, and the ugly. Second, you'll develop the *ability* to fairly and correctly assess who you are and how you function in the world. And finally, you will acquire the *tools and techniques* to function more effectively as an integrated person with acknowledged strengths *and* weaknesses. Believe it or not—and I fully expect you to believe it by the end of this chapter—even your weaknesses can work in your favor.

As you continue to recognize and develop an understanding of the many facets of the three selves we began discussing in the previous chapter—the Real Self, Ideal Self, and Imposed Self—you will also deepen your knowledge of how these three selves can work for or against you. You'll begin to identify the ways in which you experience "self-conflict" between who you truly *are*, who you *want* to be, and who you feel you *must* be in various contexts. Satisfaction and success can only come when you learn to merge these three selves into an integrated whole, thereby decreasing—and eventually eliminating—this conflict.

In this chapter, we will explore how you present yourself; the effectiveness of your choices about whether to present your Real, Ideal, or Imposed Self; and the ways in which you create or complicate life challenges through these choices. As a result. you'll develop an effective new problem-solving method to *identify* and *clarify,* problems and solutions in a highly personalized manner that takes into account the actual *context, content,* and *concept* of the situation, interaction, or life challenge you face at any given moment.

I can't stress strongly enough that reaching a state of contented effectiveness in life requires that you accept both your strengths *and* weaknesses. Identifying and taking credit for your strengths empowers you to grow these strengths in new ways, eliminating the myths that chip away at your strengths—that you'll seem arrogant, for instance, or that others won't like you if you brag.

Do you have a problem writing a résumé or filling out a self-evaluation at work, where you have to talk about your accomplishments? If you do, you're in the right chapter now. Identifying and taking responsibility for your flaws and weaknesses is essential to being comfortable and effective at being yourself and operating in a productive, potent manner. Learning to be nonjudgmental and frank as you assess these flaws, as well as developing an acceptance for those weaknesses that you don't intend to change, will make you all the more powerful. As I briefly mentioned, it is ironic that when you identify the extent to which your flaws are deeply rooted and unlikely to change, you emerge with a clarification of the ways in which the flaws work *for* you.

By way of illustration, consider the well-known film star, Marlon Brando. When Brando was just starting out as an actor, he was a handsome young man with a perfectly straight nose. He had an accident, however, that resulted in a broken nose, and his friends urged him to have it corrected with plastic surgery so it wouldn't mar his looks. Brando, it's said, looked at himself in the mirror, inspected the broken nose, and decided it provided character to his formerly perfect face. Remember how he looked in *On the Waterfront*? The broken nose not only didn't hurt, but Brando got an Academy Award for that film—and even today, that sensitive tough guy look he had—much of it created once the nose was broken—is held up as a standard to which young men aspire.

Determining and then accepting the many sides of your "real" self *and* reaching a state of alignment between your self-concept and how you present yourself to others is some of the most important work you will ever do. Let's not delay, then, in exploring the dynamics of accepting yourself, warts and all!

WHERE YOU'VE BEEN

OFT TIMES NOTHING PROFITS MORE
THAN SELF-ESTEEM, GROUNDED ON JUST AND RIGHT
WELL MANAG'D . . .

John Milton, Paradise Lost

Milton had it right: Few things will bring you greater life satisfaction, success, and contentment than a clear, positive, and realistic sense of yourself. And yet, if this is so, why is this clear sense of self so rare, so hard-won? Clients enter my office every day, saying they're searching for any number of things—better relationships, greater productivity at work, and less anxiety or depression, to name a few—and yet beneath the surface, the vast majority are *looking for themselves*. Does this sound familiar to you? Not only are they searching for themselves, but often they're afraid of what they might discover if they ever do find themselves. Perhaps this too resonates with you.

This is what I see, far too often: you come to me presenting one problem or another, but within minutes the real issue—or a significant contributor to the real issue—emerges. The real issue? You haven't learned to accept yourself, and as a result you've been beating yourself up, engaging in an endless search for what's wrong with you and a fruitless and repetitive examination of what needs fixing. Any energy you might otherwise have for responding to the challenges in your life, the ups and downs of relationships, the moral and ethical dilemmas, the daily demands, is eaten up by this search-and-destroy mission you're engaged in.

You describe all of the things about you that aren't good enough. You list the myriad ways in which you don't measure up to expectations put on you. When I try to pin you down about exactly who is imposing these unrealistic expectations, you're often unable to name the guilty parties—until I suggest that perhaps *you* are the culprit, the one demanding so much of yourself, even while you expect so little. You engage in constant comparisons between yourself and others, most of whom you perceive to be better, brighter, more attractive, or otherwise possessing magical abilities that you *don't* possess. You're not alone in doing these things, by the way—it turns out that even those people whom you might think would have nothing but good things to say about themselves do the same thing.

Perhaps you've learned to be subtle about this practice of self-deprecation. In fact, I'll bet that you have. Most people finesse the self-bashing because they're aware that others won't like them if they freely and openly present themselves as losers, to put it bluntly, or if they whine about the ways in which they are ineffective, unsuccessful and otherwise unlucky in love and life. There's no reason to think you haven't developed this same skill at presenting yourself negatively without sounding like you loathe yourself. In my office, though, your guard is down and so you're less subtle about your shortcomings. Besides, I'm experienced at recognizing even subtle self-defeating messages, and again, if you're like most people, you pepper your self-description with negativity aplenty, no matter how subtle.

You explain to me that you've been trying to eliminate what's wrong with you instead of accepting your shortcomings and working around or with them, and you present this with some degree of pride: after all, aren't you supposed to eliminate the negative aspects of who you are? In a word, no. Or at least not always. That is, it is not always necessary to try to change your flaws and faults. If they end up being roadblocks to your happiness or success, then some change is necessary—but that change it isn't necessarily the *elimination* of those faults.

We're looking for balance here, so you must put both your strengths and weaknesses in perspective, and you must accept that some of both will always be in your life. That knowledge must not stop you in your tracks. For example, consider a client of mine whom I suspect could have had almost anything she wanted out of life, except for one devastating problem: she had never learned to accept her real self, warts and all.

Maggie was one of those women who turned the heads of both men and women when she walked into a room or passed them on the sidewalk. Her hair was honey-colored and her eyes were a startling cornflower blue; any larger and they might have looked odd, but they seemed to draw others into their lovely, expressive depths. She taught aerobics, so you can imagine the figure she had, and she dressed in exquisitely tailored clothes that seemed as if they'd been made for her alone.

When Maggie came in for her first appointment, she described her frustration and sadness over the lack of a central relationship in her life. As time passed, it became clear to me that the reason she didn't have a satisfying love life was because she had spent every spare moment of her life since she was a little girl trying desperately to maintain the image of perfection she projected. I learned that when she was only four years old, her mother and father had enrolled her in beauty pageants, an activity Maggie had continued with into her twenties, winning several significant titles. Now that she was in her late thirties, however, with no pageants to win in order to confirm her perfection, she was becoming more desperate; there were always younger, prettier girls in her aerobics classes, and everywhere else, for that matter. Between exercising, half starving herself, and chasing every new trend that held out hope for maintaining the "perfect" body, Maggie didn't have time for a relationship. She also couldn't bear for anyone to see what we came to call her "Miss America" self: made-up, elaborately coiffed, dressed impeccably, and speaking in modulated tones.

Had she allowed a lover close enough to drive away the loneliness and lack of intimacy she experienced, that lover would also have been close enough to see the real Maggie. He would have seen how her hair looked in the morning before she spent 30 minutes fixing it, and the circles under her eyes or the blemish on her chin before she spent another 30 minutes applying makeup each morning. He would have seen Maggie's lovely 37-year-old figure—and not the 21-year-old body Maggie expected herself to have. He would have heard her voice grow harsh if she was angry and hoarse if she had a bad cold. In short, he wouldn't have seen Miss America, he would have seen Maggie, and that was something she just couldn't tolerate.

HOW YOU GOT THERE

Just like my client Maggie, you undoubtedly received any number of messages from your earliest days about who you were supposed to be. These messages typically take two forms:

Here is what you *must* do and be . . .
            and
Here is what you *should* do and be . . .

Both types of messages are imperatives: insistent arguments that attempt to control and maintain behavior. Meanwhile, even as you were (and are) receiving these messages, you were probably saying to yourself:

If only I *could* do and be . . .

The distance between the "musts" and "shoulds" and the "coulds" can be immense, and it can often seem as if there's no way to cross it. In a sense, you can feel defeat before even beginning your journey toward change, since you see this towering inferno of expectations blocking your path. Because you aim to please—as do all children, and many adults—you get started on a path that doesn't reflect the authentic you, and once you're on that path, it can be very difficult to back up, retrace your steps, or abandon it altogether. And yet this is precisely what you must do. You must determine the real you, the hopes and needs and expectations and dreams that will create a sense of authenticity and satisfaction inside of you. Simultaneously, you must develop a sense of acceptance for that real self, letting go of the judgments, criticisms, and expectations imposed by others.

Making these changes has a great deal to do with maturation and development. Defining yourself is part of your developmental work, work that must be done by everyone in order to achieve any degree of autonomy and life satisfaction. Think of it this way: If you allow others to define who you are and who you will be, it's highly unlikely that they will chance upon the same "you" that you would design and define if left to your own devices. Those whom you allow to define you—parents, close family members, friends, and teachers, to name a few—are bound to impose their own needs, desires, and expectations on you unconsciously, resulting in a far different you than might otherwise emerge. Some of this process is both natural and unavoidable, of course; in your earliest years, you're shaped by those closest to you. You absorb many of your parents' values, beliefs, and behaviors as a result of mere proximity. You are, after all, being socialized during those formative years.

Early in life you feel not only the pressures of expectations from others, but also the first stirrings of nonacceptance and criticism. From the first moment that a parent responds negatively, as you express your creative self by festooning your highchair with spaghetti noodles, for example, through the angst that occurs over adolescent separation processes and beyond, others—including but hardly limited to your parents—are always attempting to shape you in one way or another. This shaping, which can be seen between parents and infants, but moves into high gear around the age of six, is a maturational process. It is a typical and expected part of the developmental stages that occur for everyone, and as you age, the shaping is brought into ever-higher relief. From parents to peers, from the media to the most casual acquaintance, pressure to be a certain way is a part of your life. Who was your role model at age 12? Does that person still influence your life in some way?

You might ask why this is a problem, if it's typical and part of everyone's developmental journey. Couldn't you just shrug off the pressure and be yourself, knowing that others are imposing their expectations on you for their own reasons, rather than for your well-being?

Unfortunately, while it would be nice if you could simply look the other way, secure in yourself and unaffected by others' expectations of you, it's not that easy. Earlier, we spoke about self-concept—your view of yourself—and that it is in part formed, by the way that others see you. This fact alone makes it difficult to treat others' expectations lightly. There are myriad other reasons, as well, that contribute to why it's difficult to define yourself independent of others' definitions, and also why it works against you when you don't have your own self-definitions.

ON PARENTS AND PARENTING

It would be remiss of me not to turn the microscope around and point at you the parent, after discussing the influence parents can have on you the child. It's important to remember that children have a strong desire to please, and will often try very hard to live up to the expectations of others. You should also keep in mind that children will live *down* to others' expectations. The are forming the self and are therefore most vulnerable to influences, so you as a parent—or as any other adult or authoritative influence—must be conscious of whether you're asking a child to strive to be the best person possible or unconsciously telling him or her that you don't believe they're capable of being who or what they wish.

If there is only one destructive choice that you make as a parent, it's to attempt to shape or motivate your children by telling them they're not good enough. This is emotional sandpaper: In the process of trying to smooth out your child's rough edges, you'll end up making that self disintegrate and disappear. If your own parents used this approach, acknowledge it and then get over it. It's too late to go back and change the past (see next chapter, "Fire Your Parents"). Blaming your parents is never the answer. Move on and put your energy where it can actually make a difference—in uncovering and accepting the authentic you that went into hiding when the sandpaper came out.

WHY THE OLD WAY DOESN'T WORK

THE SQUARE ONE DILEMMA.   This is a common problem that I see with clients, and since I've often found myself saying, "You can't seem to move past square one!" I've named this trend the "Square One Dilemma." If you believe that you must respond to the vast expectations of others—whether they're high or low is immaterial—you'll soon find yourself frozen, unable to move forward past square one. It is unrealistic for a short, pear-shaped man to meet the societal expectation of having a tall, barrel-chested Arnold Schwarzenegger body. It's equally unreasonable for a smart young girl to hide her smarts in order to appeal to boys, who may feel threatened by her if she towers over them academically. Think of times when you've felt the pressure to be or do something that is out of alignment for you, and you'll know that one of the most common results is a sense of being stuck. If you can't move forward in the expected direction, you often feel as if you can't move at all.

THE BALL AND CHAINS DILEMMA. Not only are you often unable to move past square one, but you're often dragged down by the expectations of others, unable to look at the wide range of options available to you. Part of being "frozen" is a sort of tunnel vision, a narrowing view of what your potential might be. Perhaps you're familiar with Emmé, the "plus-size" model who has recently appeared on magazine covers and even hosts her own modeling show on television. Because of her size, I imagine it must have been very difficult for Emmé to imagine herself as a supermodel; our society does not tend to give "big girls" permission to see themselves as beautiful, sexy, or alluring. She has received a fair amount of media attention because she has been successful despite—or perhaps because of—her size. Imagine what potential might exist if the fuss stopped! If magazines used plus-size models, who represent a significant percentage of the population, without imposing the judgment that doing so is unusual in some way, imagine the options that might open up for larger women. Similarly, think of the chains that would disintegrate if we ceased imposing limiting expectations on people with disabilities, or on people based on race or ethnicity or religious background.

THE OBSESSION DILEMMA. Many people also become focused on the expectations and judgments of others to the exclusion of their own wants, needs, and choices. Whether this is because it's difficult to refuse others, because you believe that others are in a better position to know who and what you should be, or for some other reason altogether, buying into others' needs for you burns you out. You're wasting energy negatively evaluating and suppressing your authentic self—energy that could be far better used accepting and "growing" yourself. As a result, your energy is drained off, burned out, and used up—all with nothing to show for it.

THE WORTHLESSNESS DILEMMA. There is only one way to say this, and that is with brutal honesty: When you accept the expectations and self-definitions others have for you, over your own expectations and self-definitions, you're basically saying you're worthless. Your real self, the authentic you, loses out because it can't compete with the "you" others want and need you to be. You"re telling the world that the real you can't compete and doesn't deserve to share the stage with the manufactured, imposed self others expect. What results from this, as you can imagine, is damage to your self-esteem and a muddying of your self-concept.

THE SADNESS DILEMMA.   It's sad when you subvert your authentic self in favor of the imposed self that others want or expect from you. I can't help but think of cosmetic surgery "junkies" when I think of the sadness associated with failing to live *your* chosen life in fulfillment of *your* chosen potential. Perhaps the most famous cosmetic surgery devotee is Cindy Jackson, the "Barbie Woman" who has spent over $100,000 on 20 surgeries to transform her figure and face into a representation of the original Barbie Doll.[2] The doll, if you weren't aware, has distinctly *in*human measurements; the human equivalent to Barbie measures 36–18–33.[3] While Jackson's story might sound funny at first read, think about it. Is she fulfilling her true, human potential?

Perhaps those who make similar choices are trying to shock others, or perhaps their choices are a bid for attention of another sort. But you can be sure that they're *not* at peace or content with themselves. Elective cosmetic surgery is evidence of this, and 20 elective, unnecessary surgeries is just excess evidence. Jackson's example is extreme, of course, but even in more ordinary cases, failing to accept yourself is sad for you, sad for others around you (since they don't benefit from the by-products of your unique authenticity), and sad for the larger world for the same reason. These by-products— the stifling of your creativity, and the inhibition of your ability to love yourself, among other outcomes—keep you from fulfilling anything even remotely close to your potential. If you ask me, few things are sadder.

On Parents and Parenting...

When Evelyn, a mid-forties mother of three teenagers, came to see me, she felt guilty, frustrated, and angry. She told me that she felt incapable of being the kind of mother she wanted to be. Evelyn confided that her children often seemed ungrateful, resentful, and downright rude. She "knew" it was "wrong" for her to feel so negatively about her own children, she admitted. "Feelings *can't* be wrong," I commented, but she had an answer ready. "A good mother," she insisted, "doesn't dislike her own children—*ever.*"

Evelyn began to talk about her relationship with her own mother; she said, "I can sum it up in one sentence: nothing I do is *ever* right." I asked Evelyn to consider the possibility that she hadn't let go of her own guilt, frustration, and feelings of anger at her mother, and that she was repeating the relationship with

her own children: unconsciously expecting them to disappoint her, in a sense. While Evelyn's logical self insisted for a time that this couldn't possibly be so— after all, she wanted "good" children—it was clear to me that a light came on for her as she began to think about the link between parents and parenting. Having never experienced being good enough, Evelyn hadn't learned how to see and expect the goodness in others. In learning to let go of seeing herself as a bad daughter, she discovered the secret to being a good mother.

ROOTS

You know now how you got to this point of self-judgment and out-of-sync existence, and you also know why it doesn't work to remain in this place. Before we move on to what you can do about it, let's briefly discuss how failing to accept yourself affects you systemically.

When others want you to be someone or something you're not, the underlying message you receive is that the real you just isn't good enough. Sometimes people will urge you to meet various expectations as a means of motivating or encouraging you, but this is a dangerous business because it still sends the potential message that you don't measure up. However, it's important to make a distinction between healthy expectations and unhealthy ones. I'm not saying, for example, that you should never have expectations of others, including your own children. To leave all expectations by the wayside would be disastrous.

The distinction between healthy and unhealthy expectations is actually quite simple: There is nothing wrong with expecting—and even demanding—certain *behavior* of others. The problem occurs when you expect—and demand—that another person *be* someone else. The key here is in the difference between *doing and being*. When you insist that another adopt certain values, beliefs, thoughts, or feelings, you've crossed the line. Likewise, you have lost yourself if you give in to demands or expectations that you do work that meets another's needs rather than your own, if you abandon creative efforts that bring you pleasure, or if you otherwise give up unique characteristics that make you special. Your life is about you; it's a simple concept, if difficult to execute at times.

ASSESSMENT

On the following pages you will be integrating what you have learned about the balance between your real, ideal, and imposed selves—work you began in the previous chapter—with what you're learning about accepting yourself. You will be using a figurative approach I have designed, creating a home in order to look at the important aspects of your life and the extent to which these aspects are ruled by others' expectations versus your own expectations and desires. Seeing the ways in which the needs and wants of others enter into your picture of yourself—and, more important, your acceptance of yourself—lays the foundation for separating the authentic "you" from the imposed "you." This is essential work that you must do, and work that will have profound effects on your life.

BUILDING
MYSELF

Your self-concept, as we have discussed, is a blend of perceptions. It contains the view you have of yourself and the view others have of you. Whether the perception comes from within or from others, it is made up of a blend of your physical, social, vocational, spiritual, and other selves. These selves that comprise the larger "you" can be represented by symbols, and there are any number of psychological tests that use symbols to help you identify the aspects of yourself. This assessment is a simple version I have created of just such a test. You are asked to draw or sketch or outline a house that best represents the real you, and once you have done so, we will examine the meaning of the choices you made in terms of the symbols you've selected. It doesn't matter if you "can't draw" or have no confidence in yourself as an artist or draftsman. No one will be judging your sketch. What's important is to focus in on which symbols best represent you, and to faithfully create a house that reflects who you are. In the field of psychology, certain symbols are generally accepted representations of feelings, beliefs, thoughts, and the like; as you choose these symbols, you will be making a statement about who you are.

There are several steps to this exercise. First, for each item listed on the left margin (i.e., "Windows"""), you will select one choice from Column A, B, or C. Second, you will draw this selection on the house outline provided (see page 146). Remember, your house may be a bit different from the outline we've provided, but for now let's just stick to this one outline. Then, once you have completed the items, you will examine your choices to learn more about yourself and the ways in which you are living life authentically or in the shadow of others' expectations.

HOUSE EXTERIOR

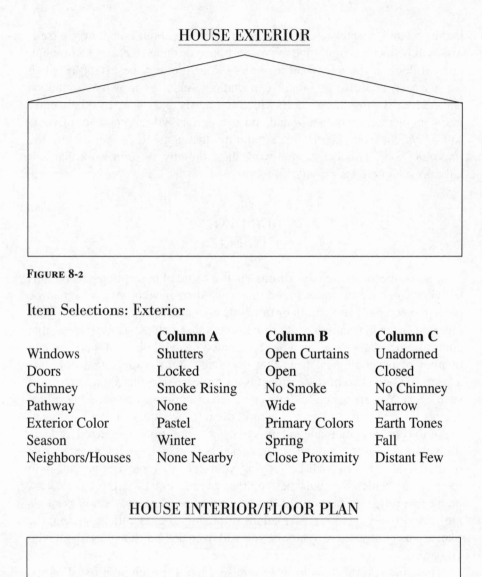

FIGURE 8-2

Item Selections: Exterior

	Column A	Column B	Column C
Windows	Shutters	Open Curtains	Unadorned
Doors	Locked	Open	Closed
Chimney	Smoke Rising	No Smoke	No Chimney
Pathway	None	Wide	Narrow
Exterior Color	Pastel	Primary Colors	Earth Tones
Season	Winter	Spring	Fall
Neighbors/Houses	None Nearby	Close Proximity	Distant Few

HOUSE INTERIOR/FLOOR PLAN

FIGURE 8-3

Item Selections: Interior

	Column A	Column B	Column C
Number of Rooms	3 to 4	8 or more	5 to 7
Layout	Private/Closed Off	Great Room Style	Integrated Mix
Interior Colors	Pastel	Primary Colors	Earth Tones
Hallways	Few/Narrow	Many/Open	Central to Plan
Living Rm. Furnishings	Minimal	Cluttered	Mix of Types
Temperature	Coats Needed	Slight Warmth	Slight Chill

UNDERSTANDING THE ASSESSMENT

Once you have completed your sketch of both the interior and exterior of your house, read the material that follows, checking back to examine your selections in light of the information provided.

On the Exterior: Seasons and Connections

Two of the most telling indications of who you are can be examined by looking at your choices of season and the proximity of neighbors.

Seasons

FALL. If you chose fall, there may be a "closing down" process at work in your psyche. This does not have to be a negative; indeed, it can indicate that you place a premium on preparedness, on readying yourself for whatever lies ahead. Conversely, it may indicate that you are in the process of withdrawing from people and activities around you or from the growth that you need to do. Fall signals a time of no-growth: the earth prepares itself for the long winter, for animals to hibernate and for growing things to burrow in and either die or hide until spring. You know yourself best; which is true for you? Are you like a squirrel, a gatherer of nuts in anticipation of the long winter, or are you a flower that cannot survive the cold? It may be that you are always on red-alert status, prepared to shut down at the first indication of "winter" (at the first sign of someone's withdrawal of affection, for instance, or at an indication of disapproval, coldness, or another hard-to-handle response).

WINTER. If instead you selected winter, many of the same observations made about fall may be true—yet more so. You have hibernated already; you have dug yourself in to survive the cold. Again, as with the autumn, this may not signal a negative; there are many people who are extremely self-sufficient, and they would be likely to choose winter as the season for their home since it indicates a separateness and ability to survive upon which the self-sufficient person thrives.

SPRING. The third choice carries a different meaning altogether. There is a positivity and hopefulness about spring, a sense of coming growth and blossoming that indicates that you are aware of your aliveness and your potential.

Why not summer? Summer was not offered as a choice because it has highly contradictory meanings. However, if you naturally would be drawn to summer, you're likely to be open, someone who enjoys engaging with others and keeping active. At the same time, the person drawn to summer might be somewhat more laidback than the fall or spring types, both of whom are engaged in planning and activity, one in preparation for closing down and the other in preparation for opening up.

Connections

How close you allowed your neighbors is also of much significance. This can convey your willingness to engage with and connect to others. Many close-by neighbors, obviously, indicates that you're comfortable with a higher degree of engagement with others. However, it can also indicate that you blur the line between self and others; in other words, you may not have clear boundaries. Does this sound familiar? Choosing to have no neighbors indicates just the opposite. Your boundaries are clear and firm, perhaps too much so—you do not have enough of the connection with others that feeds the soul. The third choice, some neighbors, indicates a balance: you have need for both engagement and space and would choose to balance these two needs, given the opportunity.

Other Exterior Choices

Now that you have examined your choices in terms of seasons and connections, you have established a groundwork, of sorts, that defines the fibers that bind you to the world around you. You can better understand the ways in which you connect to the outer world by examining whether your choices tended to be chosen from Column A, Column B, or Column C.

If you find that most of your selections came from Column A, you have made a decision to hold yourself distant from the world around you, as if it were unsafe. Your doors are locked, your windows shuttered, and you have no path leading others to you. The smoke that comes from your chimney is believed by psychologists to indicate anger—and it's no wonder if you do feel angry, considering the disconnection you've experienced and chosen. The pastels you've chosen for your exterior paint suggest a meek quality, a fearfulness, that goes hand-in-hand with the other indications of fear you've shown in your choices.

If you've chosen mostly selections from Column B, however, you are in many ways just the opposite. Your windows have curtains—but they are open. Others can see in. Your doors are open, and although you have a chimney, indicating that the warmth represented by a fireplace is available in your home, there is no smoke suggesting anger. The pathway to you is wide—others are welcome to approach, because you're comfortable with yourself and others. The bright, primary colors you've chosen indicate happiness and boldness.

With the Column C choices, you bridge a distance between A and B. You are not entirely settled with yourself, as indicated by the lack of curtains and the earth tones that allow you to blend into the background like an animal seeking to hide. There is no chimney—indicating no anger, perhaps, but also no warmth toward yourself—and while a path exists to your door (which is closed, indicating that it can either be opened or not, locked or unlocked), the path is narrow; you are not always easy to approach.

On the Interior: A Plan for Living

When you look at your choices for the interior of your home, perhaps the most compelling element of who you are is the layout of the house.

Walls and Floors

You won't be surprised to learn that a "Private/Closed Off" floor plan indicates something similar in terms of personality and choices: you have chosen to hide yourself keeping distant from and closed to others. A Great Room style, on the other hand, where there is a large, central gathering place with a constellation of more private rooms surrounding it, indicates a comfort with yourself, a confidence that the size and acceptability of your personality can sustain you and others. The third selection, where there is an integrated mix of types, indicates that you have not truly settled into yourself or into your choices for who you are and who you should be.

Another aspect of this house you've constructed is the floors. What type are they; wooden, stone, carpeted? What does the type of flooring you've selected say about you? Usually, the more luxuriant the floor, the greater degree of comfort you allow yourself or those around you. Carpeting can be both a luxury item or a means to keep noise down and allow yourself a quiet place.

It would be unusual for someone in this culture to have earthen floors, but that might have been your selection, and that could be seen in a number of ways. You might be someone who loves being close to nature and wants to get away from the life most of us lead. You might be a "free spirit" who enjoys communing with nature.

If you've chosen to carpet your floors, is it wall-to-wall or area rug, and, no matter which, what type design or weave have you selected? What does this particular type of carpeting represent for you? What does it remind you of and where might you have seen it? Interesting, how flooring can bring back memories and people or places that have influenced us.

Other Interior Choices

As with the choices for the exterior of the house, the interior choices fall into three categories. The first choices, located in Column A, generally indicate a closed-off self and a sense of discomfort with and disapproval of who you are. There are few rooms with which to accommodate yourself; the hallways are narrow and the furnishings minimalist. The temperature is kept so cold that coats are needed. In Column B, the bright colors, large number of rooms, open and abundant hallways, and warmth indicate a comfort with yourself and a settled quality of acceptance for who you are. An unsettled quality, however, is suggested by significant selections from Column C, where there is a slight chill to the air and the furnishings don't match, despite the fact that the layout is largely integrated and the hallways are central to the plan. In other words, you are at times accepting and at times not, at times comfortable in your skin and at times not. It will be important for you to examine these areas carefully so you can begin to eliminate the judgmental or critical parts of yourself.

A Last Note on Building Yourself

Each of these selections, both exterior and interior, symbolize something you perceive about yourself, something you have come to believe is true within yourself and within your relationships with others and the larger world around you. It is worth looking at each choice carefully in order to determine which of these choices you can change—and which you want to change—in order to learn to accept yourself more readily. Remember, however, *you won't fit perfectly into any one* of the three models we've provided, and if you don't, that's fine. This is an exercise to get you to begin thinking about who you are and who you might want to become—within reason. If you're comfortable with whichever choice you've made, that's okay too. The idea is to understand and accept yourself, not remake yourself into someone who will fit you like an itchy wool suit in the middle of summer.

PRESENT TENSE

What will happen to you if you decide to accept yourself? Is it possible that the world truly won't turn its back on you, or suggest that you're narcissistic, arrogant, and generally not someone to spend time with? Based on my experience and training, I'd argue that the opposite will occur. Others may envy you, and they may act out toward you at times because of that envy. But isn't it better to be envied and satisfied with yourself than to be self-critical and unaccepting of who you truly are? Of course it is.

When you choose to accept yourself, you eliminate the impediments to a happy, healthy life. You become comfortable with yourself, and comfortable people roll with the punches better. Your sense of inadequacy will be eliminated. Because you won't be wasting time on judging yourself negatively—which eats up huge amounts of energy—you can, and will, devote your energies to more productive activities. You will discover that you are freed up in any number of ways: emotionally, timewise, spiritually, intellectually, creatively. In fact, just name the area of your life—you'll experience changes in it.

When it comes to letting go of your critical self and becoming comfortable within your own life and your own skin, there really is only one way to do it: Accept yourself . . . warts and all.

CHAPTER 9

Fire Your Parents

I WAS A TERRIBLY UNHAPPY BOY. . . MY FAMILY WAS A MISERABLE
FAMILY AND MY MOTHER WAS A HORRIBLE CREATURE . . .
I GREW UP IN LIBRARIES AND AMONG BOOKS, WITHOUT FRIENDS.
WITH MY CHILDHOOD, IT'S A WONDER I'M NOT PSYCHOTIC.

Abraham Maslow[1]

Find a small object from a place where you've frequently felt calm and good.
A seashell is perfect; the sea often reminds us of the rhythms of life, providing a larger perspective when we lose our ability to see the forest for the
trees—or the ocean for the waves. We sometimes forget that life is not guaranteed to be smooth sailing or an easy voyage, and so we become focused on
the hardships to the exclusion of all else. Keep the object you've found with
you, thinking of it as a talisman against difficulty and as a reminder of the
ebb and flow of the hard times with the easy moments. At difficult times, at
moments of celebration, at any times, tune into this talisman, remembering
that you have invested it with the power to soothe as it takes you back to the
place where you have experienced ease and calm. Allow the object to support and sustain you through your memories and senses. Whether you keep
it in your pocket or on your desk, or whether you wear it as jewelry or hang
it from a key ring, keep it in sight whenever you can—and nearby always.

GET OVER THE PAST AND LIVE IN THE PRESENT

I've got some bad news for you—but it's the best bad news you're ever going to
get, if you'll just hear me out, reserving any judgments you have until I'm done.
　You can't go home again. I've learned that and plenty else in the 25 years
I've been working side by side with people through the challenges of their

lives. But if there's one thing I've learned that is *absolute* it is that no bliss-ful second childhood awaits you, patiently preparing for your return so it can nurture you, reparent you, or give you the happiness you missed out on the first time around.

One of the most damaging myths that psychotherapists have perpetrated over the past 20 years or so is that a childhood like Maslow's—or that was slightly better or far worse—can be repeated, somehow, if they didn't go as you'd hoped on the first run-through. I'd say I'm sorry to be the one to break the news to you, but I'm not; it's time you learn, if you haven't already, that the myth of the second childhood has no place in reality. You've seen the bumper stickers: THIS ISN'T A DRESS REHEARSAL. Maslow, who would be a brilliant motivational psychologist as an adult, knew the misery of a painful childhood and spent a lifetime creating a theory of psychology that we can theorize he hoped might ease, or at least explain, his own harsh memories. Countless others have had similar trials and traumas and spent their time on the therapy couch hoping for some combination of absolution and release.

Perhaps you're one of those very seekers, and if you are, be assured that it's true: There are therapists who will take your money and climb into a hot tub with you, simulating your birth so you can "work out the birth traumas" that keep you stuck. Other therapists will take your money and listen to you week after week as you sob out the tortured story of being the forgotten mid-dle child, while others will take your money and sympathize with you end-lessly about just how bad you've got it. You notice the common thread, I'm sure, regardless of the content or type of the therapy offered.

Don't misunderstand me: I'm not suggesting that you don't have issues, traumas, and even tragedies in your past. You're a person, and that means you've undoubtedly got a collection of grief and anger and disappointments, like everyone else. So let's assume that you did suffer birth trauma, or that you were ignored, stuck between two siblings, one an overachieving first-born and the other a Mommy's favorite baby of the family. Whether you've suffered is not the point; you have. We all have. The point is *how you go about healing yourself*—and *how long* you take along the way.

It's your prerogative to take weeks, months, and even years to find the cure for what ails you, but if you've read this far, I suspect that's not your style—not anymore, at least—and I know it's not mine. You want change, and you want it sooner rather than later. Like most people, you've probably tried the leisurely approach to self-understanding and discovered that when all the exploration was done, you were still left holding the baggage.

It's time for a change—a sweeping, immediate change—and that change will come about with the 10 tools for creating the life you want and the life you deserve. And of all the tools, "Fire Your Parents" is one of the most liberating and powerful you will encounter. Not surprisingly, though, and in part *because* of the very powerful results it creates, it can also be one of the most challenging tools you'll use.

"Fire Your Parents" gives you the means to create change in every aspect of your life—in your self-esteem, your self-concept, and your degree of helplessness and hopelessness—by focusing on three major areas.

This chapter will help you assess and understand the power of your past by examining the beliefs you absorbed from your earliest days—the same beliefs you still cling to, whether they work or not. Imagine a drowning man holding onto a block of concrete as if it is a life preserver, not realizing that the very thing he thought would protect and save him is pulling him under. The outdated roles and rules from your family of origin can be just that way. The beliefs you hold, most of which are about the roles you've taken on in your family and the rules you've unconsciously followed, show up throughout your life in any "system" of two or more people: work groups, social cliques, and the like. It's common to mimic your earliest family-of-origin roles and rules in later systems, from the workplace to the family you create as an adult. After all, we tend to veer toward the familiar, because of comfort, ease, or because it represents the path of least resistance. This is not always negative, but it *does* always have a tremendous impact on how you feel about yourself and how you relate to others.

In addition to assessing how the powerful past can rule your present and future, in this chapter we'll identify the ways in which your focus on the past, both conscious and unconscious, continues to keep you stuck in unworkable beliefs and behaviors. And finally, we'll illustrate concrete methods for breaking free from your past and for creating a new present and future of your own design.

But first, as you set out to purge the past and embrace the future, you have a task in front of you that cannot be ignored or delayed. Before you can stop looking in wistfully at each warm, lamplit window for a rescuer's face—which is a seductive hope——before you can take on the adult behaviors and truly relate to others as an adult, instead of in imitation of your parents, you must accept this one basic truth: *once you leave childhood, you will never again find anyone who can make it* all *right.*

DISMANTLING THE MYTH

It's time now to dismantle the myth that a second childhood awaits, complete with perfect nurturing, gentle acceptance, and unconditional support. If

you're going to be your own therapist, you must let go of what has happened
to you in the past—no matter how tragic or traumatic—and focus your energies in *only two directions*: the present and the future. Let's spend a moment
in the past, then, understanding its impact upon you and recognizing your
strength and the lessons you've learned, before leaving it behind for good.

Where You've Been: Redeemable Moments

Precious few of us reach adulthood without scars, bruises, and baggage. By
the time you were delivered at the doorstep of your 20s, you probably had
plenty of suffering tucked away in your memory, some buried, festering in
silence, and some exposed, out there, bloody and raw. Add a decade or so,
along with job changes, losses, marriage, and parenthood that so many
Americans first experience in their 20s, and you can guarantee yet more
scars; whether we experience "good stress" or "bad stress," it still leaves its
mark. In fact, Holmes and Rahe's Social Readjustment Scale[2] gives a higher
stress rating to certain events that are traditionally thought of in positive
terms—such as becoming a parent—than it does to some negative events like
being the victim of a crime! If you've been a parent, this is perhaps no surprise, but even if you haven't, it still should make sense: If the stressful event
is one that pervades every area of your life—as does parenthood—it will
have a profound effect on you.

Back before the stressful events of adolescence, the teen years, and adulthood, there was the cocoon of family. Even if you didn't have a happy childhood, and if you're like the majority of people, you'll say—and believe—
that you felt safe in the bosom of family. You'll probably also say that things
seemed simpler to you back then. Sure, Mom was a little high-strung, and
Dad didn't ever want to talk about feelings, but no one lied, cheated, or stole
in your family, not as far as you knew—and if they did, it was what you
knew, the norm, and so it didn't carry the weight that such things would have
when you encountered them later in life. Because they were all you knew, the
rules were clear and the roles were all right. Everyone danced their particular dance according to some pattern that seemed long established and somehow safe.

If safety and simplicity were hallmarks of most childhoods, that is not to
say that everyone remembers *happiness*—these qualities are hardly the
same. Some people remember only the good times, and some remember only
the bad. *The challenge is in finding a balance rather than telling a war story*,
an occupation that makes up the bulk of so much therapy. What is forgotten
in the recounting of wounds or in the competition to see whose scars are

worst is that even in war stories there is poignancy and beauty. There are always redeemable moments. Look at the Holocaust as an example—could there be a story in which a redeemable moment is less likely? And yet, in even those dark years there are war stories containing the most haunting beauty and kindness, virtues brought into stark relief against the backdrop of so much horror.

What you must do as you return to your past is *not* perform a careful accounting of your damages; instead, if you're to benefit from the past and then leave it behind—and make no mistake, the past is exactly where your baggage belongs—you must search for the grace, the lessons learned, the themes that you can excavate carefully and carry as beacons. These would be the redeemable moments made up of people and events that shine, however dim, up from the distance of your history.

Maria was raised in a coldwater flat in Brooklyn, and her earliest memories—all of her memories through young adulthood, in fact—seem to include a sea of familiar faces, aunts and uncles, grandparents and babies and more, filling that flat with their loud, angry voices. The voices rang with the disappointment and hopelessness and outrage of never-enough—money, silence, space, warmth—making a siren song that filled the hallways of the tenement, cutting into the quiet Maria so envied in the less crowded flats on either side. As an adult Maria lived alone—and lonely—often bitterly lamenting her loneliness even as she complained of her childhood and the noise and chaos that had never stopped. A very patient friend who had listened to Maria's story many times one day became impatient and asked her if she'd ever felt lonely as a child. In that moment Maria—who had the gift of being honest with herself, even if full of complaints to others—began to see her history in a different, softer light. She realized that she had let the past own her present and future.

From Then to Now: Leaving the Past Behind

As you prepare to leave your past behind, taking with you those things that will be of value to you in your new life—just as you would if you were leaving your parents' home as a young adult—you'll need to consider two sets of needs and feelings.

The Terminated

One of the two sets of needs and feelings you must take into account are those of "the terminated"—your parents or other authority figure(s). The wise supervisor doesn't fire an employee without regard for his or her feelings, and you are in an even trickier position, since years or even a lifetime of patterned behavior, including love and admiration, have been involved. This is no lower-rung employee you run into in the cafeteria now and then. As often as not it's the person who literally *gave you life*, the person who helped you believe in yourself when you were most unsure, the person who encouraged you to take brave new chances when you were most fearful. It's easy to slip into a sense of guilt over the decision you've made to change this relationship, and this is something to guard against. Guilt has never been a sound basis for a decision, let alone a relationship. At the same time, though, it is important to honor the value the relationship has held for you at times in the past, and possibly even now.

Remember that even though the relationship is not working for you now—or will not work, not if you're to lead a truly adult, responsible life— it *did* work for you, more or less, perhaps over many years. And so, though you've chosen to redefine the relationship to fit who and what you are and want to be, and there's no reason for you to feel guilt about it, your decision does not erase the positive aspects you once experienced. Your parents will recall those positive aspects as well, and so your decision to redefine the roles in the relationship might well feel like a betrayal to them. In all likelihood you will appear suddenly disloyal and ungrateful, a Judas who is betraying the very person (or people) you have admired unquestioningly for so long. This is a shock for those who were authority figures in your life, and it's bound to result in painful feelings and difficult moments, during which it will be hard to know just what to do.

Perhaps the most effective and soothing thing you can do is to acknowledge—to yourself and to your authority figures—that the changes you are making are about growth and forward movement, not rejection and disavowal of the role or roles they once played in your life.

The Terminator

At the same time that you're considering the feelings and needs of those you have looked to as an authority figures, you must also keep a watchful eye on yourself. After all, you can't overlook the fact that letting go of the familiar dynamic of having a rescuer hovering nearby is also a major change for you. It can be worrisome to think about losing the safety net you've relied upon, and to know that the endless well of answers—even if they might have done more harm than good—will dry up because of your choice to make changes. Many people choose the difficult familiar over the unfamiliar, even though the unfamiliar may bring an incredible wealth of positive energy and change.

By the way, if you're thinking that it won't be difficult changing the terms of your relationship since there's no love lost between you and your authority figure(s)— usually a parent—I would disagree. In fact, I wouldn't believe any insistence on your part that the love you feel for a parent or other authority figure is dead and gone. The more anger and hate you hold onto, the more love is lurking in the recesses of your heart. When homicide detectives investigate murders, they know that the most violent crimes are committed against loved ones, not against sworn enemies or distant strangers—they call this phenomenon "overkill" and it's what you're trying to do when you deny any remaining glimmer of positive feeling for your authority figure. Your heart follows the overkill maxim: the more anger you hold toward someone, the more thoroughly you try to blanket and hide the many wounded surfaces of your heart—and hearts don't get wounded by people you don't care about.

The fact is, if you're like most people, you'll find that firing your parents isn't easy or simple at first—and perhaps not at all. That's all right; it's not meant to be. After all, you're making drastic changes to what may be the longest-standing relationship you've had. And you're also taking back the authority in a relationship where the authority has always been assumed to belong to the authority figure by default. This can be confusing and difficult for the terminated and the terminator, and we'll talk more about the how-to's a bit later in the chapter. For now, though, it is useful for you to be prepared for mixed feelings as you explore how you reached this point and as you contemplate making these changes.

Because of the challenges posed by these major changes, at this point you'll want to do more than simply acknowledging the "gray area" of positives and negatives that the relationship has offered. It will also be helpful to consider how you ended up in this position. Exploring this issue has two major benefits. First, it will help you trace the path you've taken from independence to dependence—because there was a time, undoubtedly, when you relied less heavily on your parent or authority figure. I will talk about this and the theory of "learned helplessness" in the next chapter, but for now, suffice it to say that learned helplessness means that when someone exhibits power over you and underscores your dependence, you become more and more helpless—or less and less capable of helping yourself—out of habit and out of disuse of the "self-rescuing" skills that are typically developed over a lifetime.

Self-rescuing skills include the ability to stick up for yourself and the commitment to squarely face your strengths and weaknesses. They also include the courage to be truthful with yourself and others about your feelings, needs and beliefs, and the willingness to reach out for support from others when you are struggling. These tools, like any, rust when they're unused and poorly maintained. That's exactly what is happening here when you rely on a parent or authority figure—a guru of sorts—to "solve your life" for you.

Exploring how you ended up in this relationship with these dynamics gives you the building blocks to understanding how to avoid repeating the mistake again, whether with the same person or a different one.

A second major benefit of exploring the roots of this relationship—whether or not you're firing your *literal* parent—is that you can look to your actual parent-child relationship for an understanding of how you developed your views toward and interaction style with people in authority positions in general.

Authority and Dependency

Undoubtedly you'll come up with reasons, specific to you, that explain how your relationship became one of dependence and "guruism." What follows are three of the most common categories of explanations I've seen in my practice when I've worked with people who were feeling stuck in the guru–grateful receiver role.

Role/Rule Issues

In relationships based upon one person taking responsibility for another, the most common roots are typically planted in role and rule issues. We are all raised according to certain rules, often the same rules our parents were also expected to obey without question as children and young adults. We are also steeped in roles: Dad is the authority figure and breadwinner; Mom is the artist and the soft touch if Dad is unyielding; a younger brother is the math whiz and troublemaker; and so on. No doubt you can identify one or two roles that each member of your family occupies.

You were raised with certain rules and roles echoing around you, reflecting the attitudes and practices of your parents regarding authority and responsibility for yourself. These rules and roles taught you, from your earliest days, that you should not challenge authority because if you did:

- You would make your parents look bad.

- The neighbors would judge you/your parents harshly.

- You would annoy, inconvenience, and anger your parents.

Furthermore, the roles may have taught you that "children are to be seen and not heard,'" that "good girls" don't challenge authority figures or that "good boys" don't challenge adults (who are presumed to be better informed).

These and dozens of other spoken and unspoken rules and roles can have a powerful impact on how you interact with authority. While there is nothing wrong with instilling a healthy respect for authority in children—and, in fact, to have no respect for authority is equally disastrous—this respect can go overboard and become an unquestioning, Stepford-wife type of acceptance and acquiescence, whatever the authority figure is saying.

Authority Issues

Along with issues surrounding the rules and roles taught in your earliest significant relationships, lessons learned about authority can be at the root of your rescuing interactions with others later in life as well.

The primary authority issue I've encountered is a misguided belief that it's easier to be an autocrat—a parent who hands down pronouncements from on high as if democracy was just a passing failed experiment from some long-distant age. Think of boot camp and the armed forces and you'll be on track with an autocrat's leadership style.

Hand in hand with this belief, to which many subscribe, is an approach to independence and self-responsibility that emphasizes "staying inside the box," following the rules, and obeying authority without question. In other words, a strong emphasis on authority works at cross purposes to developing independent thought and self-responsibility. Unwavering faith in authority probably works in the trenches—after all, you can't have half your soldiers popping up out of the troop's hiding place announcing that they've got a better idea while enemy bullets whiz past. In normal circumstances, though, blind faith in authority is an invitation to trouble: think Hitler; think Nixon; think Ted Bundy assuring a trusting young woman that she's safe in his car.

Safety Issues

The other major category of root causes for abdicating one's responsibility and blindly following another authority concerns safety issues. You often hear veiled or outright warnings—particularly in childhood and adolescence—about the many dangers of straying from the tried-and-true path. Making a decision of your own, a decision that may not correspond to your parents' beliefs or wishes, can create anxiety for them—and as a result, for you. Like most people, you were probably taught that the safest choice is to follow the rules ("Better safe than sorry!") and that trouble accrues to those who insist on operating outside of the generally accepted norms. Depending on the society in which you live, these norms may leave you space for individuality or they may limit you. Either way, however, repeated warnings will leave you with an expectation of danger resulting from your own choices—and that can't help but influence the choices you make about taking responsibility for yourself and being your own powerful authority.

The Roots: Muddying the Waters of Self-Concept

One of the distinctions that sets us apart from all other animals is our ability to conceive of "the self" as a tangible, authentic being. Dogs, birds, and worms do not know that they exist, and they certainly do not wonder about the meaning of life or the consequences of the choices they make. You, though, must form a picture of yourself; this is one of your earliest, most important, and ongoing life tasks. And while this self-portrait can change over time, it is remarkably stable through the years, in large part because you find ways to reinforce your existing beliefs about yourself. You surround yourself with friends who view you much as you view yourself, and you choose activities and behaviors that are consistent with your beliefs about yourself. The result of all the careful creating and maintaining of self-image is a fairly static self-concept.

The self-concept had its earliest roots, however, in a time before you were making many choices. By the age of three you had a well-established, though not unyielding, sense of self which you expressed by your answering "No" to requests adults made of you. Much of what would come in the years ahead was simply additional layering that confirmed the underlying foundation formed so early on.

Firing your parents—or making substantial shifts in any authority-based relationship, for that matter—is related to self-concept more heavily than to the other two roots we've discussed: self-esteem and helplessness/hopelessness.

The connection to self-concept has some of its origins in gender differences, which are part of your earliest unconscious lessons. Women tend to see themselves in relationship to others, for example, while men tend to view themselves in terms of what they do, and so women are more likely to adopt a guru and bow to his or her opinions and beliefs. Men will be more likely to do so if they determine that abdicating responsibility is the most logical or expedient path to resolving a situation. These are generalizations, of course, and should be taken as such—there are exceptions to every rule, and exceptions to every exception, as well.

You should be aware, however, that your self-concept is behind your decision to cede authority to others rather than retain it yourself. A clear self-concept that includes a view of yourself as powerful, strong, intelligent, competent, and confident will not permit you to turn your self-responsibility over to another. A red flag is being waved—one you should not ignore—if you *do* give up authority. You can consider it a message from your self-concept telling you that there is damage, but room for healing in how you view yourself.

Recall the difference we discussed earlier in the book: self-concept is who you believe yourself to be, while self-esteem is how you feel about yourself, but also remember that the two are inextricably connected. The third root issue, helplessness, may also eventually result from these self-concept and self-esteem difficulties.

A self-concept that permits you to abdicate responsibility also spells self-esteem trouble. Think about it: With a negative self-view you're going to approach life's challenges with self-defeating behaviors; there's no way around it—except to do some major renovation work on your self-concept.Let's talk a bit more, though, about how self-concept and self-esteem are connected, and about why letting the first drive the second—when the first is negative—is so ineffective.

WHY THE OLD WAY DOESN'T WORK

By now you're well aware that I'm not fond of getting bogged down in the past. While someone else is slowly, painstakingly deconstructing—and then reconstructing—her history, I'd much rather be charging ahead, focusing on discoveries that count today and making changes that impact tomorrow. The past is the past is the past. In real estate they say that the three key features of any property are "location, location, location." In my brand of therapy—the brand that will make me obsolete, since you can learn to do it for yourself—the key features are "now, now, now!" If it happened yesterday, by all means tell me about it (undoubtedly we'll learn something), but then let's move on!

We can spend five percent of our time on what went wrong, but from this point on, let's save 95 percent for figuring out what to do right, and how to do it. In keeping with that equation, then, let's talk about why the old ways, the established habits and unconscious patterns, don't work, and then we'll figure out what you can do right now in terms of authority and self-responsibility to make your life work spectacularly for you.

There are two general types of messages you'll receive throughout life that are intended to keep you "in line"—whatever and wherever that line might be. Those messages are either external—the kind that come from *others* in positions of authority or influence in your life—or they're internal, the "self talk" that *you* send to keep yourself on a certain path. Within these two message categories you'll discover some of the following reasons for why giving over your authority to others doesn't work.

Messages from on High

The authority figures around you cannot remain on the throne unless you agree to keep them there. For that reason, many authority figures will find a way to inhibit you or stop you altogether from rebelling against the pronouncements they hand down. This can be effective for the authority figure, but it doesn't help you. The power struggles that naturally occur in a one-up one-down relationship don't benefit you because the bottom line is that if you're busy rebelling—or if you're busy suppressing the desire to rebel—then you're not learning.

Another reason the "old ways" don't work is that they depend on static authority figures. In other words, if your authority figure changes in certain ways, you're sunk. Maybe the guru doesn't want to be a guru anymore; maybe the guru takes a philosophical nose-dive to the right and you've always been left-leaning. Whatever the change or changes made by the authority figure, you can be left guruless—and as a result, without answers that work even marginally anymore. Another problem is that you don't want the authority to change because it will leave you floundering. So you play a role by helping to define and keep Mom and Dad ogres or your therapist an infallible expert.

Messages from the Inner You

Viewing your choice from the inside, choosing to rely on another person to make the decisions and to come up with answers for you, is also damaging, particularly over the long run. If you suddenly find that you don't have someone in this role, you will become heavily engaged in the search for a new guru, and meanwhile feel empty and lost without the guidance to which you're accustomed. You will also find that your creativity is sidetracked and increasingly "toothless" over time, your unused creativity shrivels up.

Relying on someone else to handle your life—to come up with options, evaluate those options, and make decisions for you—also *puts up walls.* You are willingly placing yourself in the role of helpless sycophant, and you're placing the authority figure in the role of expert, roles that are inaccurate, inauthentic, unnatural, and distancing. In addition, life demands flexibility, and while you know this in your heart, if you are rigidly following proscribed rules and roles, you'll find precious little flexibility. *Without flexibility, taking responsibility for yourself and being the power in your own life is impossible.* All that *is* possible, in fact, is falling back on the established behaviors you've used before, the ones that leave you relying on someone else rather than piling up experience running your own life, and building up confidence in yourself as you do so.

From this point forward, you need to be the architect of your own life, not the day laborer who does someone else's bidding.

ASSESSMENT

Ideally, you would live in a balance of the past, present, and future. If you were able to achieve this balance, one foot would be anchored in the past so you would always have the benefit of your experience, and two feet would be planted firmly in the present since that's where you exist. At the same time, you would keep an eye toward where you would set your foot in the future so that you were always striving/growing. There are many obstacles to achieving this balance, however, not least of which is that you probably don't have three feet. Let's overlook that, though—you're clever and will come up with something—and look at the real obstacles. This balance requires the equilibrium of a high-wire artist, the insight of a seer, and the courage and wisdom of a sage. But *you can start and grow in skill from here.* You may feel like a klutz, blinded by confusion, scared and unwise. *And so... you can only improve from here!*

You can also look inside your experience, using the assessment tool below, in order to achieve a clear picture of the factors that impact on your relationship with authority. Examining the ways in which you relate to authority, both intellectually and emotionally, you will begin to form an understanding of not only the role authority plays in your life, but the many insidious ways it influences your choices, from moment to moment.

Take a few minutes to read through the following scenarios, answering each quickly and "from the gut." All are based on the idea of you returning home for a holiday celebration. If this isn't a scenario that seems likely to you, do the best you can of playing out what you would do. Also look at the italicized responses to each situation; they offer an alternative for how you might handle a similar situation in a way that is supportive of your independence and well-being.

GOING HOME AGAIN: FIRING YOUR PARENTS ASSESSMENT

You've heard the saying that "You can't go home again," but rare is the person who doesn't try. In your attempt to resolve past issues and revisit fond memories alike, you can discover unplumbed depths about the nature and quality of your relationship with your parents or other authority figures.

Read the following scenarios and then choose the answer that feels *closest* to how you would be most likely to react, or to how you have reacted when you tried to return home. Circle the number (this represents points assigned) at the end of each answer you select; select only one answer per scenario. Although no response may feel exactly right, *pick the one closest to your typical response.*

Scenario: You are returning home to celebrate the holidays. Your mom wants you to stay with her and your siblings, who are also returning home, but past experience tells you that tempers will flare by the second day. You know that if you stay at a hotel, your mother will, as always, be offended and hurt, and she will say that the conflict is either in your mind or something you bring on yourself. You:

1. Figure it's not worth upsetting your mother and just bear the miserable nights together. (2)

2. Tell your mother you're staying in a hotel and will not listen to her complaints about it, and that if she can't accept that, you just won't come to the celebration at all. (5)

(continued)

3. Decide that you take things too personally, as your mother always says, and agree to stay at home with everyone, accepting that you need to work harder at getting along. (3)

4. Explain to your mother that it's best if you stay in a hotel—and why—and let her know that it's nothing personal, but that you're very firm about doing it this way. (0)

Scenario: At the holiday meal, you choose food carefully; you've lost considerable weight, a fact you're proud of, and you don't want to slip up over the holidays. When your mother urges you to eat more and you politely decline, your father says, "Nonsense! You're way too skinny!" and begins to pile more food on your plate. You:

1. Clench your teeth and keep quiet, figuring you'll just leave what you can't eat and not cause a big scene in front of everyone. (2)

2. Get up from the table and make an announcement about your weight loss—that you've achieved with no thanks to anyone at the table—and let your family know that if they can't support you in this, you'll just go eat at a restaurant. (6)

3. Take the filled plate and matter-of-factly return portions to the serving dishes, saying you were just trying to avoid wasting food since you've been watching what you eat. You add, perhaps, that you don't want to quit now, when you're feeling so good about your success. (1)

4. Take the full plate, feeling guilty for upsetting things, and accepting that perhaps you've lost enough weight for now, since they're describing you as skinny. (4)

Scenario: Birthday gifts are being opened and you wait excitedly. Although you haven't spent much money—which family members usually do, in a competitive spirit you dislike—you have spent long hours compiling a scrapbook of memories for your brother. The result is a beautiful and irreplaceable history of his childhood. When he opens the gift, he makes a strange face and his response is lackluster. Your older sister pointedly says, "I didn't realize we were on a budget this year." You:

1. Feel hurt and angry that she's implying you're cheap, but swallow your feelings since it will turn into an unpleasant scene if you say anything. (3)

2. Respond to your sister by commenting that you've realized over the years that the best gifts you've gotten are ones from the heart, and so you've

(continued)

changed how you value gifts, putting your focus into labors of love instead of expensive quick gifts. You also (perhaps) pull her aside privately later to let her know that you felt hurt and/or attacked by her comment. (1)

3. Angrily let your sister know that you spent far more hours of effort on your gift than she's ever spent on any gift—especially the tacky thing she gave your brother this year. You also make sure your brother knows that you didn't miss his lackluster display of appreciation. (6)

4. Berate yourself silently or out loud since you know how your family is about spending on gifts; it's the only thing that really counts. (4)

Scenario: You bought a home with your romantic partner and let your parents know you'll be attending the holiday gathering together. Your parents let you know that you won't be welcome to share a bedroom in their home, even though you're an adult. You:

1. Let your parents know that you respect their right to make the rules in their own home, and tell them you think everyone would be more comfortable if you and your partner were in the house for all of the festivities but stayed elsewhere at night. (1)

2. Think of lots of cutting things to say to your parents about how old-fashioned they are, but you don't since they'll just ignore you anyway. Instead you mutter, "Fine," and spend a bizarre three nights across the hall from the person you sleep with 362 nights a year. (2)

3. Finally have it out with your parents, informing them in no uncertain terms that you live with this person and share a bed, among other things, every other night. You let them know that you're not a child anymore and that you're tired of being treated like one: either you share a room or they just won't see you over the holidays. (7)

4. Listen to why your parents don't want you sharing a room and then decide that since they've lived longer or have more experience at life than you, they're right about this—and stay in the separate rooms, defending your parents' position to your partner. (3)

Scoring Your Answers

Once you've responded to each scenario, add up the numbers at the end of each response you selected. You should add up a total of four scores. Look for

(continued)

your total in the rating scale below. If you find that your score is on the bor-
derline of two categories (within one or two points of the range), the myths in
each of those two categories are likely to be ones you subscribe to at various
times. For instance, a score of 14 would indicate your discomfort with rock-
ing the boat and a semipervasive sense that you may mess up your life or that
your family knows more than you do.

Interpretations

Score of 0 to 6: *I'm Okay, You're Okay . . .*

- It's okay to have needs and wants of my own.
- The sky will not crumble if I have views that differ from others' views.
- I don't have to treat others with kid gloves; they can handle me being me.

Score of 7 to 12: *I shouldn't rock the boat . . .*

- If I make waves in my family, I'll be left alone and unhappy.
- If I don't live up to the expectations of others, I'll be miserable.

Score of 13 to 17: *I'll screw up my life/They know more than I do,
even about me . . .*

- I need to depend on others to help guide me in my life.
- My parents/doctors/teachers are more capable than I am.
- I'll never be able to stand on my own two feet.
- If my parents think poorly of me, I must be doing something wrong.
- Only my parent/guru/etc. understand me.
- My parents only have my best interests at heart.
- No one really loves me for who I am (if they really knew me they wouldn't
  love me).

Score of 18 to 24: *There ain't enough room in this town for both of us . . .*

- It's not wrong to question authority figures and to do it in a stinging manner no matter how destructive it is.
- If I question their answers, they'll stop rescuing me or helping me but I'll
  suffer the consequences.
- If I disagree with them, they'll be angry with me and not love me anymore,
  but if I give in, I'm sunk for good and I don't care if I'm burning my
  bridges.

PRESENT TENSE

Where You Are Now: Understanding Your Choices

Now that you have identified where you stand on the "Self-Authority Scale," let's talk first about some of the major benefits to making the changes that will nudge you off the scale and into your life—a life of immediate, powerful self-authority. There are three primary benefits to taking back the authority in your life.

First, when you abdicate responsibility for the decisions and behaviors you choose, you also give up the pleasure and pride that accompany difficult decisions you've made. If someone else is responsible for the choices in your life, you can bet that they will expect the benefits and rewards to accrue to them as well, since you've remained in the background, in a no-risk position. No guts, no glory—if you aren't willing to take risks and step forward into the harsh glare of the lights, you don't get the benefit of the warm illumination when choices are well made either.

A second benefit to taking control of your personal authority is that you will immediately experience an increase in self-confidence, self-esteem, and sense of competence. You'll be amazed—wonderfully, magically so—when you feel the rush of independence that swells inside you after you shrug off the heavy weight of others' approval and disapproval. This negativity is one of the reasons many people give up claiming their own authority to begin with, in a defeatist move that goes something like this: *Fine!* If you don't trust me to make a good decision for myself, *you* make the decision . . . but I'm warning you—it's all on *your* shoulders then. You can see that it's a petulant, ineffective move, but sometimes everyone acts this way, even if the behaviors are highly unsuccessful and self-defeating.

Charting Your Course

I met Max when he was nearing the end of medical school. He wasn't a client of mine; he was a student doing his psychiatry rotation, and we fell into an easy banter about our lives for the three months he worked with my patients. I admired his empathy toward people, how he seemed to accept them without judgment, a rare quality for anyone. In one of our earliest conversations he told me about his love for the sea, and I could see it in his face as he spoke; he had that traveling gene that some have and some don't. You can't invent it, but if

you've got it, you can't outrun it, either. Quickly I learned that he was in medical school meeting his parents' dreams, not his own, and that he had always
done so, not uncommon among the high-achievers in medicine. For such high
achievers, the issue of who owned the dream became easily confused early in life.
Max knew he liked medicine well enough, yet wanted to be at sea on a ship. In
fact, it was all he really ever wanted. When the opportunity came—Max would
be able to spend the year after graduating on a ship traveling the world—his
parents felt betrayed and angry. They took the only real power they had, their
money, and held it out as a carrot or a stick; Max would get no help in repaying
his loans if he went to sea; he would breeze through med school in a luxury co-
op if he didn't.

There were a few dicey days there where it seemed as if the lights had
blinked out in Max's eyes. His expression seemed dull, flat, like the depressed
patients we saw. And then graduation came, and the next day I heard he had
done it—he had taken his degree, proudly waving it, and while the party was still
raging that night, he'd slipped away and reported to the ship, which set out at
dawn. I heard echoes of him from time to time, but just recently, I heard he'd
fashioned a career—one he loved, as a cruise ship doctor. It just took letting go
of the gurus who were never guiding his life to begin with.

The third benefit of taking back the authority for your own life is a
favor to your authority figure, although she or he is initially not likely to
see it that way—or perhaps never will. Nonetheless, whether the other
person realizes or accepts it, in taking back your own power you're freeing up the other for a life of his or her own, without the burden and weight
of feeling they have to take care of you. Just as you sometimes take a bite
or two of dinner and realize with surprise how ravenously hungry you are,
when you remove yourself from the other's balancing act of spinning
plates you become as much a nonissue as possible—and this happens all
at once.

Obstacles to Growth: Stumbling Blocks Along the Path

The benefits to taking back your authority seem to offer powerful induce-
ments to doing so—and yet many people remain stuck, insisting that they
cannot move forward for one reason or another. These obstacles in your path
must be identified, understood, and set aside before you can truly introduce
change your life.

If you think of firing your parents or other authority figures as resembling the act of firing someone in the workplace, you'll see that there are numerous similarities, and they can serve as a helpful guide to examining the obstacles that may stand in your way. Perhaps the most powerful way to identify with and experience these obstacles is to imagine yourself being fired.

Imagine, then, that you've just been summoned into your supervisor's office at a job you value and enjoy—and need. Without warning, you've been summarily fired. What are some of the reactions you might have?

Obstacle of . . . Feelings

Fear is a primary and primal response to threat, and few things are as threatening to an adult as losing a job. Whether your job involves producing widgets or—as we are discussing—taking responsibility for someone else, rampant fear arrives when you're dismissed. Another typical feeling is embarrassment: being fired is a rejection, and rejection can feel humiliating. It may be difficult for you to separate the "job"—taking care of someone else—from who you are, and if the two are intertwined, losing the job will feel like a direct attack on your own worthiness. Shock is also common; despite warning signs along the way, it's often hard to believe the unthinkable has happened. You may have told yourself that you would never really get fired—that it was just an empty threat—or you may have believed that you had more time to change matters.

Imagine these feelings in the context of the relationship with your authority figure: he or she has been helping you, making decisions for you, and telling you what to do, and suddenly, shockingly, you are rejecting that help. Not only does this create shock, but it is also a formula for anger, or even rage. The authority figure may be outraged that you would dare to reject the help after all the good he or she has done for you. This is a distorted view, of course—what the helper defines as helpful has been hemming you in and contributing to keeping you help*less*, but that is unlikely to be the helper's perspective.

Obstacle of . . . Change

A second type of obstacle relates to routine and change. You may be the type of person who likes new adventures, new surroundings, and new people in your life . . . but I'd guess not to a great extent since letting someone else maintain control over your life, is a strong, silent statement that you don't feel confident and courageous enough to venture out into the rapids of life. So you're probably more comfortable with the familiar—as many people are—and find routine soothing. Another area of change that may create obstacles for you or for your authority figure has to do with time; for the authority figure, particularly, taking care of you may have taken up a great deal of actual and emotional and intellectual time. The caretaker may wonder what he or she will do now, if not run your life for you. And you may wonder what you will do now, if not run yourself ragged trying to please your caretaker!

Obstacle of . . . Appearances

Although you might prefer to deny that appearances play a significant role in your decisions, it would be unusual if this were actually the case. When someone is fired, it's typical to worry about losing status in the eyes of others, and it's also common to wonder how to explain to others that you've been fired. At a deeper level, you are likely to find yourself wondering who you are now, and what role you play. If you aren't your adult son's savior, your spouse's caretaker, or your friend's rescuer, who *are* you? Redefining a relationship is not only a cumbersome business at times, it can also be emotionally painful.

Whatever the obstacles that appear before you, keep in mind that a large number of them are designed to keep you from feeling the to-be-expected fear, anxiety, and uncertainty that comes about when you make changes, regardless of the type or size of those changes. Even when the change signals positive forward growth, the fear of change often convinces you to go along with the tricks of your conscious and subconscious selves—just as the smoker tricks him- or herself into believing they now have enough control to smoke just one cigarette without starting up again. Humans have an incredible facility for chicanery, particularly when it comes to the self. We fall for our own scams even when we would scoff at them if another person tried to get them over on us. Be vigilant with yourself, and if you find that you're producing obstacle after obstacle that interferes with stepping into the authority role in your own life, you can be sure that what you are actually avoiding is the new, challenging responsibility, not the obstacle itself.

INTO THE FUTURE

With your new understanding about the choices you've made regarding authority and responsibility, it's time to climb back up onto the throne, to give up the abdication plans and take back authority in your life. You are the ultimate monarch in your life, and it's time to stop treating the subconscious voices and old, worthless behaviors as if you're running a democracy. When it comes to running your life, it can't be one voice, one vote—not if some of those voices are the ones from deep down in your subconscious, trying to steer you clear of growth and change.

Remember, as you begin to disentangle yourself from the authority figures you've propped up like puppet dictators, you bear full responsibility for having placed the puppeteers in that position; and while they have undoubtedly been meeting their own needs by taking over authority in your life, your responsibility is to extricate yourself gently but firmly. Think of the medical creed: "First, do no harm." Though your guru may shriek and storm at the changes you're making—something we'll discuss in a bit—you can be assured that you're doing the right thing as long as you do not handle the firing with cruelty, mean-spirited glee, or spite.

Making Change: Eight Steps to a Clean Break

You have reached a point in your life where you must make this change; you cannot have someone else making your decisions for you or interfering heavily in how you run your life. Getting your life together means taking over its management.

Although we've been using the metaphor of "firing" in this chapter, the reality is that you're reorganizing, just as a business does in bankruptcy. There's a second reality as well, which is even more important. Firing your parents is easier said than done, if what you're envisioning is actually severing the relationship. But that's not what I'm recommending. While there are certainly situations in which that is necessary and even preferable, doing so goes well beyond the scope of what we're discussing here, and if you were considering a clean break, be wise to think it through carefully. This caution would also apply if it's your intention to end your relationship with a significant person in your life.

When I refer to changing your relationship with a parent or another authority figure, I'm suggesting that you divest the authority figure of the Ozlike power that he or she wields. When you reach the point where you feel like less of a person because of the relationship or a point where you're stretched too thin or tapped out, it's time to make this change. Recognize that this won't be easy; after all, your authority figure has been good to you at times, and useful to you as well, but the roles of authority figure and supplicant have outlived their usefulness. Knowing this, the kindest and smartest thing you can do with your guru is to let them go—

graciously, appreciatively, but decisively. Again, this doesn't mean "breaking up" with your parent or other authority figure. It means rebalancing the scales.

Use some of the standard adages from firing an employee as metaphors as you begin to make this change. This will give you a framework for how to proceed, as well as how to make the change smooth, effective—and less painful for both of you.

- *Allow the other to save face.* Remember that being ""let go," whatever the reasons, can awaken a powerful sense of humiliation. There is no need to compound this; make it easier and less painful for your authority figure.

- *Make it a quick, clean break.* Don't drag out the changes over weeks or months or longer. Be kind and firm, and don't backtrack on your decision.

- *Honor the other with a metaphorical gold watch.* Recognize the powerful source for good your guru has been at times, and appreciate him or her with a gift, whether tangible or emotional. Let them know that you're grateful.

- *Don't break off all ties, if possible.* Just as you'd keep an honored former employee on the holiday party list, remember that you're redefining the relationship with your authority figure, not ending it. Let them know they're valued and aren't being abandoned.

- *Enroll the other in your "continuing emotional benefits" (companies call it COBRA and it's for continuing health benefits) plan.* An employee would be eligible for benefits for some time after leaving a company—so consider how you might show this person that you recognize their value by maintaining emotional "benefits" in the new relationship you're creating with him or her.

- *Reinforce the terms of the separation.* Be sure that the new relationship is clearly defined. You'd get back the keys from a former employee, and you wouldn't encourage him to drop in constantly. Take back mom or dad's key to your apartment? Maybe. Think in advance about the perimeters you want to impose on the newly reorganized relationship.

- *Clear up any unfinished business.* An employee would clean out the desk and take home any personal belongings. You and your authority figure should talk through the changes you're making and directly address the feelings that arise.

- *Use the other as a consultant in the future.* Just because you're reorganizing the relationship and taking back your authority doesn't mean you can't continue to find ways in which to rely upon the experience and expertise of your former guru. Doing so will also go a long way toward healing any sadness or resentment left from the ""firing."

What to Expect: Post-Firing Tendencies

You can do everything "right" when you fire your parents or other authority figure and still find a grieving or angry person on your hands. In fact, you can almost count on it, at least temporarily, because it goes against the grain for many people to accept rejection easily. Rejection cuts too close to the bone, bringing in humiliation and its milder cousin, embarrassment, plus anger and its tougher cousin, rage. If you're prepared for a range of responses, however, you'll be better able to handle those reactions.

The first and most common reaction you can expect when you fire your parents is simple resistance. It may take a passive form, with your authority figure ignoring you and continuing to deliver advice and decisions as if you'd never raised the subject. Or they'll drop guilt bombs on you at inopportune moments—as if there were any good moments for guilt!—when you may be most vulnerable. Or they'll argue with you, insisting that you aren't competent to handle your life. Or they'll even enlist others to plead their case.

A host of feelings may be the response you receive: anger expressed in dozens of different ways; sadness arriving with tears or sorrowful speeches; frustration at the sudden lack of control being indicated, accompanied by name-calling (a good trick here is to try to brainstorm any and all names you might get called first; this will help remove the sting).

Another likely set of responses might find the other person running hot and cold, going from perfectly friendly to cold as ice in the space of a moment, or switching alliances to someone else: a sibling, a colleague, a competitor.

CONCLUSION

It's not always easy or simple to make a clean break from the conscious and unconscious beliefs you hold about yourself as a result of the parenting you received. No one—from the least evolved person to an enlightened seeker sitting cross-legged atop a mountain—is immune to the potent power, let alone the subtle forces, of parenting.

Being influenced by authority figures, whether parents or others, is not an inherently bad thing, nor is it something you can eliminate from your life. You are who you are in large part because of your interactions with others in your life. What you *can* do, however, is step back from the unconscious edge that keeps you making ineffective choices and engaging in self-defeating behaviors, and step into a consciousness of how you're affected by your parents and other authority figures. Once you have this awareness, you're halfway to freedom from the endless, futile journey home again—and well on your way to personal power and authentic adulthood.

Challenge Authority

How can we be sure that a benefactor is a genuine
supporter who respects his beneficiary?
Who shall guard the guardian?

Thomas Szasz, The Myth of Psychotherapy

Listen to yourself—literally—by taking your hands and cupping them behind your ears, pushing forward with your hands: you will hear yourself as other people hear you. Are you speaking in a child's voice of uncertainty? If the voice you hear isn't one that matches how you view yourself, make a conscious effort to change it: lower the pitch, slow down your rate of speech, modulate your words so they sound gentler. In other words, replace the negative voice characteristics with the ones you want. Until you achieve the changes you want, formally build this into your day: write it three times on your calendar; put Post-its up on your refrigerator, computer screen and bathroom mirror to remind you to keep listening to yourself.

MANAGING YOUR OWN LIFE

First, let's define *authority*. According to the dictionary, it's someone who is an acceptable source of reliable information on a subject. Now, when that "subject" is you, and you take authority, you accept, and let others know, that you're the expert when it comes to your life. It makes perfect sense that the root word in *authority* is "author," since to author something means to write it, to create, shape, and record your perceptions, thoughts, and feelings. Claim authority, and you claim the power to write your life as you desire.

If you want to be more effective at managing your life, you have an important decision to make. Are you truly ready—right now, no wistful glances back, no half steps or maybes—to stop looking to someone else for your answers, rescue. and salvation?

This chapter will give you every tool you need to decide, and every tool you need to make the changes necessary once you've made your decision. It will illuminate the answers to other questions too, questions you must answer to make an informed decision about taking back your power. You will examine the role that authority plays in your life, and the ways in which you give your power to others. Meet the victim inside of you—and before you say "Not me! *I'm* no victim!" read on, because the fact is, we *all* have a victim-in-waiting lurking inside, just looking for a chance to come out and wreak havoc. As you learn how to recognize and vanquish the victim, you'll also begin to see what's in it for you—and the answer isn't small potatoes. You'll discover how taking back your power and asserting your authority can—and *will*—change your life into something infinitely better.

Along the way you'll also learn new methods for recognizing when you're in danger of slipping out of authority, and you'll learn a practical, concrete set of tools that stop you from making this destructive move in five simple, powerful steps. When all is said and done, you will know *exactly how to step into your life in a totally new and powerful way*, claiming your authority and interacting with others.

First, accept that you are in charge of who takes the responsibility in and for your life. Second, assess your choices and behaviors truthfully. And finally, learn and apply the concrete, practical, and instantly effective P.O.W.E.R. tools—five steps for permanently rejecting victimhood.

MAKING A COMMITMENT TO BEING
YOUR OWN AUTHORITY

Let's begin by taking a step back. Think for a moment about the first question I asked: Are you ready to give up the simple salvations, the temporary rescues, and the easy answers? The commitment is one you are going to be fulfilling alone, but on these pages I want to be your "other half" (if not your better half!), the (pleasantly) nagging voice challenging you to be everything you can be. Now, out loud, say, "I'm ready and I will work to change."

Try this: Take a moment before you continue to find a quiet place where you're sure you won't be interrupted and you're comfortable. Turn down the lights, close your eyes, and slowly take several deep breaths. Think of a time when you relied on yourself in a challenging situation. As you continue taking deep, slow breaths, let yourself feel the positive emotions your self-reliance brought: pride, a sense of strength, new self-respect, and growing self-confidence. As you embark on this commitment to increasing your authority, use these positive feelings to buoy you.

You must quit searching for gurus, saviors, and stunt doubles to take your falls for you. *You* are the best expert in your own life. You will make mistakes and suffer the bruises that come with change, sometimes feeling confused, trapped, and overwhelmed as you try to overcome challenges without someone else running interference for you. However, the most effective and lasting way to understand your issues and overcome your struggles is to *create the answers for yourself.* We will examine this in detail.

UNDERSTANDING VICTIMHOOD: WHO IS AUTHORING YOUR LIFE?

If you're like many people, you believe that you already take a fairly large share of responsibility for your life. Sure, you ask others for advice at times; you run ideas past trusted friends or family members, and you'll even follow others' recommendations if what they say makes good sense or if they have special knowledge of some sort about your situation. After all, that's what anyone with common sense would do, and there's nothing wrong with seeking out the wisdom and experiences others have to offer. Beware, though—it's easy to fool yourself into thinking that you seek help less than you really do, or that you're less dependent than you really are.

Beneath the surface, you may rely on others more than you realize. To determine this, you need to honestly evaluate how much you count on others for specific answers, how much general authority you invest in others, and how free you feel to challenge the authority of the "experts" around you. When you ask yourself who has the "situational power," the "planning power," and the "challenge power" in your life—or in a particular situation in your life—what you find may lead you to realize that you're not quite as in charge of your life as you think.

Read about each of the types of power below, and then use the questions with each to consider any situations in your life in which you experience two or more of the most common warning signs that you are overrelying on others for answers or solutions.

EIGHT WARNING SIGNS OF OVER-RELIANCE ON POWER

Read each thought/belief below. If you have had this thought at least once in the past week or if you actively hold this belief at this time in your life, circle the corresponding score in the right-hand column. Add up all of the individual scores you have circled to come up with your Total Feelings Score.

THOUGHTS	EMOTIONS	SCORE
Others are more powerful than I am	Resentment	1
I'm helpless to solve this problem/situation	Anger/Frustration	2
She/he is so much smarter/better than I am	Inferiority	1
I never know how to handle anything	Incompetence	2
I must be a bother to other people	Embarrassment	1
I can't begin to figure out this problem	Confusion	1
I can't do anything about this situation	Powerless	2
If I were more competent I could solve this	Ashamed	2
	Total Feelings Score	____

IF YOU SCORED:

0-4   You feel powerful in most situations, and this creates yet greater power in your life. Continue to reinforce your sense of competence and confidence.

5-8   You feel powerless in significant ways, and this creates yet more powerlessness as your beliefs contribute to the kinds of choices and behaviors that keep you powerless and dependent. Focus on increasing positive messages to yourself.

9-12   You feel almost totally powerless in your life and seek out situations and solutions that keep you powerless, trapped and miserable almost all of the time. Start with small goals to increase your confidence, and build to bigger ones.

Examine the feelings that comprise your score and consider how approaching challenges with these feelings in place creates negative outcomes. Anger begets angry responses from others, confusion begets confused solutions, shame results in a failure to openly address your problems, and so on. The bad news: Your beliefs create the responses and results in your life through self-fulfilling prophecies. The good news: You can create positive outcomes by shifting your beliefs and behaviors!

Situational Power

When you face a situation that feels unfamiliar or difficult, it's critical that you discover the balance between how often you rely on *you* and how often you rely on others to actually solve your problems (situational power). Once you have a clear picture of the balance of situational power in your life, you take on a greater degree of control. Ask yourself these questions:

- Do friends make most of the decisions and plans when you're together?

- Do you frequently "poll" friends before making most decisions?

- Do you give polling results of others more weight than your own views?

- Do you have difficulty making a decision or arguing in a way that goes against significant others' arguments and recommendations?

- Do others express surprise if you announce a decision when they haven't first weighed in with an opinion?

If you can answer yes to any of these questions, you're in danger of assigning your power to others—or you've already done so. You'll want to pay particular attention to methods given throughout the book, and particularly to the P.O.W.E.R. method, to learn ways to take back your authority.

Planning Power

While situational power is about allowing others to solve *specific problems*, planning power is about how much expertise and authority you believe you have—and how much you relinquish—in your life. For instance, do you believe that others are smarter than you? Do you generally assume that others have more spirituality, greater problem-solving abilities, superior wit, better physical strength, and so on, through most or all areas of life? In other words, to what extent are you confident in your personal power, compared with others? Having little faith in your ability to direct and determine outcomes in your life keeps you from having to take responsibility for any fallout from the moves you make—after all, you didn't know what you were doing to begin with! Others should have warned you, advised you, helped you, or otherwise guided you—right? Wrong, of course. Your life is up to you, and you're competent to handle it! Consider:

- Do you feel safest/most comfortable if you check decisions and plans first with a therapist, spiritual adviser, or other significant guide?

- Do you believe that advisers usually have the right answers for you?

- Do you tend to question your thoughts/decisions if they conflict with the adviser's thoughts/recommendations?

Again, if you answered yes to any of these questions, you're giving up too much authority. As you read on, focus on the methods for taking back your power and authority.

Challenge Power

Challenge power refers to the extent to which you feel confident and comfortable questioning—and disagreeing with—those in positions of authority and control in your life, whether they have situational power or planning power. It would be simpler to challenge authority if you remembered that you were the one who *gave* that authority to that other person (or people), of course, but this is not always so simple. You've been taught to respect and obey authority, and old habits die hard. When you recognize the ways in which you hold yourself back from challenging others, you let yourself in on an important secret about authority and your life: *until you're the one making the decisions, you will not live the life you want.* Consider these questions to determine how you feel about challenging authority:

- Do you find that you rarely question anyone in authority?

- When an authority figure disagrees with you, do you back down quickly?

- Do you feel you don't have a right to question authority?

As with the previous types of power, beware of yes answers. They're danger signs on this journey, signs you'll want to watch for vigilantly from now on.

When Victims Meet Authority

The questions you just answered have probably shown you that, like everyone, you have hidden areas of insecurity, places in your life where you're not sure of yourself. Regularly giving authority to others is a sure sign of this; in moderation, it's certainly no cause for concern. In fact, allowing others to see your weaker or less secure self can be a sign of great strength. Drug addicts learn that the first step in overcoming addiction is admitting that the drug has become bigger than they are, and the supervisor who admits to not knowing an answer and then locates the information—rather than making something up—wins the respect and admiration of his or her employees.

The truly intelligent person knows that learning about yourself is a life-long journey. When you admit to someone else that you're unsure about something, you'll discover that your disclosure allows for reassurance *from* others—and greater self-esteem and security *for* you. As self-disclosure allows you to more clearly see your tendency to take the victim role, it also helps you move out of it! Beware, though. When telling others about your insecurity, gauge their reactions as well as *your* feelings about what you've shared. If you experience repeated feelings of anxiety and/or anger if others don't respond with "rescuer" moves, it strongly indicates that if you are not a victim yet, you are well on your way.

When you disclose to others, you do so along two dimensions: depth and breadth of information.[1] *Breadth* of disclosure refers to the fact that as you begin sharing about yourself, you do so at a surface level, covering many subjects without any significant intimacy. This allows for people to get to know each other. As the *depth* of disclosure increases, however—as you share more intimate information about yourself with another person—and *as the other person reciprocates*, the result is affirmation. When someone listens to your feelings without reacting negatively, you're being told that your feelings are within the range of what is normal, and that you are not wrong, bad, or inferior as a result of what you feel. This has the benefit of creating a sense of security. If you know that others accept you, you feel more secure about not only your relationships, but about *who you are*. Unfortunately, victims don't tend to disclose these feelings in a way that encourages or allows a positive—or even neutral—response. In a victim stance you might *say* you're fearful, but the blame that accompanies your disclosure—blame of others, of situations, or of the big, bad world—creates defensiveness or pity in others, not affirmation.

Presenting yourself truthfully—as weak and strong, competent and less so—makes room for honest, equal relationships. Victimhood, on the other hand, shuts doors: it narrowly defines others (as being there to help or save you) and paints you as incompetent or inferior, since you present yourself as needing others more than they need you. You behave as a dependent when you have problems, create excuses when things don't go as planned, or seek others as targets to blame for your mistakes. It's like the graduate student who blames the typist for *his plagiarism* on a research paper. Graduate student or not, he's a *self-assigned* victim of other people's capricious actions *in his mind*.

The Menendez brothers did it when they blamed their father for abusing them, and employees do it when they blame an alarm clock for their late arrival to work. This behavior is what lies behind the "excuse abuse" that began getting so much press a few years back. Many people don't want to step up to the plate and "own" their problems or issues. It seems easier, in the short run, to find someone or something else to blame or to solve matters. The key phrase here is "in the short run," because abdicating responsibility has far-reaching, negative results. Relationships suffer when the rescuer doesn't want to be burdened anymore, and *you* suffer when you don't learn how to take care of yourself *by* yourself—and these are just two of the damaging results of over reliance on others for solutions and answers.

Failure to take responsibility, at both an individual and societal level, is one of the major problems facing individuals, corporations, the judiciary, and just about every other system today. *This underlying failure to claim your power shows up in the hundreds of seemingly small decisions you make every day in your life.*

As you examine the discoveries you made about your relationship with situational, planning, and challenge power, you'll expose the roots of your own tendency toward victimhood. It's likely that this will leave you feeling at least somewhat defensive, which is normal. After all, it's hard to think of yourself as a victim—a word that has gotten a bad rap, and deservedly so— even if you spend the better (or worse!) part of your life in just that position. The "Blame Game," the assessment tool in the final chapter, will further help you discover your tendencies toward victimhood and to explore the ways in which you assign responsibility to others and avoid it within yourself.

The bottom line on who falls prey to the lure of victimhood: at some point, *everyone* does. *Even you.* One or more of the weak spots in your life begins to fray, either because you're facing a specific challenge or because of day-to-day challenges that grab hold and don't shake loose. When either happens, it's easier than you might think to slip back into the familiar habits and past "successes" of blaming others.

For instance, imagine, if you're a woman, that it's "Prince Charming" time again as you begin a new relationship full of hope and excitement, convinced that *this* partner will be different from the others, the ones who "let you down" (a victim stance in itself, since there is no awareness of what *you* contributed). Despite that, the first time the new love doesn't call when he has promised, you instantly give up your challenge power—afraid to call him and hold him accountable for not keeping his commitment. Or, at a time in your life when you're searching for a sense of meaning, you encounter a spiritualist whose teachings strike a chord in you. Soon you're consulting her regularly, even holding off on decisions before getting her advice. The adviser takes on a central role in your choices, even those that seem insignificant to others, but you feel safer knowing that she has given approval to your plans. In ways both large and small, your weak spots aid you in giving up bits of your authority incrementally, until *you* are all gone, swallowed up by your abdication of planning power.

The definition of authority includes having the power to act on behalf of some-one: when you take back the authority in your life, you reclaim the power to act on your own behalf. An authority is also someone who is an accepted source of reliable information on a subject; the subject is you, and when you take author-ity, you accept—and let others know—that you are the expert when it comes to your life. It makes perfect sense that the root word in authority is author: to author something means to write it, to create, shape and record your percep-tions, ideas, thoughts and feelings. Claim authority and you claim the power to write your life as you desire.

To identify the areas in your life where you're giving up your power—or the areas where you're most likely to do so—figure out your "Victim M.O." with the assessment that follows. In assessing yourself, the aim is to begin to identify with the idea of "Victim, heal thyself." Identify ways in which you're most vulnerable to victimhood, and you'll develop the clues you'll need to shift out of the victim stance and into a take-charge position.

THE VICTIM STORY

Taking a pass on victimhood probably sounds good in principle, but take a step back and consider this: There are reasons *why* you seek to give others more authority than you should, and if those reasons are strong enough, leav-ing the victim role isn't simple. This is why knowing what you receive from victimhood is essential; becoming familiar with this will help you dodge its attractions as it helps you claim the authority in your life. The victim and the victimizer share one thing in common—they both participate in the "dance" of victimhood.

You can positively address the needs that the victim stance meets—albeit destructively—and you can more gently lead yourself through the rough feelings that create victims, but *only if you know what these needs and feel-ings are.*

THE VICTIM M.O.

Move rapidly through the checklist below, reading and scoring each statement about yourself. Do not change your answers or consider them at length; use your gut response to answer. Use this scale to score each statement as it relates to your own behavior:

$$
\begin{array}{lll}
1 & = & \text{Almost never} \\
2 & = & \text{Infrequently} \\
3 & = & \text{Sometimes} \\
4 & = & \text{Frequently} \\
5 & = & \text{Almost always}
\end{array}
$$

1. ___ I believe that I have the right to be happy.
2. ___ I feel I should be in control of my life.
3. ___ I believe that I am a worthwhile person.
4. ___ I feel proud of myself.
5. ___ I believe I am as smart as others.
6. ___ I feel good about the decisions I make in my life.
7. ___ I believe it's okay for me to say no to people.
8. ___ I feel confident in standing up for myself.
9. ___ I believe I don't have to give in on what others want.
10. ___ I feel good about myself, in general.
11. ___ I believe that I am a good person.
12. ___ I feel I contribute to other peoples' lives.
13. ___ I believe my ideas are as good as ideas others have.
14. ___ I feel glad that I was born.
15. ___ I believe each day holds something to look forward to.
16. ___ I feel happy when I think about my future.
17. ___ I believe my decisions are the right ones for me.
18. ___ I feel confident that others want to be with me.
19. ___ I feel happy much of the time.
20. ___ I believe that my life has a purpose.

SCORING:

___ Total of ODD items (a correct score should be between 10 and 50)

___ Total of EVEN items (a correct score should be between 10 and 50)

When I think about victims and the powerful gains to be made by taking the victim role, I invariably remember Beth, a woman in her mid-30s with whom I had the good fortune to work. She was referred by an internist treating her for severe headaches; they were resistant to treatment yet seemed to have no clear physical cause.

Case Study: Creating a Victim Story

"It's been that kind of year," Beth said. "I don't know how I'd have gotten through it without my savior, Steve. Dr. Nauman hasn't been any help; he still hasn't made these headaches stop. My marriage started falling apart two years ago—we realized we weren't going to be able to conceive and I guess the infertility damaged a lot between us. Mark doesn't want to adopt and is being unreasonable and unfair—I'm suffering yet he's furious at me since I do want to adopt. Mark's the problem, now—as long as he refuses to be reasonable I'm stuck and miserable. I met Steve at the adoption place—he runs it—and he's given me more hope than I've had in five years. Even though Mark still opposes adoption, Steve—my savior—has helped me fill out the paperwork just in case. It has gotten to the point where I really just rely on him for everything; he's smart where I'm not, and he's just got such an incredible ability to see what's the right thing for me to do. He's halfway convinced me to go ahead with the adoption—it's a private agency, and they'll allow a divorced woman to adopt if it comes to that with Mark. I'd be lost, I tell you, without Steve's guidance, and that makes Mark even angrier, but what does he expect? He says I used to share everything with him and lean on him, and it's true, but I can't count on him anymore, and if he wanted me to still go to him to solve everything he should have handled it differently."

After Beth finished filling me in on her situation, I realized I'd lost count of the "victim statements" she'd made, which told me there were plenty. I knew she was blaming Mark for her misery—and probably for the headaches too—and it was also clear that Beth was looking to Steve as some sort of magician-cum-guru, the answer man. She'd even called him her "savior" twice—a dead giveaway! Beth's words, her tone, and her take on the situation all fairly reeked of victimhood, and it didn't take a rocket scientist—or an internist, for that matter—to see why she was having headaches. While Beth diagnosed her headaches as symptoms of marital problems, I was sure they were the result of breathing in too many toxic fumes from a virtual dumping ground of blame and self-pity.

The Victim Story: Plot

An interesting thing happens to people who are in a situation that feels out of control. You'll probably recognize this from your own life: you quickly begin to create a "story" about the situation, complete with a theme, a cast of characters and motivations, and plot points that paint the circumstances in the best light possible. The "best" light varies from person to person, of course, depending upon their experiences and usual patterns of behavior. Recognizing and understanding this story goes a long way toward revealing why you're cloaked in victimhood.

The story doesn't always "fit" each of us in exactly the same way. For some of us it involves *self-blame*—even when the events are beyond our control. The teenager who hears his parents arguing about his school tuition days before they announce their separation may blame himself, for instance. If he weren't so expensive and so much trouble, his parents would still be married. In another case the story involves blaming someone else. An employee, newly fired, insists that nothing she did ever satisfied her boss; she ignores the warnings and the advice of others to quit being late, shorten the lunches, and pitch in more. She *knows*: her boss just couldn't be pleased. The other situation involves denial: we will deny, deny, deny, *refusing to acknowledge the reality* of a situation even when it is absurd to continue in the denial. Think, for instance, of the stereotypical mistress who makes herself available on weekdays in hidden hotels and restaurants, but never sees her lover on holidays or weekends—yet continues to insist that he is leaving his wife any day.

Whichever story you create, the "backstory"—behind-the-scenes information that rarely gets out—is that you are *also taking on the victim role*. Whether you blame yourself, blame someone else, or deny reality, victimhood goes hand in hand.

One of the most powerful ways to see your own victimhood is to write your *own* victim story. Whether in the past or present, you've already created much of the story; writing it simply illuminates its powerful storyline.

What you will discover goes far beyond the players and the theme. As you create your story and answer the questions posed, you'll begin to see inside the "cover stories" you have created about your powerlessness, the powers others wield, and the ways in which your life isn't of your own design.

The Victim Story: Action

Once you're in the victim role, you're likely to do one of two things—and sometimes both. You may focus increasingly on your helplessness, *turning negative feelings inward and denying your power*—and along come headaches, stomach ailments, and a host of other physical complaints. Beth did this, and her stress and helpless feelings began to come out in the form of headaches that couldn't be controlled.

The other typical response is to *turn positive feelings outward, giving your power to someone else.* Beth did this as well. She turned over to Steve what little power she believed she had, reinforcing her sense of helplessness even as she gained false reassurance on some level because she had vested to Steve the authority and answers for which she was so desperate.

More on Beth in a moment; but first, think about whether either of the action responses above sound familiar to you. Do you suffer from physical complaints frequently? Do you give up authority to others so you won't have to deal with the consequences if things go wrong? If so, you already know— from unpleasant experience—that these two responses are actually traps masquerading as ways to cope with helplessness. Their real result is a collection of combined feelings that lead to *learned helplessness.*

As I noted in the previous chapter, the phrase "learned helplessness," first coined by Martin Seligman, Ph.D., refers to the mind-set that results as you seek out help from others time and again and as a consequence gradually become less competent at handling your own problems. Seligman wanted to reduce the number of dropouts at his university, and he began to research *who* dropped out in order to do so. He discovered that the students mostly likely to quit college were those who came from families where they had rarely been challenged to solve problems. Instead, these students had parents who rushed in with solutions, ran interference for them, and gave them little reason to develop independence or personal authority.[2]

As a result, when these students were faced with inevitable problems and challenges at college, they didn't know what to do. Their helpers weren't there to rescue them, and the students didn't have the skills or the confidence to take on their own rescues. The only ability the students had developed was knowing who to approach for the answers, and how to approach them.

Beth had learned something similar: she first relied on her husband to rescue her, and when a situation arose that was more than he could solve alone—the infertility—she turned to Steve. As I questioned Beth further, I wasn't surprised to discover that she met many of the criteria for learned helplessness. Victims typically do. While you might feel grateful, on one hand, for the solutions and saves that others offer you, it's not unusual to feel angry, depressed, and resentful at the same time. After all, when you decide you can't handle your own life or the situations that arise in it, you're also making a statement about your low level of competence and confidence—and that can't help but feel lousy.

Journaling: Your Victim Story

Set aside at least an hour—and maybe more—to write your story. Don't rush this exercise; if you need to complete it in several sittings by all means do so. The key is to tell your whole story. Don't judge yourself, edit your experiences or change anything: this is for your eyes only and it relies on the truth if you are to gain any benefit and insight from it.

Writing on every third line (skipping two lines after each line), take 10 to 15 minutes to write about a time when someone else victimized you—when someone behaved outrageously toward you, harming you in some way. Include their bad behavior, your shock, the ways in which you were harmed and all of the negative character traits, feelings and motives you can brainstorm explaining why she/he did this to you. Blame freely. This should be a situation in which someone really did a number on you, and you are under no obligation to take any responsibility!

With a different ink color, go back and rewrite the story on the two empty lines below each original line. In this version, however, tell the story as if you are 100 percent responsible for everything that happened. If the other person hurt you ("He called me lazy") follow it with how you participated ("I often use name-calling, too, when I'm angry"). Explain why you were motivated to allow such a betrayal or hurt, and be sure that no behavior remains unexplained or blamed on the other.

When you finish the second story, identify at least three specific things in the first story that were truly inaccurate, and three things in the second story that were accurate.

Continue to look at your victim stories from all angles, taking responsibility for your part(s). Finally, make a commitment to take responsibility for one of the inaccuracies with the other person.

Do you feel any of the Symptoms of Learned Helplessness?
√ Feelings of incompetence
√ Feelings of helplessness/hopelessness
√ Feelings of fear and anxiety
√ Feelings of shame and embarrassment
√ Feelings of depression
√ Feelings of confusion/disorientation
√ Feelings of resentfulness toward helpers

√   **Feelings of anger toward helpers**
√   **Feeling cornered/trapped by problems**
√   **A desire to run away/avoid problems**

The Victim Story: Roles

In order to do the victim dance, there must be two additional and complementary players: the "Victimizer" and the Rescuer. If either or both are present, you'll know you're at the Dance. For Beth, "Steve the Savior" was the rescuer while Mark, Beth's husband, was the victimizer.

The Victimizer

You can't have a victim without a victimizer. Although it's usually another person, the victimizer can be a situation, an event, a process or a system. For instance, a victim may claim to be victimized by the corporation that employs him; another victim may blame the weather for her late arrival. In order to identify your victimizer, simply look for the source of your blame. The "benefits" to having a victimizer are clear—and clearly harmful: Victimizers allow you to duck responsibility, avoid hard work and sidestep the feelings that can accompany not knowing what to do. These benefits are harmful because they damage relationships and keep you from learning to be your own authority.

The Rescuer

The Rescuer is most often a person, but—like the victimizer—you can sometimes assign the rescuer role to a process, group or other non-person. Jim, for instance, works on commission and is low on funds; he goes to his company for an advance against income whenever he finds himself in this position. Barbara invests her all in new romantic relationships, and friends rarely hear from her or see her when she has a new love in her life. When the relationships go sour, though, she expects her friends to be available day and night with rescues in the form of comfort and words of wisdom. The rescuer gets to feel powerful and competent—but also often catches the blame if the rescue move backfires in some way. And, the rescuer can end up feeling used. For the victim, the rescuer becomes a central figure, and dependency often grows. As is always true in the Victim Dance, however, the

victim learns nothing about taking on power or solving problems.

Soon Beth had acknowledged examples of three primary areas in her victim story:

The Plot: her tendencies toward victimhood (low self-confidence)

The Action: ways in which she abdicated responsibility (her headaches)

The Roles: the restraining behaviors she sought and allowed

VICTIMHOOD AND AUTHORITY: WHAT'S IN IT FOR YOU?

As I worked with Beth, I did several things to help her see how the victim story she had created could tell her everything she needed to know about how she was abdicating responsibility for her life. As she considered her story, she was armed with the knowledge of her own tendencies for victimhood, just as you'll be armed by completing the "Blame Game," the "Victim M.O.," and the "Victim Story." By examining the roles assigned to significant others, Beth reinforced this knowledge, and so can you.

I then asked Beth to consider a very powerful question, which you should consider too: *What are the benefits in being a victim, and what are the benefits in taking back authority?* And please, no "yes, but" answers!

Declining an Invitation to the Victim Dance

You've seen many of the feelings associated with abdicating authority for your life, and you know about its negative effects—the way it creates dependency, learned helplessness, resentment, anxiety, depression, and dysfunctional relationships. Why, then, would you *choose* to be a victim?

That question says it all. Victims don't believe they have a choice. They're victims, after all—things happen *to* them, not *because* of them! However, deep inside in a little secret place, victims do derive "benefits" from their failure to take authority and power into their own hands. Remember, though, "benefits" is a highly subjective term; what one person sees as a benefit is someone else's drawback.

Here are seven proposed benefits of giving up your authority:

1. It's an easy out if someone solves your problem.

2. There's no need to take responsibility for the solution.

3. There are new solutions or plans.

4. Others will take care of you in various ways.

5. It makes the helper feel good and like you more.

6. It removes the fear of making the wrong decision.

7. You gain the benefit of experience others have.

Although it might sound surprising, if any of the benefits of giving up your authority sound familiar to you, it's a good sign. How? You, along with everyone else, have areas where you're likely to get into the victim stance. The wish to give up authority isn't a question of "if" but "when." *You are the agent of your own emotional handicaps: you set things up so you will end up failing, and in effect you are your own undoing.* If you recognize any of the benefits above, it means that you are not only acknowledging this—a critical step in taking on more authority—but also that your insight is strong regarding the payoffs you'll get if you succeed.

Why Be Your Own Authority?

* There are dozens of reasons to take back your authority, and what they all add up to is taking back the power that belongs with you. Broken down, however, the numerous reasons build a powerful foundation for change: *Being helpless is miserable.* When you give up your authority, whether it's by vesting it in someone else or denying it in yourself, or both, you increase your helplessness. Imagine the moment when your car skids on ice or rain, before you tighten your grip on the wheel, pump the brakes, and steer into the skid. The panic that results from that instant of helplessness is abject misery and seems to go on forever, in slow motion.

* *Being helpless means no or little control over outcomes.* If you're helpless, you are by definition accepting that you are unable to help yourself. This is a self-fulfilling prophecy; if you believe that you're helpless, you will behave in ways that are consistent—and guarantee the outcome.

* *Being helpless means accepting others as experts.* Some others are experts, of course, but beware the gurus and chieftains who hold themselves up as experts in *you.* The only expert on your life is you, and others who pretend to be are in it for reasons that often have little to do with

you or *your needs.*

- *Being helpless creates and maintains poor self-esteem.* If you give up your power, you lose, lose, lose. Making decisions, achieving, and even making mistakes goes along with being powerful and contributes to healthy self-esteem.

- *Being helpless interferes with adult relationships.* In order to relate as adult to adult, you must give up any hold on victimhood or helplessness. When two adults relate without blame or a need for rescue, the relationship has infinite possibilities for growth and learning.

- *Being helpless interferes with competent parenting.* In order to relate adult to child, you must also give up your attachment to helplessness. This is true in practical terms, of course, but even more important, you must step up to the plate and accept responsibility for the emotional health, well-being and growth of your children—and an adult who has one foot in childhood cannot handle this responsibility.

- *Being helpless interferes with professional authority.* In order to reach your career goals, you need a center of authority. Denying this authority and power in yourself makes this impossible.

- *Being helpless interferes with achievement and success.* Your dreams, hopes, and plans will go only as far as your power to realize them. Helpless people have hopes and dreams but not the drive and energy to increase their skills.

TAKING BACK AND TAKING ON AUTHORITY

Once you recognize your tendencies toward victimhood and take a clear look at who you invest with authority in your life, and once you've made an honest assessment of the benefits you've gained by abdicating authority—and the benefits you'll accrue by ceasing to do so—there are three steps remaining in taking on or taking back your power.

First, you must *accept that the distribution of power is in your hands.* Second, you must *honestly evaluate your role (and related behaviors) in each situation,* whether victim, victimizer, or rescuer, remaining conscious at all times of the warning moves, emotions, and damaging outcomes. And finally, you must choose to *operate from a position of P.O.W.E.R.,* an authoritative stance built upon five concrete, practical, and instantly effective methods for rejecting victimhood and embracing your power.

If a Guru Falls in the Forest

The first step in challenging authority is to be able to see that it's *you* who give your authorities all of their power. It's a common misconception that authority exists independently. It doesn't. Without you *handing over* some degree of control to someone else, that control continues to reside in *you*. A guru is only a guru when you invest him or her with a guru's power—and if you make the choice to retain that power within yourself, it naturally follows that you're the guru for yourself!

You have had different authorities throughout your life: you started with parental authority, and you moved on to the other types of legitimate authority held by teachers, peer groups, employers, and so on. What all authority has in common, once you're an adult and capable of independent living, is that *it is only as powerful as you allow it to be*.

Why do we accept others' expertise without question, buying into the strange belief that others know better than we do about our lives? The answer is at the very heart of why you haven't fully taken over management of your life. Understanding your motivations for seeking quick cures and easy answers while challenging the authorities who *have* their authority only because you *gave* it to them, is one of your biggest tasks as you embark upon changing your life. And both are essential to taking the initial step of commitment toward recognizing how, when, and why you give up authority.

If you continue to blindly believe that you've got everything under control and that you *never* look to others for the easy out, you won't see the need for changing how you relate to authority. This is why it is so essential to go *beyond* the first step of recognizing that you invest authorities with their power and into the second: truthfully and searchingly evaluating the way in which you take—or reject—authority in each situation.

Evaluating Your Role: Victim, Victimizer, Rescuer or . . . ?

You have learned a number of ways to look inside of the feelings, behaviors, and motivations that combine to create a victim—and conspire to deny you authority.

These many methods—the checklists and the Victim M.O. and the Blame Game and more—can be used again and again as you check back with yourself to see how you're doing when it comes to taking on authority. These are general methods for determining if and when you are taking on the victim role. When you examine behaviors such as your tendency to get sick instead of feeling angry, or your tendency to blame others or to repeatedly rely on others for answers, you begin to see where your victim traps are. Finally, and ironically, the more discomfort you initially experience with the final P.O.W.E.R. step, the more likely it is that you've been bogged down in victimhood, often fleeing from authority. The great news is that your discomfort can be a motivator. Allow it to tell you that you need to make these changes *now*, and *in as many ways as you possibly can*—and as a result you will experience profound positive changes as you discover the remarkable distance you've come.

Taking It to the Streets

The final step in challenging authority and taking on power in your life is a set of moves that give you the specific behaviors to operate from a position of power. Therefore they are called the P.O.W.E.R. tools:

Prepare for challenges

Own your feelings

Weigh your options

Evaluate outcomes

Reclaim your truth

The P.O.W.E.R. tools are five steps designed to help you move rapidly and accurately through the process of rejecting victimhood and taking on authority in any situation. They are simple to remember and simple to incorporate as you consider issues facing you, examine the "players" and the elements, and determine the most powerful way for you to take ownership.

Prepare for Challenges

Whether a specific situation faces you or you're considering general life changes and challenges, you must prepare yourself. The way to do this is to be fully equipped with the understanding and tools you need, i.e., reading this book and thinking long and hard about your choices and behaviors. Preparing for challenges goes beyond this, though. You must also learn to expect that others will challenge you if you change your behavior in any significant way. The key here is to recognize that others have an investment in you continuing to behave just as you always have—and so when you change, you are likely to experience resistance and interference. Being prepared keeps you from being blindsided and allows you to think through how you will overcome the obstacles others place along your path.

Own Your Feelings

As you consider making a decision or embarking on a life-planning process, you need to know that one of the chief determinants of whether you succeed will be the extent to which you accept and "own" your feelings. Owning your feelings means taking responsibility for what you feel, not blaming others for "making" you feel certain ways, and not judging yourself harshly for your emotions. You will feel a degree of fear and some reluctance as you make this and the other changes—that's natural. You need to accept these feelings—and simultaneously reject them, if they're keeping you from making the moves you need to make. You feel what you feel, and when you reach a state of acceptance and nonchalance about this, you focus your energy and attention on problem solving versus wasting it on denying or explaining your feelings.

Weigh Your Options

When you're face-to-face with a problem that needs a solution, it's easy to remain stuck in tried-and-true solutions. One of the most frequently reused options is going to someone else for the solution. Widen your perspective, seek out others for *ideas* (but not solutions!), and then carefully weigh your solutions in terms of what works for you, not what keeps the peace, what works for others, or what is the easiest out.

Evaluate Outcomes

Brainstorm a list of all of the possible outcomes that could result for each of the options you weigh. Set a minimum of five, 10, or more outcomes for yourself so you do not limit your imagination. Push! Don't worry about whether the outcomes you imagine are reasonable or sensible. In brainstorming, you discover what you most hope for, what you most fear—and what is most likely. You can then tailor your choices far more effectively so you end up with an outcome that takes likelihood, fears, and hopes into account to arrive at a solution that works for you.

Reclaim Your Truth

It's a cliché that "The truth shall set you free," but it's a cliché because it's true and often repeated! When you're in the process of examining a situation, considering the options and outcomes, and interacting with others on the solution, the most powerful thing you can do is to remain truthful to yourself: to how you feel, what you believe, what you value, what you know, and what you want. It's when you abandon one or more of these areas that you shift out of authority. Reclaim your truth and live powerfully.

CONCLUSION: THERE IS NO PERFECT ANSWER, BUT THERE IS A POWERFUL YOU

In a scene from William Shakespeare's play, *Macbeth*, the title character calls upon a physician to heal the ailing Lady Macbeth, who is suffering mightily from a guilty conscience and appears quite ill. After the physician examines her and insists that he does not hold the answers that will heal her, Macbeth argues with the doctor:

Canst thou not minister to a mind diseased

Pluck from the memory a rooted sorrow

Raze out the written troubles of the brain

And with some sweet oblivious antidote

Cleanse the stuff'd bosom of that perilous stuff

Which weighs upon her heart?

The physician, who knows that Lady Macbeth suffers from sorrow and unrest in her soul rather than an illness of physiological origins, continues to insist that he cannot solve her ailment, telling Macbeth, "Therein the patient must minister to himself."

Thomas Szasz, who has authored over 20 books about psychiatry, psychotherapy, and the potential damage to patients inherent in "professional" therapy, referred to this scene from Shakespeare in one of his books, making the point that there is no guardian—*save the guardian that exists within you*—who can change the course of your life or make your challenges disappear. The task of diagnosing and healing yourself, his argument suggests, is simplest, clearest, and best if *you* are guiding the process.

That no one holds the magic potion or the perfect answer seems obvious, and yet psychotherapy is established on a virtual mountain of myths that dispute this simple truth. Degrees in psychology are granted just like degrees in engineering or computer technology, as if you could see—and even more absurdly, as if you could *fix*—the mass of misfires and misconnections in another human being. Classroom hours and limited one-on-one experience with patients, the degrees seem to imply, create experts who are better healers for you than you are for yourself. As a society we long for wisdom; in any religion or philosophy the wisest become powerful because we believe they possess the answers we search for throughout our lives. The rest simply follow, hoping for discarded bits of wisdom distributed like extra fortune cookies.

While it's true that some people know more than others, and that some people have greater insight or a greater ability to learn, I want to repeat the clear distinction: The knowledge the therapists possess is *not about you*. Socrates knew about the philosophy of persuasion and Mozart knew about piano playing, but their genius in those areas didn't extend to the beating of the human heart. And yet that's exactly the myth that has formed: The wise are thought to be wise in all ways—or, at the very least, in the *way you need them to be*.

The antidote to this is challenging authority, and placing it squarely where it belongs: in your own hands.

GIVE A MAN A FISH AND HE EATS FOR A DAY;
TEACH A MAN TO FISH AND HE EATS FOR A LIFETIME.

Native American proverb

When you provide your own therapy, you create the new skills and changed behaviors that allow you to give up your gurus and solve your own problems, issues, and challenges—and as you do so successfully, you will explode the myth of the easy answer or the perfect therapist, coach, or guru. Once you redirect your focus to *your* competence and *your* power, you create a new reality that initiates powerful self-healing.

Stick Up
for Yourself

PEOPLE WHO HAVE WHAT THEY WANT
ARE VERY FOND OF TELLING PEOPLE
WHO HAVEN'T WHAT THEY WANT THAT THEY
REALLY DON'T WANT IT.

Ogden Nash,
"The Terrible People"

Over the course of my career, I have worked with thousands of people, including my individual therapy clients. From inpatient psychiatric units to plush offices in "designer" therapy setups, I've seen the damage caused when people—rich, poor, and at all points in between—fail to stick up for themselves. It's the Doormat Syndrome, and if it doesn't start early in life, it certainly has its roots in countless old messages that you were inadequate, worth less than others, and undeserving of good treatment. It's time to unearth the messages, replay the tapes, and start hearing good things, not the least of which is that you're going to have to stick up for yourself now if you're ever going to make a go of this thing called happiness.

You simply cannot walk around, tail tucked between your legs like a beaten dog, and expect others to treat you well. You can't criticize yourself before others do it and expect them to hold their tongues. You can't present a wall of shame to the world and expect to see a reflection of pride. That's just reality, and it's time to do something about it.

Go to a high-end store that cheerfully accepts returns—Nordstrom comes to mind; they pride themselves on their no-hassle returns. Buy something and then return it within the next day or two (be sure to save your receipt and use a credit card!). There are several reasons for—and benefits derived from—doing this. First, you can gauge your level of discomfort, and that can tell you something about how difficult it will be to "exchange" parts of yourself, at times. Second, and most essentially, this Quick Fix will give you a chance to stand up for yourself, get something that is due to you—and succeed at focusing on your needs and wants.

WHERE YOU'VE BEEN

Maybe it started before you even understood the words: your mother sighed and muttered something as she threw you a look of frustration when you wet your bed again. Or perhaps the message came from your father when he made a disparaging comment and grimaced as he yanked at your shoelace, the one you hadn't yet learned to tie. All of us receive this type of message— after all, there are no perfect or frustration-proof parents, teachers, or human beings, period. Therefore, at times all of us are on the receiving end of the criticisms and judgments of others. However, when you receive more than your share of judgments and criticisms, a common outcome is self-criticism, and what grows out of this is a failure to stick up for yourself. Because the significant others in your life did not stick up for you in your formative years—or because significant others did the same later in life at a vulnerable time—you learned that you were not worth sticking up *for*. If others couldn't be bothered to do it, neither could you, if you even knew how, which is doubtful. After all, where would you have learned? While everyone else was absorbing lessons in standing strong, and were sending out signals that they were not to be treated poorly, you were learning to absorb criticisms. It's not an auspicious beginning to a life of confidence and competence, let me assure you!

In essence, what you learned is that you had to take whatever others dished out. If you didn't take it, so the reasoning went—often unconsciously, of course—you believed that others would not like you, spend time with you, or even acknowledge your existence. Your needs and feelings had to come second (or last) at all times, while others always had to be first. It doesn't matter whether this principle applied to family, friends, colleagues, or the most casual of acquaintances; the bottom line was that you suppressed and repressed what you needed in order to survive your interactions with others with the smallest possible damage. The problem, as it turns out, is that the damage wasn't so small, after all. A minute or an hour or a lifetime of being someone's whipping boy or girl is a minute, an hour, or a lifetime too long.

HOW YOU GOT THERE

Perhaps it's obvious to you that the fear of being disliked, which we have already discussed briefly, is at the root of the tendency to avoid sticking up for yourself. But there are many other reasons that feed into this behavior, and each is wrapped up in the behavior so tightly that it can be difficult to distinguish it in order to move in a new direction. Even the fear of being disliked has a number of layers, making it more complex than it might seem at first glance.

If you are to move forward in a new and confident direction, you must take apart the layers in each of the reasons that contribute to your failure to stick up for yourself. You must understand how you arrived here in the first place so you can begin to deconstruct the damage done and rebuild on a new, stronger foundation

Fear of Being Disliked

This fear, often introduced in earliest childhood, is then reinforced in any number of interactions and situations throughout childhood, adolescence, and beyond. At some point it will be unnecessary for the negative adults around you to reinforce the fear, since it will exist independently within you.

Young children naturally expect to be liked and to be treated positively. It is not within their realm of experience that others will criticize or judge them—until others do so and introduce the fear of a repeat. When the first criticism occurs, it causes distress in a child, just as it does in an adult, except that children have fewer resources with which to deflect the criticism. Since it typically comes from a central figure in your life—a parent, another relative, or a teacher, for instance—the criticism has extra power.

The criticisms children receive aren't always packaged as obvious remarks or judgments, of course. One of the most insidious forms is teasing;

a particularly powerful way to treat a child negatively without having to take responsibility for it. How many times have you heard someone tease another and then insist "I was just teasing!" if the other reacts with distress? The teaser is evading responsibility for having caused harm or uncomfortable feelings, and meanwhile you're left holding the bag, straining to believe in the trusted adult yet knowing that your feelings are hurt.

It is in this manner that adults first introduce children to the uncomfortable experience of not knowing how or whether to trust their own feelings. As a child you feel one thing yet are told that you *should* feel another. What is particularly hard to understand is that many people seem to think teasing is funny. An adult brings in the mail, for instance, and the child asks, "Is there anything for me?" In response, someone says, "No, nothing for you. I guess nobody must like you!" It's "just a joke," right? But how can something hurtful and harmful be a joke? Instead, a parent could have made a kinder choice, taking the junk mail addressed to "Occupant" and saying, "Yes, this one is for you! You're very popular around here, aren't you?" Even a simple move like this builds self-esteem and self-worth rather than tearing it down.

I'm not suggesting that there is no place for playfulness and gentle teasing, but it's important to look at the results of the choices others make—and the choices we make. Particularly when a trend of such teasing exists, the seed planted will contribute to you becoming a person who's treated poorly by others (and by yourself), because you are accustomed to it.

Susan laughs as she describes it, but the experience resonates with every woman at the table and they all groan and laugh simultaneously. When she goes to a hairdresser, Sue explains, if the stylist is unpleasant or outrageous, she won't challenge her; won't disagree with her or correct her, not even if the stylist says something egregious. She's too afraid of the woman wreaking revenge on her hair.

Benign Neglect

Everyone agrees that life is busier than ever; parents rush off to work in the morning, come home just in time to throw together dinner, stuff some laundry in the washer, and hustle everyone back out the door to Scouts, church meetings, sports events, or a school activity. In addition, parents are often distracted by their own "stuff"—their needs, their feelings, and their experiences. This is understandable, and to a large part it can't be changed. What can be changed is the common result: the benign neglect of children. In this kind of lifestyle, you often have to take care of yourself as a child; you're only noticed when you do something out of the ordinary, whether that something is very positive or very negative. In between times, little or even nothing is done to shape and build up your self-esteem, as if it's enough to simply feed, clothe, and house you.

I often think this is why a large percentage of therapy clients are in therapy to seek the attention and acceptance—without having to make the big sale, win the big race, or secure the big contract—that were lacking in childhood. The therapist sitting across from you is giving you the gift of time, which suggests that you are valued. The problem, of course, is that the therapist surreptitiously eyes his or her watch after 45 or 50 minutes, or forgets something important you've told her, and you're back at square one, feeling undervalued and ignored. The best way to deal with this is to build the therapist—and the parent—within. Unlike the therapist who glances at his watch, when you can sit comfortably with yourself—in other words, when you can treat yourself, your experiences and your feelings worth your own time—you can heal these wounds. Your accepting and respectful attention to yourself will make huge inroads into the failure to stick up for yourself that results from benign neglect.

Delia loves her children—you can see it in everything from how she cares for them physically—dressing them in neat, clean clothes—to how she reaches over and strokes their hair or touches their arms while she's talking, to how she describes them. Her husband Jim, though, is an alcoholic, and this occupies much of Delia's time and energy. He's unreliable, unsteady, someone Delia must watch out for. As a result, although she's a sweet woman, her attention is often elsewhere. For Jim and Delia's two children, home life is like living on a boat of questionable seaworthiness. One moment the waters are calm and reassuring, with Delia in charge, and it seems that they will all stay afloat. In the next moment Delia seems to disappear in the violent, storm-tossed waves of Jim's presence. The children can never be sure what's coming next. You can see it in their eyes; they have grown terrified, giving in to every whim of both parents in order to keep from drowning.

Failure to Foster Independent Differences

A third contributing factor to not sticking up for yourself is the failure of significant others to foster your independence and to respond positively to your differences. When you express an independent opinion, instead of an adult drawing you out, encouraging you, or complimenting you on having a mind of your own, your opinion is shot down and criticized. It may not even be allowed; in some families there is a strict embargo on independent opinion. The "family" is Republican, a parent announces, or liberal, or religious. Any family member who wavers or strays from the party line is met with discouragement and even punishment. In some cases, divergence of thoughts and feelings can be met even by parental violence, a sure sign to the child that it's unsafe to have independent thoughts and dangerous to stick up for yourself.

Stuart developed a social conscience early on, perhaps an unusual thing in a family where apathy was the order of the day. He couldn't wait to be old enough to vote for the president, and he read the newspapers as soon as he could understand the words. He soon learned to keep his political views to himself, though, after his father backhanded him when he announced in sixth grade that he thought the United States ought to help educate immigrants. His father told him he'd have a different view when it was his tax money being poured down the drain for people who were stealing jobs from hardworking Americans. Stuart didn't change his views—but he did shut up. Even years later, long after his father died, Stuart had great difficulty expressing a political opinion—or any opinion, for that matter—if it differed from the opinion held by the person with whom he was speaking.

Worship of Authorities

A fourth factor that contributes to not sticking up for yourself is that you may have been taught to treat adults and/or authority figures as gods. These unapproachable scions—physicians, experts in a field, and religious leaders, for instance—were not to be questioned. Instead, you may have been taught to follow them blindly, regardless of your beliefs, your contradictory opinions, or even evidence suggesting they were in the wrong. Of course, authority figures themselves contribute to this at times, becoming angry if questioned. We discussed this in detail in the last chapter, "Challenge Authority," but it's relevant here, as well (and keep in mind one of the conclusions reached: if an expert gets defensive, you should rethink following that expert!).

> Evan was only in therapy for five minutes when he realized that the therapist was not the one for him. There was something arrogant and preening about the man sitting across from him, and his observations were shallow and obvious. Although Evan tried to focus on his issues during that first session, his negative gut reaction to the therapist made it difficult. Once or twice early on, and repeatedly in later sessions, Evan tried to raise the issue, something that felt nearly impossible for him to do. The therapist's response was to raise the subject of resistance, telling Evan he was clearly struggling with his own unwillingness and inability to disclose, substituting artificial obstacles for the real reason why he didn't want to continue in the therapy. The sessions continued for almost two years before Evan finally got up the courage to leave—and even then he felt cowardly and embarrassed about how he went about it: he simply paid off his bill, stopped showing up for the sessions, and refused to return the therapist's calls.

There are any number of factors that contribute to the failure to stick up for yourself, with these four among them. You can see, by reading the examples and by examining the effects in your own life, that there are also negative results when you don't present a face of self-confidence and self-worth to the world. Let's talk about those results before we move on to discussing letting go of allowing others to treat you as a doormat.

WHY THE OLD WAY DOESN'T WORK

When you fail to stick up for yourself, there are several typical outcomes. First, you always end up with the short end of the stick. Second, if others always get what they want first, you fail to get what you want. Third, you're often left with negative, uncomfortable feelings that drain you of energy you could use in more productive ways. And finally, when you don't stick up for yourself, you leave yourself unprotected in numerous ways. Whether you're at home, at work, or in some other context of your life, not reaching out for what is yours is like wearing a sign on your forehead: "I don't deserve it, so don't let me have it!"

- At the dinner table you insist that you don't care for seconds, even though you're still hungry, because you don't want to risk the possibility that others won't have all they want. *The leftovers grow cold as your stomach growls.*

- On the racquetball court you make a great shot, winning the game—but your partner says it was out of bounds. You know it wasn't, but you don't argue because you don't want to rock the boat and risk being disliked. *Your partner ends up winning the game . . . by one point.*

- Your physician gives you a prescription. Although you're curious about its side effects and interactions, you don't question the doctor, who seems busy and rushed. *You spend a long night being ill before discovering, through the pharmacist the next morning, that the new drug you've started interacts negatively with a daily prescription you take.*

- Your coworker begins talking about the bombing of the World Trade Center and makes several disparaging comments about Muslims. You want to say that most Muslims are peace-loving and nonviolent, but you remain silent because you're afraid of what might happen if you speak up. *Another coworker, a Muslim, feels unsupported and hurt.*

In just these four brief examples you lose out on four things: enough food to fill your stomach, the satisfaction of triumphing in a hard-won game, your health and well-being, and the good feeling that comes from doing the right thing. As if that weren't bad enough, you're also left with negatives: hunger, anger, illness, embarrassment, and a host of other feelings that drain you of energy and reinforce your belief that you don't deserve better.

In essence, if you are to get by in life staying under the radar that detects needs and desire, you must deny yourself constantly and be a chameleon, not wanting something one moment (if others want it) and wanting it the next (if they don't). It's a tricky existence, an exhausting existence, and a futile way to live when there is so much richness, so much offered to you out in the world.

ASSESSMENT TOOL

This is a good point at which to determine how much you stick up for yourself, as well as the extent to which you allow others to walk over you like the proverbial doormat. If you find that you're allowing others to use, abuse, or otherwise treat you poorly, don't jump on the bandwagon and use it as an excuse to beat up on yourself. Instead, make the changes I recommend in "Moving Forward," following the assessment.

DOORMAT INDICATOR

Answer the following questions with *True* or *False*, choosing the answer that most closely matches the choice you would make most often:

____ 1. You are at a restaurant and the rare steak you ordered is delivered medium well done. You tell the waiter you'd like a new steak, cooked correctly. (**1**)

____ 2. An old friend asks you to cover for her by telling her husband she was with you when she wasn't. You don't know where she was, but you tell her you're not willing to do this. (**3**)

____ 3. While taking a professional class, another student approaches you and asks you for the answers to an assignment. You refuse. (**2**)

____ 4. You hire a friend to paint your house and are dissatisfied with the results: a mediocre job that may meet the terms of the contract but is also plainly sloppy. You insist that the painter improve the results before you pay in full. (**3**)

____ 5. You are at an outdoor café eating a meal, and the man at the next table lights up a foul-smelling cigar; smoke blows in your direction repeatedly. You politely ask the man to find a way to keep the smoke from spoiling your meal. (**2**)

____ 6. While parked at a convenience store, the occupants of the car next to yours sit in their car, doors open, making it very difficult for you to get back in your own car. You ask the driver to please allow you to pass by. (**2**)

____ 7. Your colleague repeatedly takes the credit for work you have done. You tell her that you will report the problem to your supervisor if it occurs again. (**2**)

____ 8. You suspect that a repair person is charging you for a car part that wasn't actually replaced. You call the manager and insist on proof before you pay the bill. (**2**)

____ 9. A friend you socialize with often is always 20 or more minutes late. You tell him that you feel annoyed and insist that he be more punctual if you are to continue to get together. (**2**)

____ 10. Although your hotel room is lovely, you notice many small areas overlooked by staff: the tub is not clean, the dresser is dusty, and the carpet only partially vacuumed. You call the desk and request that housekeeping come promptly. (**1**)

(continued)

Scoring

After each question there is a point value in parentheses. Points are assigned based on the difficulty of the situation. Add up the points for each question, including them under *either* the True or the False column, depending on which answer you chose for each question. For instance, if you chose *False* for Question #1, you will enter 1 point under the *False* category. Add the points in each column when all have been entered.

	TRUE		FALSE
1.	_____	1.	_____
2.	_____	2.	_____
3.	_____	3.	_____
4.	_____	4.	_____
5.	_____	5.	_____
6.	_____	6.	_____
7.	_____	7.	_____
8.	_____	8.	_____
9.	_____	9.	_____
10.	_____	10.	_____
TOTAL	_____		_____

Note: you should have no more than a total of 10 entries above; all 10 may be in one column, or they may be divided between the columns. You should have a maximum score of 20 points, total.

If your True *score was 15 points or more:*

You're no doormat. You stick up for yourself in social, work, and other contexts and situations, making sure that others don't walk all over you. Remember to finesse the way you take care of yourself: you might come across as pushy and too self-focused if you don't.

If your True *score was between 10 and 15 points:*

You're doing pretty well on sticking up for yourself but you need to be careful; about one-third to one-half of the time you're letting others take advantage of you and/or treat you poorly. Pay attention to the types of situations in which you allow this, and be on the lookout in the future for this tendency.

If your False *score was between 10 and 15 points:*

Take your cue from the scoring category just above; about one-third to one-half of the time, you're allowing others to walk all over you. This isn't healthy

(continued)

for body, mind, or soul, and it's not going to take you where you want to go, regardless of your destination. Pay careful attention to the "homework" and development tools ahead.

If your False *score was 15 points or more:*

It's likely you have a serious self-esteem issue, with a score in this range. Somewhere along the line you learned that you didn't deserve to be treated well or respected. As a result, you allowed others to take advantage of you and treat you poorly, which reinforced your beliefs. You not only need to focus on the homework and development tools, but to do serious work on your self-esteem. As you work your way through the tool chapters, focus in particular on the assessments and interventions geared toward increasing and reinforcing self-esteem. You can do it—and now is the time.

MOVING FORWARD

By examining the results of your assessment tool and being truthful with yourself about the choices you've made and continue to make, you know whether you stand up for yourself or not. Many people don't in one context or another, and so we're going to spend our energy on making changes to the self-defeating patterns of behavior that will reinforce poor self-esteem and insecurity. It's time to let go of the cringing, cowering approach that will cause you to lose so much.

Eleanor Roosevelt, a woman of uncommon courage who stood up for her convictions and created great change in any number of areas, was not always so powerful—at least, she didn't believe she was. She conquered a limiting sense of insecurity and a stifling inability to stand up for herself *in mighty fashion.* I mention this because it's easy to slip into believing that the courageous and the secure are somehow different—as if they're born with different genes, with superior innate abilities and skills. This simply isn't true. What they *do* have is the courage of their convictions and the willingness to *take a risk.* Eleanor Roosevelt said, "If you have to compromise, be sure to compromise *up!*"[1]

As you begin the "homework" on the coming pages, I'd like you to keep this in mind. Don't settle! Don't allow others to always get the second helping, the credit, the best of this or the first of that. Throw your hat into the ring as a contender instead of looking back regretfully, as Marlon Brando did in *On the Waterfront,*[2] when he sadly mused, "I coulda been a contenda . . . " Be a contender. Better yet, *be a winner.*

HOMEWORK ASSIGNMENTS

There are three central domains in your life: work, family, and friends. I've provided an assignment that will help you begin standing up for yourself in each of these domains. You may discover that there is an imbalance, with one domain more difficult either because of longstanding traditions against which you must struggle or because of a lopsided power differential. For instance, you may be up against a family tradition of repressing feelings, and if everyone but you continues to observe this tradition, you'll face greater difficulty. What you need to do, in this case, is arm yourself with the knowledge that others are steeped in this tradition and not yet willing to let it go— but that doesn't mean *you* can't.

The imbalances and struggles that occur may take place at work or in your family role, but even your friends, whom you've *chosen* to be in your life, are not always above keeping you in a lesser position in order to further their needs. In what I call the "Prince and the Patient Syndrome," I've seen as much in families where one child succeeds masterfully (the prince) and one is the chosen "patient" who always needs help just getting through life. A similar pairing can be seen in friendships. The "Prince/Princess and the Pardoner Syndrome" operates when one friend is always forgiving the offenses committed by the other (the prince/princess). You fail to see that this not only perpetuates the power imbalance but is also *not* in your favor.

In the Workplace ...

During the next several days, choose one small area where you feel you can *stand up for yourself.* For example:

- Don't offer to collect the money for an office gift.

- Don't agree to be the one to decide how to split the bill at an office luncheon.

- Don't agree to let someone else have the bagel, cupcake, or Danish you like.

- Don't allow the company to schedule a trip on your child's birthday.

- Don't allow yourself to feel pressured to schedule client phone calls during dinner or during the time you usually reserve for the family.

- Don't give up the parking space you and another driver arrived at simultaneously

- Don't agree with the boss just because everyone else sits back in silence.

- Tell your clients that you don't accept weekend meetings.

- Schedule your vacation first before others so that you don't get the "leftovers."

- Learn to say "I'll consider it and see if I can accommodate you" when asked to take on an overload of assignments.

- Don't allow yourself to respond to requests with a kneejerk "Okay" statement.

You are learning to build your abilities with a series of small personal accomplishments. The word "small," however, shouldn't be construed as "insignificant" because no personal, positive move for you is less than significant. The idea here is to pull yourself back from the practice of giving in while you create the opportunities to "compromise up." Each of these examples of ways in which you can stick up for yourself may seem small—or, if you're not accustomed to standing up for yourself, they may seem larger and more anxiety-producing—but their sum is greater than the parts. You don't have to do exactly what I've outlined in the examples. They're "mind joggers" to help you find ones that fit into your personal situation. Over time, making these small changes will increase your confidence, give you greater skill in negotiating and sticking up for yourself, and give you the power to make even larger, more significant changes down the road. *How* you compromise is up to you, but it must be a compromise that gives you a "win" of some sort. You can decide what the magnitude of the "win" needs to be for you to feel satisfied. Remember, *you're* keeping score here.

In the Home ...

Because the outcome of this exercise depends in part on how many people live in your home and what the relationships are between them, the instructions have to remain somewhat fluid and flexible. However, no matter who is in your home, there's someone who always wants you to pick up after them—whether literally or figuratively. In order to begin to make changes in these expectations and in your response to them, practice the following do's and don'ts:

1. *Don't* offer to put someone else's wash in with yours just because you're doing your laundry.

2. *Do* set up a schedule for yourself, and if someone needs an errand run, consider it only if it's convenient for *you*. Decide if you will do it then or not at all. Mom's bank run doesn't have to be *your* emergency if you're running around doing errands already.

3. *Don't* assume all of the cooking, cleaning, and shopping chores. Everyone eats, so everyone needs to know how to shop for and prepare foods. Likewise, if you're the money-handler, the mechanic, or the lawn service in your home, take a step back and figure out who can contribute and how. Then see that it happens: make the request, and if that doesn't work, make it a demand. Remember the Nike ad? *Just do it!*

4. *Don't* lend something if you don't want to lend it.

5. *Do* insist on taking time for yourself: to work out, to go to a movie, to lie on the sofa and stare at the ceiling—it doesn't matter what you do, as long as you do it for yourself.

In Your Friendships . . .

Let's look at lopsided friendships and examine some ways in which you can handle the dissatisfaction, frustration, and reinforcement of poor self-esteem that results when you don't stick up for yourself. Try doing one or more of the following:

- Don't agree to go to a particular restaurant, movie, or play just because your friend wants to go. Do it because you want to or there's a compromise in it for you.

- Don't continue to pay for coffee when your friend says that he or she "doesn't have any change" or "forgot my money."

- Don't allow your friends to make negative comments about you or your life unless they offer something constructive too. A possible rejoinder with which you could respond is this: "And that is constructive for me in what way . . . ?"

Each of these can be tempered to fit your comfort level, but however you temper them, at least try these approaches out in some fashion. Remember the discussion earlier in the book about changing your behavior and allowing your beliefs to follow. Here's your opportunity to stand up for yourself and then watch as you begin to believe that in fact you can stand up for yourself. Time's a-wasting; go to it!

WHERE YOU ARE NOW

If you've reached adulthood without learning to stick up for yourself, you already know a great deal about the things we've been discussing. You've also just read through the "homework" and may have even tried out a few of these new behaviors. As a result of all of these factors—except the homework, which will yield positive results—you've been through the losses, endured the indignities, and experienced the other ill effects of not sticking up for yourself. On paper, in any case, it would seem an open-and-shut case: not sticking up for yourself just doesn't make sense. Nothing good comes of it, and plenty of bad accumulates. Why, then, would anyone *choose* this path?

We've already discussed the roots: the poor self-esteem that results from negative messages and neglect and the like, and how this creates the "choice" of not sticking up for yourself. There is an additional element to the story, though; there are two categories of obstacles that can hold you back from standing strong even when you know you should stick up for yourself.

Emotional Discomfort

It can be terribly threatening and uncomfortable to stand up to others, and particularly to others who will arouse those old childhood feelings of inadequacy, fear, or humiliation when you try to challenge them. Remember, it's often in the best interests of others that you don't get what you want and that you don't stand up for yourself. It means more of those second helpings, more racquetball games won, and so on, if you don't stick up for yourself, and for some people, the cleanness of the win doesn't matter; it's all about getting the win itself.

Physical Discomfort

Hand in hand with those emotional responses that come when you try to stick up for yourself is a collection of physical messages. From sweating to an increased heart rate and pulse to clammy palms and stomach cramps, you may well experience a somatic reaction to the feelings that arise when

you challenge others by standing up for yourself. Some people even integrate these physical symptoms into their long-term way of responding to
and functioning within a world that seems dangerous: they develop clusters
of migraines, back spasms, ulcers, or some other recurrent physical problem that manifests when their stress levels are highest. If this is true for
you—if you have any chronic condition—it would pay to examine it closely to determine the role stress plays in your life. No longer is the mind-
body connection considered voodoo medicine; even the most conservative
physicians now understand and accept that stress and wellness are inextricably related.

   If there are emotional and physical obstacles that keep you from standing
up for yourself—and there undoubtedly are—there are also plenty of benefits you need to be aware of to counterbalance the power of those obstacles.

BENEFITS

Perhaps the most potent benefit of sticking up for yourself is the infusion of
power it brings you—and the way this infusion creates unexpected change in
all sorts of areas of your life. When you become powerful, you can begin to
see yourself as powerful; the belief can follow the behavior, you'll recall,
which is exactly what will happen in this instance. You will firmly insist that
the person in front of you in the express line—the person with 45 items—
move to a regular grocery line. You'll take that second helping when you're
hungry. You will politely but definitively tell your neighbor that you'd prefer
it if he no longer walked his dog in your yard. Besides the outcomes you
might expect—the cooperation of others, even if grudging—you'll begin to
stand taller, both literally *and* figuratively! In figurative terms, this means
that you will feel emboldened to stand up for yourself in other ways and in
additional settings. Once the ball is rolling, you'll soon discover that it's not
so difficult after all—and that the results are well worth any risk you may
run. This power you acquire will bring a wealth of other new feelings and
experiences to your life as well, including the sense that you can now:

CONTROL AND DIRECT YOUR OWN LIFE.   Once you stop devoting all that
time and energy to downplaying your importance, you'll have energy available for the really important things, such as deciding how you want your life
to be. This new available energy can be used to make decisions, direct yourself in new endeavors, and control what occurs in your life. Not a bad result
just from reaching out for a second helping, is it?

Do What You Want to Do.   How would it feel to be the one to decide what (and when, where, and how) you want to do with your life? From the smallest decision (bowling or a movie tonight?) to the largest (marriage?), sticking up for yourself is the first step in taking over management of your life. There's nothing wrong with doing what you want to do—recognizing, of course, that compromise is important in relationships and that you cannot walk over another to get your wants and needs satisfied without harming them. Barring the kind of selfishness that such behavior indicates, it is not only all right, but essential, that you decide what makes you happy and satisfied—and that you pursue it.

Have More Balanced Relationships.   By standing up for yourself, not only will you get what you want and learn to direct your own life, but you'll also notice that your relationships begin to become more balanced. The honesty will increase as you clearly state what you want and need—and as you insist upon receiving it. Again, this is not to say that you should become some taller version of a me-me-me three-year-old, demanding that others give freely to her while she simply basks in the glory of being herself. This is charming—for a little while—in a three-year-old, but highly annoying in an adult.

Let Go of Those Somatic Complaints.   That's right—when you begin standing up for yourself, you will rapidly shrink the physical problems that were related to the self-esteem and other issues that caused you not to stick up for yourself. Having illness or pain is a major drain on energy, and of course it can also be physically limiting. Somatic complaints keep you from directing your full energies toward your own health and well-being.

Upsetting the Staus Quo

Keep in mind that, implicit in the changes you make, standing up for yourself can be threatening to others. You're upsetting the status quo by causing shifts in the entire network around you. However, this does not mean you shouldn't make these changes. To the contrary! If sticking up for yourself is the goal, the only way to meet it is to forge ahead, and I encourage you to do just that. Just be aware that when you do so, you may well encounter discouragement from others initially or, in some cases, even over the long haul.

You may also find that some relationships end; there are selfish people who have kept you around because they always got their way, and once this situation changes, your utility expires. Even if the relationship doesn't end, you can expect anger, resentment, or passive-aggressive behavior from some people in an attempt to control you. Just remember that your goals now diverge. You want to be powerful, and the other does not want you to be, and so he or she may pull out all of the stops to get what they want. Of course, you'll want to reconsider whether it serves you to stay in any relationships that continue to try to punish you for sticking up for yourself or control you.

CONCLUSION

You have choices to make, and you can make them now or delay making them, telling yourself that the risks are too great, the obstacles too many, the benefits too sparse. For someone who is committed to remaining in a rut, there's always a reason to stay there. For someone committed to change, though, there is—fortunately—also always a reason that supports the change. Choose to stick up for yourself, and you're making a dozen or a hundred other changes too: you are sending the power to be happy filtering downward and outward through your life. What better reason could there be?

Live Dangerously

'TIS BETTER TO HAVE LOVED AND LOST
THAN NEVER TO HAVE LOVED AT ALL.

Alfred, Lord Tennyson, "In Memoriam A.H.H."

Regardless of where you are when you find yourself backing down, disappearing from fear or wimping out, take one to two minutes to develop and access feelings of focus and courage inside of you. There are three steps to doing so. First, breathe slowly in through your nose, taking in as much oxygen as you comfortably can. Second, hold the air for a few seconds, then breathe this air back out through your mouth. Third, become conscious of your shoulders by focusing on them, tightening and then releasing them briefly and gently during your breaths. Each breath should take about five slow counts. This Quick Fix will relax you and help you to replace self-defeating negative thoughts and feelings of fear as you instead concentrate on your breathing and on the sensation in your shoulders. This, then, will prepare you to live dangerously!

QUIT THE REHEARSALS
AND LIVE YOUR REAL LIFE

I've seen it in the laboratory of the therapy office far too many times. It begins innocently enough as an experiment—you come in seeking help in understanding your choices, your behaviors, your feelings. So far, so good. We get out the microscope and start looking into the hypotheses and beliefs that define your life. Still no problem. The longer you continue with the hypotheses, though, exploring this childhood trauma and that adolescent angst, this old wound and that ancient sorrow—instead of moving toward the experiment of living—the more it seems that you haven't come for therapy; but to avoid your real life. The analogy that takes hold for me is that of a mold growing in a Petri dish, interesting for a moment but not something anyone wants to have to clean up, and it seems as if even looking too close-ly at the tender mold might cause untold damage.

I'm talking about the hiding out that far too many people do in therapy. They use the controlled, safe, and comprehensible life on the couch to sub-stitute for the uncontrolled, scary, messy, and confusing life that occurs out in the real world. In fact, it's something we all do at times—though perhaps not with the assistance of a therapist—and it doesn't have to be negative.

Before we talk about living dangerously, I want to be clear that when feel-ings or experiences are overwhelming, there's nothing wrong with taking a temporary break, a time-out to adjust and adapt. A perfect example of this is grief. Earlier we discussed the steps involved in grieving. Denial is the very first, and it's just one way of shutting down, tuning out, or otherwise avoid-ing reality—*until you can handle it*. *That's* the critical point: you must *return to the reality that faces you*, no matter how unpleasant or even unbearable it may seem.

Unfortunately, the longer you stay in traditional therapy, talking your reality to death, the easier it will be to remain withdrawn from *dealing* with that reality. You'll be able to convince yourself that you're making progress, of course—after all, you *are* "dealing with" your issues . . . aren't you? *No!* In fact, you're just marking time. While talking about your problems or chal-lenges can certainly help you create a game plan for addressing and over-coming them, it cannot take the place of the action steps you must implement if you're going to make changes in your life.

In this chapter we'll focus on how you can identify areas in your life that you're avoiding, what the costs and benefits are of coming out of hiding, and how to go about living dangerously. Amazingly, you can do so without creating any danger for yourself or others! We will discuss how you can revisit your past without getting stuck and a way to live in your present without needing to flee. Finally, you'll read about an approach that will let you imagine your future as one containing endless possibilities—*except* for those possibilities generated by fear. They have no place here, and it's time to let them go.

Outside of the too-often-inauthentic setting of traditional therapy, you *can* rid yourself of the paralyzing fears that keep you treading water, and you *can* generate the energy and gain the real-time skills to zero in on the changes that will create the life you want. It's time for you to come out of hiding—not tomorrow, and not next week, and definitely not next year, but *today*. What are we waiting for? Let's get started.

WHERE YOU'VE BEEN

A few chapters back we talked about the critical importance of accepting yourself, and in the previous chapter we talked about sticking up for yourself. These two rules of good living are central to this topic too. If you're going to have a satisfying, rich life, you cannot go about trying to avoid risk. You must accept yourself when others don't, stick up for yourself when others won't, and live dangerously—taking risks in every area of life—even when you want to hide. In fact, you must do so especially when you want to hide! Living authentically and with satisfaction and living "safe" cannot peacefully coexist.

Instead of living dangerously, you've been trying to avoid making mistakes—in other words, you've been in hiding. As you've attempted to minimize the chances that you might get hurt, you've been in hiding. As you've accommodated others when it caused you inconvenience and pain, keeping your mouth shut when it made you seethe to remain silent, or denying your truth when you felt as if you might burst from the pain of pretense, you've been in hiding.

You haven't lived dangerously because you've been avoiding a real life, avoiding making waves, and therefore keeping yourself in a protective cocoon. Without realizing it, though, every day you spend in that cocoon adds another layer of thickness to the walls; over time they can begin to seem impenetrable to you and to others. When that happens, you may feel so separate from others and from your real self that you lose touch with the need to take risks. I'm knocking on the sides of the cocoon; whether it protects one small corner of your life or your entire existence, it's time to break out. You've also assumed that the cost of living dangerously is too high. In truth, the cost of living any other way will impoverish you faster—and for longer—than anything else. Whether you've hidden out in the privacy of your own life or under the guise of "dealing with things" in traditional therapy, where the neutral furnishings and therapist's soothing voice have lulled you into a false sense of progress, let's shake things up. As long as you've been saying you'll take risks tomorrow, you were working on that cocoon. Tomorrow may have always offered another day to Scarlett O'Hara, but *you* can't be guaranteed an endless supply of tomorrows.

HOW YOU GOT THERE

I'm willing to bet that somewhere along the line you learned that it's better to be safe than sorry. Maybe it happened early, when you took a risk and failed, and an adored parent criticized you rather than sympathizing, comforting, and supporting you. Safety could have been the word put in cross-stitch on your layette, you heard about it so often. It wasn't just about crossing streets while holding Mommy's hand and exploring in the kitchen only when Daddy was watching. It went way beyond obeying the crossing guard and listening to teachers. Instead, you were taught that the world is a train hurtling at you at top speed, and you're the wreck waiting to happen. *No, don't do that! Be careful! Watch out! You could get hurt! You will get hurt!* Sound familiar? If it does, you have internalized those voices, and their powerful presence keeps you in line, and avoiding even necessary risks, as an adult.

Maybe, though, you didn't pick up the danger lessons until later. Perhaps it happened when you experienced your first romantic relationship, when you loved and lost and, unlike Tennyson, decided it would have been better to have never loved at all. Or perhaps it happened when you entered a competition, applied to an exclusive school, or set a goal you didn't meet.

Whether it happened earlier or later, the grooves that were established in your brain, the ones that call out *Danger! Danger!* repeatedly as you go about living, are going to take some effort to smooth out. It's going to be hard to even *try* to live dangerously at first—because you've been taught that it's foolhardy to do so, and a guarantee for pain. The real pain comes from avoiding risk and staying hidden away in that suffocating, stultifying cocoon.

All I ask for now is that you try. You don't need to succeed at first. It's okay to try and not succeed; there is learning in the trying.

WHY OLD WAY DOESN'T WORK

The bottom line is this: *you should live dangerously because life is meant to be experienced*, and taking risks means experiencing life. You can talk about life until you're blue in the face but the only thing that will ultimately give you satisfaction is *living* it. That involves going out on limbs and taking risks. The pounds won't roll off if you only *talk* about not eating those pastries, and the Olympics won't come calling you for the butterfly stroke if all you've been doing is talking about how the water might feel. Close your mouth (no more eclairs) and jump in (get your feet wet)! You will never know or understand the options and possibilities that exist until you do. Live dangerously, because in order for you to truly exist in any meaningful way, you must participate *fully* in your life. You won't *learn* anything if you don't experience life, nor will you *feel* the abundance of emotions possible, *think* the depth of thoughts conceivable, or *create* the kind of life that is possible.

Okay, so certainly life must be experienced. Equally true is this: *live dangerously because when you limit the options and possibilities experience brings, you limit hope.* And few things are sadder than a person who lives without hope. Your vision becomes narrowed; you view the world through a long tunnel that provides no glimpse of the potential that exists for you. It is a vicious cycle: the options and possibilities seem limited, so you strive for less; as you strive for less, the options and possibilities become more limited. Break out of this cycle; do not risk letting it run your life as if you're a hamster on a wheel, always exerting tremendous energy . . . and always ending up in the same place.

If I haven't yet convinced you that it doesn't work to "live safe," try this reason: *live dangerously because living fully opens up your creativity—and your sexuality.* Living dangerously means becoming engaged with your life and with the world around you on all levels: emotionally, physically, spiritually, intellectually, and more. If you can learn to be more engaged in your everyday actions, you'll become more comfortable when you're engaged in intimate relationships with others. There's a turning inward that happens if you're not involving *all of yourself* in living your life.

I remember a job I had years ago—you'll see how *many* years ago when you hear this story! I was a secretary and had to wear not only a hat to work, which was de rigeur at the time, but also gloves. The rules were rigid and we didn't dare break them—it seemed too "dangerous" to do so. Even a simple interaction like shaking hands with others, though, can feed your self-esteem, and as your self-esteem grows, you present yourself differently (and more powerfully) in the world. Unfortunately, as women at that time in the work world, we were denied that, and I think the gloves served to reinforce the distance that was artificially created.

Let's do a brief assessment so you can get a handle on where you stand when it comes to connecting with others in a real, albeit sometimes "dangerous" way—and when it comes to standing tall, walking proudly, and moving through your life with confidence. I call this assessment tool the "Safety-Danger Continuum," and it will give you a better read on how willing you are to live dangerously.

THE SAFETY-DANGER CONTINUUM

As you read the brief scenarios below, choose your most likely response. If there is a situation in which no response sounds like the one you'd choose, select the choice that seems closest to the choice you would most typically make.

You're single, and an attractive person is trying to establish eye contact with you in a social setting. You:

A. Avoid eye contact, wishing you felt more confident.
B. Make eye contact but take it no further.
C. Approach and strike up a conversation.
D. Approach and tell the stranger that you are attracted to him or her and want to get to know them better.

A friend of yours relies on you frequently—when she does not have a boyfriend. When she has a partner, she'll go months without even contacting you, which hurts your feelings. You:

A. Don't say anything since she might get angry.
B. Joke or vaguely mention the behavior but leave it at that.
C. Raise the subject with slight misgivings but stay firm that you're unhappy with her behavior.
D. Tell her off for her rude behavior and lack of caring.

You're teaching a class and your students are arriving increasingly late, disrupting your concentration and showing a lack of respect. You:

A. Tell yourself it's just the way students are nowadays.
B. Make occasional sarcastic or oblique comments about the behavior.
C. Take the tardy students aside after class and firmly tell them that you won't accept students entering your classroom late.
D. Explode at them the next time they're late, threatening to fail them or drop them from the class.

You have a chance to visit a country you've longed to see. It will mean two weeks away from work, and your boss is known for disliking long staff vacations. You:

A. Turn down the offer, not wanting to make waves with the boss.
B. Tentatively bring up the subject but back down instantly if your boss objects.

(continued)

C. Tell your boss about your plans, let him know that this is important to you and that you'll find a way to avoid a disruption in the workplace.

D. Let your boss know in no uncertain terms that this is a dream you've had for a long time and no one is going to interfere with it, especially not him.

Your partner wants you to take a sexuality class together, one that teaches couples to be more sexually intimate. You:

A. Refuse to discuss or even consider the idea.

B. Make jokes or avoid the subject in other ways, feeling uncomfortable and embarrassed at the thought of it.

C. Express any misgivings you have but mostly feel good about the idea of becoming more intimate with your partner, and therefore agree to participate.

D. Instantly agree and try to talk other friends into participating as well, sharing intimate details with them in the course of discussing the idea

You are accepted into several graduate programs after applying. One program is in business and doesn't excite you, but will ensure a good living. The other is in the arts, your passion, but—as others often say—so impractical. You:

A. Immediately accept the business school, reminding yourself that practicality is all-important.

B. Vacillate for a time over the decision but ultimately accept the business school, knowing that you can probably still pursue the arts as a hobby.

C. Accept the arts program despite your concerns, figuring out some alternatives for bringing in enough money to have the things you want.

D. Accept the arts program instantly—good living be damned!—figuring you'll scrape by, and if you don't, maybe friends or family will help out.

When you were a child you were bitten by a dog, and you've feared animals ever since. Your child longs for a puppy, something you denied her for several years, saying she wasn't ready for the responsibility. She has proven otherwise and raises the subject again. You:

A. Continue to say she's not ready, refusing to consider that you might be the one who hasn't been ready all this time.

B. Admit to your fear of dogs but refuse to get your daughter a puppy.

C. Discuss your fear of dogs with your child and think of ways to overcome that fear as you agree that she can have a puppy.

D. Throw caution to the wind and get her a puppy on the spur of the moment.

(continued)

Scoring Your Answers

Use the following point values to score your answers. Your total score should be within the range of 8 to 32 points when you've added up the scores

> A = 1 point
> B = 2 points
> C = 3 points
> D = 4 points

8 to 13 points

You've got to learn—and learn fast—to live life. Forget living dangerously; with a score in this range you're barely living at all. You are letting fear of failure, fear of others' responses, fear of change, and dozens of others fears rule your choices and your life. Until you step outside of your comfort zone, expanding it along the way, you will keep living a fragile shell of a life.

14 to 19 points

You are occasionally willing to consider living dangerously, but you haven't yet made the important transitions to doing so. Take those tentative thoughts you've had and act on them: state your feelings, defend your beliefs, and stand up to others, or you'll find that you always end up in a safety zone that offers you no excitement, no challenges, and no real joy.

20 to 25 points

You're doing well! You consider your choices and are willing to expand your options to include things you haven't tried before, even if you feel a bit scared when doing so. This is what it means to live dangerously, and you've got the hang of it, so keep on with what you're doing!

26 to 32 points

You've learned the lesson of living dangerously all too well—you've gone past looking out the window and are dangling from the ledge. It's great to live dangerously, but there's such a thing as foolishness: take a step back and consider the consequences before you act, and remember that having passion and potency in your life doesn't have to—and shouldn't—put you in real danger.

ROOTS

It should come as no surprise to you that lack of self-esteem are at the root of the fear of taking risks. After all, when you avoid risks you're trying to protect yourself from being found out, disappointed, shot down. Remember that message because it's coming back to haunt you: *it's better to be safe than sorry.*

Let me say it as plainly and as clearly as possible: it is *not* better to be safe than to be sorry. Being safe means keeping yourself from growing, learning, exploring, loving, and living at any level even remotely close to your potential. What a dreadful loss, and a terrible way to live your life. In fact, being safe in many ways isn't about living your life—it's about hiding carefully behind a wall, observing and perhaps commenting from time to time, but never truly participating. When opportunity knocks, you don't answer the door. When possibility beckons you turn the other way. When love presents itself, you flee—emotionally, intellectually, physically, or all three at once. Few things are sadder.

I'll grant you that it's better to look both ways before crossing the street, and that it's better to check the stove a second time if you think you may have left the burner on. It's not better to be safe than sorry, though, *whenever it involves taking an emotional, physical, or intellectual risk that you have already weighed with common sense.* Then being safe is the dangerous choice to make, because choosing safety equates to choosing a nonlife. The danger of being too safe is insidious: it will slowly build up over time, giving you a collection of experiences that didn't happen, memories never made, and report cards showing only lessons unlearned. Eventually, then, your life will become an album empty of photos you didn't take. Of all the things that can wreak havoc on your self-esteem—and plenty of things can, I assure you—the regret of an unlived life might well be the foremost.

DEVELOPMENT TOOL

Typically at this stage in the chapter I would present you with an assessment tool, but we're going to do something different this time. I call it a "development" tool rather than an assessment because it will help you to develop a new skill rather than assess or evaluate yourself. You already know about how fearful you are of living your life fully, whether this fear cripples you or merely changes your course from time to time. By now you've done a number of assessments, and I believe you know yourself better; you're ready for a development tool that relies on your "therapist within" to tell you how much or how little you need it.

I've often found homework assignments to be helpful because they provide focus and can be designed and used in increments, with you progressing step by step as you work up toward something you *want* or *need* to do. These assignments are divided into three categories: those that relate to "Mind," those that relate to "Body," and those that relate to "Social" aspects of your life.

The Mind

Perhaps you've always wanted to express your creative side, yet are afraid of failure. The fear of failure, in fact, is quite common, and it keeps many people shackled in a lock-step existence as they try to conform, getting through life by getting along. Let's explore your creative side in order to help it grow. Try the following exercise—and don't let fear, poor self-esteem, or the wish to stay "safe" stop you:

1. Take five days, setting aside time each day, to write a short story (no more than about 1500 words) on something important to you. Or, if you prefer, it can be a poem instead.

2. Do an Internet search for an on-line magazine that accepts submissions for the type of work you've created (one that doesn't charge you any fees).

3. Submit what you've written.

My guess is that you're thinking you can't possibly do it. Am I right? The risk of embarrassment, rejection, and negative self-evaluation is just too great. Nonsense! Think about it: you'll never have to face anyone when doing this, and embarrassment and rejection cannot occur independent of another. You can't be "rejected" by some faceless entity out in cyberspace! It's just not logical. You can't be embarrassed if no one is there to see you fall. It doesn't make any sense. Besides, you can do this exercise under a pseudonym if you wish, and that will help you to take the risk, as well. If your poem or short story is not accepted at one place, try another. Go on, *get out on that limb and try*.

The Body

Allowing your body to release itself from the grip of insecurity that causes it to tense up is another way to live dangerously. Remember, living dangerously doesn't mean placing yourself in physical peril. Instead, it means stepping into an area where fear is signaling "danger" to you as a means of stopping you from doing something that would probably create learning, excitement, pleasure, or a whole host of other positive outcomes. Try the following:

1. Exercise and confidence can be a "two-fer" if you plan it right. Find a t'ai chi class for beginners at a local school or Y (but not at a club where you'd have to sign a membership agreement). I suggest t'ai chi because it develops grace , tones the body, and teaches self-defense all at one time; it could be bowling, yoga, or square dancing if you prefer.

2. Promise yourself that you'll complete the class *no matter how much* your mind is telling you to stay home on those nights.

3. Don't agree to more than this one class unless you feel you want more classes when you get down to the final two class sessions in this series. In fact, do not make this decision either way before there are only two classes to go.

If you're wondering why I'm so insistent that you enroll in a class that involves a physical activity of some type, it's because I know for a fact that there is a deep, profound connection between the mind, body, and spirit. If you do not nurture all three, all three will show the negative effects of neglect. Perhaps you're a couch potato, though, or you're active but see yourself as nonathletic and unable to pull off a stunt like taking a t'ai chi class. Don't be so fast to judge or limit yourself. Even if you were always picked last for kickball in elementary school or have led a sedentary lifestyle since—in fact, especially if these things are true—you need to pay attention to your physical self. It is the vehicle carrying around all that work you've been doing throughout the book, and if you don't take care of it, it can't take care of the inner you.

The Social Self

Socializing for adults can be difficult. Unlike in childhood, when your parents arranged play dates, or in your school days, when there were plenty of prearranged social functions, adulthood requires your active participation in the planning stages. This is much easier to do—and creates far less anxiety and pressure, an added bonus—if the primary purpose of your social activity isn't social! In other words, stop worrying about meeting Mr. or Ms. Right; stop worrying about whether you'll make friends or have fun;

let go of thoughts about whether you'll appear to be a wallflower or the life of the party, lampshade and all. Focus on activities with a purpose: painting a group home in the community; feeding the homeless; shelving books at the library at the local senior citizens' center; teaching a class; bowling with a group from your church; or marching for a cause. You see? In about 20 seconds I identified six activities that are not necessarily social by definition—with the possible exception of the bowling party—and yet each will result in social interaction. But without the pressure of that interaction hanging over your head (you'll be focused on the task or activity at hand), you'll be more relaxed, more yourself, and less overwhelmed by the challenges of having to "perform" in a social situation, if that overwhelms you.

If none of those ideas appeal to you, here are a few more places and ways in which to increase your "social danger zone":

- Volunteer for Habitat for Humanity or a similar project that builds homes for needy families.

- Sign up to do stage and scenery work for a local community theater.

- Dust off your vocal cords and get involved in a choral group that travels to hospitals and nursing homes to entertain patients.

- Call Meals on Wheels or a similar program and offer to volunteer once a week or once a month.

- Volunteer to work on a local, state, or federal election campaign.

Before we move on, let's talk for a moment about a different, deeper, and more complex level of living dangerously. While the ideas above can help you begin to make this change, they're only a starting point. The real dangers in living are about relationships, success and failure, and change. Truly living dangerously means going out on an emotional limb and risking hurt—not foolishly, but wisely, knowing that in order to feel the full range of joyful and exciting and passionate emotions available to you as a person, you must also risk the full range of painful emotions. They come attached to each other, inseparable.

As you gain experience in living dangerously through the concrete and practical ideas above, begin to transfer this knowledge to your emotional life. What kind of changes can you make in order to experience more? Here are just a few possibilities:

- Decide that you will tell the truth . . . all the time.

- Commit to turning someone you dislike into a friend.

- Practice telling others how you feel, especially when you feel afraid or angry.

- Promise yourself that you'll find something good about yourself daily and acknowledge it.

- Think of something you've always been afraid of doing . . . and do it anyway.

- Do something you've been avoiding doing for too long.

- Take responsibility for something you regret having done.

- Claim the credit for something you feel good about having done.

PRESENT TENSE

You're probably too busy to read the rest of this chapter right now, between those t'ai chi classes, volunteering at the zoo, shelving books at the library, and making the complex but rewarding changes above—but try to fit it into your busy social and emotional life anyway! It's important to examine why you don't jump up to engage in the activities and suggestions I've made, and why you make the choice—even when the drawbacks have been crystal-lized—to try to live your life without risk.

Obstacles

Often, feelings alone can serve as obstacles to making emotional, relation-ship, and lifestyle changes—and at other times, simply knowing that you may *have* these feelings can serve as the obstacle. Many people avoid the hassle of having to deal with the emotional fallout that can result from change. By now, though, you know that this is not only unwise, but emo-tionally unhealthy. You must accept yourself as you are—feelings, warts, and all!—in order to live with satisfaction and to experience learning and growth.

Here, then, are several of the obstacles that present themselves when you try to step outside of life free of risk—in other words, here are the things that may send you backward, vowing not to try the experiment again, when you try to live dangerously.

You may find that you ...

Feel unskilled and foolish because you're trying something new and unfamiliar. These feelings are natural, and I'd expect them to arise as surely as I'd expect the sun to set at night or the oceans to recede at low tide. You need to adopt the same attitude: feeling foolish is just part of learning and living, and if you can go at it with a sense of wonder and a sense of humor, you'll be a better person for it.

Feel afraid and unsure because you're trying something new and unfamiliar. Of course you do! Anyone who says he or she doesn't experience some feelings of fear or some degree of uncertainty is either not telling the truth or not closely in touch with his or her feelings. Let yourself feel these things, know you are not alone, and know that you have survived similar feelings in many different contexts at many other times in your life—and still survived and thrived.

Won't know what skills you need because you're trying something new and unfamiliar. The truth is, you probably won't! Some of your skills will be transferable, of course. You'll find that leading a tour group is similar to training new employees, or you'll discover that reading blueprints for that home you're helping to build is in certain ways like reading computer programming language. Who knows what you'll discover? Where your skills do not cover you, though, relax. You can learn—and that will expand the social experience, as well.

Believe you can't learn *what you need to know* because you're trying something new and unfamiliar. Of course you can! As you engage with others, interacting and observing, you will absorb a certain amount of what must be learned simply by a sort of "osmosis." The remainder can be learned the old-fashioned way, of course, through books, questions, and study, but the fact is, there may not be too much to learn; after all, bowling isn't rocket science, and t'ai chi isn't quantum physics. Focus, observe, and don't sell yourself short, and you'll discover something magical: you won't have to chase the lessons; the *learning* will come to *you*.

Believe you can't teach an old dog new tricks because you're trying something new and unfamiliar. I disagree, and I disagree with all my heart and every bit of my experience. You're neither too old nor too young—ever—to expand your knowledge base, even if that means becoming computer literate at the age of 78 in order to begin to email with an extended family, as did a woman I know. She's a delightful grandmother of 11—and now she's a technical whiz. Let her serve as an example to you of what is possible when you believe in possibility!

Keep replaying what you've been told, that you're not safe, because you're trying something new and unfamiliar. Maybe you're not safe—maybe you will experience hurt, disappointment, or loss. Maybe you'll know feelings of sorrow, anger, or frustration. In fact, you'll feel these feelings and more if you're experiencing your life.

The other option, though, is not to feel any range of emotion at all. Read the words of poet Kahlil Gibran, writing in *The Prophet,* on this subject:

> Your joy is your sorrow unmasked.
> And the selfsame well from which your laughter rises
> was oftentimes filled with your tears.
> And how else can it be?
> The deeper that sorrow carves into your being,
> the more joy you can contain.

The more you feel, the more you *can* feel, and this is true whether what you feel is painful or full of joy. It can be difficult to remember this when you're in the midst of distressing or uncomfortable feelings, but this is exactly what I want you to try to do. Hold onto the thought that *your joy is your sorrow unmasked,* and remember Nietzsche's words, that whatever doesn't kill you—and not much does, when it comes right down to it— makes you stronger.

BENEFITS

I'm going to assume, and hope, that by now you've made the decision and even some of the initial moves toward living dangerously. Let me fill you in on the benefits of doing so, even as you're experiencing some of these benefits on your own, while making initial forays into risk-taking.

When you live dangerously—worrying less about how the world might hurt you and more about the potential that exists for learning, loving, and living—you'll discover that *you don't need your imagination to see how very capable you are.* In fact, your abilities will not only become clear, but will *expand exponentially with each new and positive risk you take.*

Discovering and expanding your abilities is only the beginning to the benefits taking risks will provide you. You'll also *broaden your horizons* in almost limitless ways. In your relationships with others and in your dealings with the universe—the events that occur around you—you'll have potential to be someone you never thought you could be. There are not walls, doors, or ceilings on you when you take risks, because you discover your strengths and potential instead of reinforcing your weakness and boundaries.

Taking risks will also *increase your self-esteem.* This is a natural, predictable outcome of living dangerously, and it makes *sense* that it is. When you're discovering your full potential and achieving new, seemingly impossible outcomes, whether they are small or large, you'll feel a surge of powerful self-confidence and good feeling. The more you achieve, the better you feel—it wouldn't be logical if it were any other way.

Last, but certainly not least, since there are nearly countless benefits, a ripple effect occurs when you take risks. I can't tell you exactly what to look for, since the positives will depend on each given situation, but the general effect of living dangerously is similar to when you skip a stone across water. The surface of the water is marked by concentric circles, each one wider, each one moving more water outside of it. When you take risks, you're making change; when you make change, even infinitesimal change, you're causing often unanticipated changes to everything around you: your relationships with others, family, or workplace colleagues, social systems and more.

CONCLUSION

It's natural to feel some measure of insecurity and fear. We all do. Whether your insecurity is about those extra five pounds, about a skill you believe you're lacking, or about something deeply hidden, unseen by the world, you feel fear when you think about exposing it—and its resulting vulnerability—to others. If this fear grows too large—as it often does, the longer you avoid doing something about the insecurity—it can begin to dwarf the original issue, and soon you're afraid to take even a tiny risk that might be necessary to make a change. Your resistance is what is keeping those five pounds on, though; your resistance is keeping that skill outside of your expertise and keeping you from letting another person truly know you as you are. As long as you allow your resistance to rule—and as long as others will impose their own desire to maintain the status quo—you will see nothing change in your life. You'll live safely, perhaps, but you'll live in a static state, never growing, never moving, never learning.

As for the old message—"it's better to be safe than sorry"—erase it, cover your ears, block it out. The longer you stay in a holding pattern in your life, and the longer you flee from possibility or hide from opportunity, the more your potential will atrophy, like muscles that have gone unused for too long. Why you began protecting yourself is no longer the issue—most of us protect ourselves in some ways at some times. We experience hurt or fear or some other emotion that scars us, and instead of allowing the scars to heal by exposing them to light, and to new, fresh air, we guard and protect them. This has the opposite effect of what we intended, though. Scars thicken and only serve to eventually numb you. Muscles loosen and become useless. Your heart and your will are far stronger and far more flexible than you may know; now is the time to discover this truth. Let go of the self-protection and grab hold of the brass ring. Learning, loving, and living: you can—and *will*—do it the moment you begin living dangerously.

Give Up
the Throne

LIBERTY MEANS RESPONSIBILITY.
THAT IS WHY MOST MEN DREAD IT.

George Bernard Shaw

George Bernard Shaw, the Anglo-Irish playwright, once said, "Liberty means responsibility. That is why most men dread it."[1] The topic of freedom and what it means to us was also captured in a book by the famous psychologist Erich Fromm,[2] who believed that freedom could cause anxiety because it created a surfeit of choices.

Faced with so many choices, many people try to decrease their anxiety and fear by limiting their options—which then limits potential. To be completely free, you must find a balance between the myriad options available and the responsibilities that exist for you. When it comes to choices and responsibilities, both as they pertain to you and to others, it's essential to know where to draw the line. *The actions and reactions of others are not your responsibility.* If you allow them to be, you will remain stuck where you are, never learning or changing in a substantial way. This final tool will help you recognize the tendencies you have for avoiding personal responsibility, while identifying how and when you take on too much other-responsibility. By helping you strike a balance, it's an essential tool for achieving happiness over the long haul.

Take an index card and cut it into thirds. Write one of the following sentences on each of the three sections: "I am not responsible for others," "It's *your* problem", and "This problem is not *MY* problem!" Place the cards in three spots where you'll see them frequently: your wallet, on the dashboard in your car, clipped to your computer, and so on. Use them to jog your memory and reinforce your beliefs: *you* are responsible for your choices and behaviors, while *others* are responsible for their own.

WHAT OTHERS DO IS NOT YOUR RESPONSIBILITY (AND VICE VERSA)

You can take 100 percent responsibility for *your* life as you let go of the need to manage or control everyone else's. This is an essential change in helping yourself. What you do, the choices you make, the behaviors you exhibit, are all on you: no one *but* you can make you *feel* or *be* a certain way.

If you are to make this change, it's important to learn to distinguish your own habit of taking responsibility for other people's choices and behaviors and to identify how the effects of blaming and crediting others for your choices impacts you negatively. Only then can you reclaim the power you gave away to others and return it squarely to where it belongs—to yourself. At the same time you do this, you'll reassign power from yourself and place it squarely with others when that's where the power belongs.

The fact is, one of the most important goals in helping yourself—and the *most likely obstacle*—is connected to taking full responsibility for who you are, for the choices you make, and for the behaviors you exhibit. If you cannot do this, you cannot change, grow, or learn in any significant way. I know that's not what you want, so step up to the plate and claim what's yours!

WHERE YOU'VE BEEN

Take a minute to see if this sounds familiar to you. You've been taking responsibility for everyone else's choices and behaviors, blaming yourself when others mess up or don't follow through, criticizing yourself when others fail in some way, and feeling superior because you'd have done whatever it was much better. Admit it—feeling superior is one of your reactions. In fact, it's a core emotion when it comes to taking responsibility for others:

they get to be incompetent or irresponsible, but in return you get to feel like the most accomplished person on earth! Of course, you can also begin to feel chained and responsible for others.

You can easily recognize if this is a tendency of yours by tuning in to your feelings. They will tell you faster than anything else whether you struggle with this issue. Here are a few significations:

- Self-pity: *Poor me for having to deal with all of these responsibilities!*

- Rage: *Bad you for forcing me to pick up after the messes you make and leave around!*

- Frustration: *It's too much to handle—why do I have to handle your stuff plus mine?*

- Disappointment: *You've let me down by not being the person I thought you were or you were supposed to be.*

I could go on, but I'm sure you've recognized yourself in these points. You'll most often feel some combination of all of these reactions and emotions: self-pity and anger are often interlocking, for instance, as are frustration and disappointment. These are all normal responses to being burdened with the responsibility for another person because it's not the natural order that you should be. While we expect that parents will be responsible for children, and adults for caring for an aging parent, at the points in between, adults are expected to take care of themselves. This is not to say that you bear no obligations to others; that would be absurd, of course. As human beings, we all have certain ways in which we're responsible to others; this is natural and right. However, what another person does is the result of a process within that other person, a process you *cannot* take credit or blame for unless you have directly and unfairly influenced the process.

There are two elements to taking on too much responsibility. One is *taking over* another's responsibility. The other is *dodging true accountability in your own life* while appearing to be accountable because of all that responsibility you're taking for others. There are a number of clues that can tell you if there's an imbalance in responsibility:

- If you begin to feel resentful toward others for what you're doing for them.

- If you feel that your life is more about taking care of others than about taking care of yourself.

- If there never seems to be any time for what you want and need.

Stepping into true adulthood means taking on responsibility for what is yours and letting go what's not.

> BY IMPOSING TOO GREAT A RESPONSIBILITY,
> or rather, all responsibility, on yourself,
> you crush yourself.
>
> _____
>
> *Franz Kafka, The Fourth Notebook*

Kafka had it right; you will ""crush yourself"" if you try to take on the responsibility that rightly belongs to others. As you read on, you'll learn more about your own imbalances in taking and assigning responsibility, but for now it's important to begin to understand the process and to become aware of when you're overstepping in either direction. Use the clues I mentioned above, and ask yourself often whether you feel a sense of balance— or a sense of resentment—when it comes to the give and take in your life. You need to separate yourself from the psychological processes within you that lead you to take on more than you should. To do this you need to understand why and *when* you take or assign responsibility The following assessment will help you do both of those things.

THE BLAME GAME

Move rapidly through the checklist below, reading and scoring each statement about yourself. Do not change your answers or consider them at length; use your gut response to answer. Use this scale to score each statement as it relates to your own behavior:

1	=	Almost always
2	=	Frequently
3	=	Sometimes
4	=	Infrequently
5	=	Almost Never

1. ____ I speak up when decisions are being made.

2. ____ I get what I want.

3. ____ I control what happens in my life.

4. ____ I deserve the things that happen to me.

(continued)

5. ___ I make good choices in my life.
6. ___ I feel others pull their weight.
7. ___ I impact on others' lives.
8. ___ I make a difference in the world.
9. ___ I cause good things to happen.
10. ___ I believe that I have the same rights as others.
11. ___ I let others know how I feel.
12. ___ I believe that I can choose my future.
13. ___ I apologize when I do something wrong.
14. ___ I believe things work out in my life.
15. ___ I try to make my life happier.
16. ___ I believe that life is fair.
17. ___ I feel glad that I'm me.
18. ___ I believe that I deserve to be happy.
19. ___ I make others feel good.
20. ___ I have good karma.

___ Total of ODD-numbered questions (Behavior Score)
___ Total of EVEN-numbered questions (Belief Score)

If your BEHAVIOR score is:

10 to 20: You behave responsibly in most situations—keep at it!
21 to 39: You try to accept responsibility, and often succeed, but work at doing it even more.
40 to 50: You rarely take responsibility and it's damaging your life and relationships.

If your BELIEF score is:

10 to 20: Your beliefs are consistent with your actions. You're no blamer—way to go!
21 to 39: Work on your beliefs—they're part of why you blame others for your troubles.
40 to 50: You don't have the beliefs OR the behaviors: you're a Major League Blamer and have to make changes fast if you're going to be successful in work and play, love and life.

HOW YOU GOT THERE

As a child you undoubtedly learned that when you take care of others, you get positive feedback. This will show up clearly in your results on the Blame Game, but let's look at an example as well.

Imagine this: Mom came home tired from work and you rubbed her feet for a moment because you'd seen someone do it on TV. In response, she smiled with pleasure and called you her "favorite person in the whole world." Your brand new sibling—probably *not* your favorite person in the whole world!—cried, and you handed him a toy to hush him, but when you did, that rush of praise from Daddy and Grandmother rapidly taught you that making others' problems disappear was a worthy pursuit. The positive feedback was immediate and powerful, teaching you that it served you to take on the problems of others and solve them.

There is another type of reward, as well. You may have learned that when you take over others' problems, the household or the company or the social event—or anything else, for that matter—runs more smoothly. Maybe you were the peacemaker in a family in turmoil, so your reward was that ruffled feathers became unruffled. Or perhaps you were the one who tried to comfort your mother and make her feel better when she was upset, handing her food if she was hungry, her drink if she seem stressed, and so on. You probably received rewards for that type of behavior. You may have learned the lesson without conflict; if you took on a chore unasked and got praise for that, but were largely ignored unless you were doing similar things, you absorbed a potent lesson in taking over problems. *Good things happen when you solve problems.* That's the lesson. As you got older you may have learned that taking over problems meant that you could assure they were solved as you wish. There's a great deal of power in that!

Were you the one in the group projects in school who always ended up pulling far more than your fair share so you could guarantee a good grade? Are you the worker in the office who always agrees to stay late and finish projects? If so, keep in mind that you're very powerful because *you* are controlling the outcome; as much as you might complain about being in the position you're in, it's a *choice,* one that makes you feel superior to others, and it handles that nagging sense of insecurity you might feel.

The Dull Edge of the Blade

Even as you were watching others evade responsibility, you may have learned to do the same thing on a personal level—ducking and dodging any strong sense of personal accountability. It might defy logic that you'd make the same choices you so scorn or disapprove of in others, yet this is often precisely what takes place. If the sharp edge of the blade feels "forced" to handle others' issues and problems, the dull edge refuses to handle your own. Both are destructive, both are habits that get developed over time with practice, and both have one positive in common: they can be changed.

They can't be changed without effort, though; you need *honest vigilance* to see these behaviors in yourself whenever they occur, and you need *commitment within yourself* to eliminate the tendency to take on too much responsibility or the tendency to dodge responsibility within your own life. Honest vigilance is about keeping an eagle eye trained on yourself to gauge your progress. Making a commitment is about making—and, most important, *keeping*—a promise to yourself. Your promise is that you will continue on your path of accountability even if it causes distress or is inconvenient, and even if you think a thousand times that you'd much prefer to return to the "old way" that is so familiar.

WHY THE OLD WAY DOESN'T WORK

Life on the throne is not the best choice you can make. It's at once as simple and as complicated as that: simple because it's *not* the best choice, and complicated because there are so *many* reasons, some of them complex, *why* it's not the best choice. As always, though, understanding these reasons is the first step in being able to identify their presence in your own life… and *that*, of course, is the first step in creating the change you want. So let's examine why the old way—*life on the throne*—just doesn't work.

When You Don't Take Responsibility for Yourself, You…

- *Damage relationships* by refusing to step up to the plate, acknowledging your accountability for mistakes, choices, and even positive aspects of the relationship. This creates a distance and damage in the relationship that only one thing can cure: taking full responsibility for every action and interaction in which you're involved.

- *Damage trust* by being irresponsible; others quickly learn that they cannot count on you to be accountable for your actions and choices.

- *Don't stretch, learn, grow, or change* because you're too busy "hiding out" behind excuses and explanations to face the truth that allows you to learn and change.

- *Feel badly about yourself and create a false sense of reality within you* because you're being dishonest with yourself and others. This has the effect of distancing you from others, which leads to negative feelings, and it also leads to distorted interactions since you're operating from a false reality.

When You Take Too Much Responsibility for others, You . . .

- *Stunt their individual growth* by taking care of everything for them. This is a dangerous road to go down; once you've set off on the journey, it can be hard to find your way back, and the other isn't likely to offer you directions.

- *Stunt the relationship growth between you* since you're relegating both of you to relationships that are out of balance. These relationships often have parent-child, teacher-student, or one up/one down power differentials, which fit in certain contexts, of course, but not in healthy, equal relationships.

- *Spend more time feeling unpleasant emotions* such as anger, frustration, disappointment, and embarrassment when others fail and you must rescue them or when others expect you to take over and clean up after them.

- *Often neglect what you need to do in your own life* because you're otherwise occupied taking care of the needs of others and don't have time for your own needs.

Obviously there are ample reasons to give up the throne. Think about how you feel and react when you find others relying on you to an unhealthy degree or when you catch yourself ducking and dodging responsibility. What do your feelings tell you? *Use these feelings* as red flags that can signal you when you're treading in unsafe territory.

In addition to using your feelings to warn you when you're taking on too much responsibility or abdicating the responsibility you should be taking in your own life, you can listen to the language you use. The words you choose can tell you a great deal about how firmly rooted you are in a healthy degree of responsibility within yourself and within your relationships with others. Listen for phrases like the following to tell you when you're:

Taking on Too Much Responsibility

- I'll take care of it.
- Don't worry, you can leave it to me.
- Don't bother yourself.
- It's not your fault.
- You didn't mean to . . .
- You couldn't help . . .
- I'll find a way to . . .
- Just put it in my hands and . . .
- You're not as good at this as I am, so . . .
- I know what we'll do . . .
- Give me some time and I'll . . .

Dodging Your Own Responsibility

- It's not my fault.
- I don't/didn't know.
- I didn't have anything to do with it.
- I don't know what you're talking about.
- I didn't mean to.
- I couldn't help it.
- I guess I just wasn't born lucky.
- How could I know that?
- I've never done this before.
- That's never been my experience.

ROOTS

A SHIRKING OF ETHICAL RESPONSIBILITY
DEPRIVES [MAN] OF HIS WHOLENESS AND
IMPOSES A PAINFUL FRAGMENTARINESS ON HIS LIFE . . .

Carl Jung, Memories, Dreams, and Reflections

Jung addressed the concept of not accepting responsibility when he talked about being deprived of "wholeness" and having a "painful fragmentariness" imposed on one's life. He understood that to shirk one's responsibilities is to take away what makes us complete, instead shattering us into disparate parts. His statement goes to the root of the problem of not taking on enough responsibility and of taking on too much of the responsibility for others. It is an issue of self-concept—it changes who you are—and also an issue of self-esteem, affecting how you feel.

How you feel about yourself is affected by the degree of responsibility you take and the take-over. The person who fails the accountability test is different than the one who steps up to the plate; he or she will necessarily feel differently about themselves. If you're to maintain and build upon your self-esteem, you must recognize what is yours and what is not—what you're responsible for and what you're not responsible for. It's unhealthy and not in the least bit productive to handle your life any other way.

However, because you've seen yourself as incapable (or unwilling) to take responsibility for the choices you've made, or because you believe that you need to take responsibility for others, you see yourself differently than you otherwise might. Your sense of *self-esteem* is irrevocably tied up with the extent to which you are able to take on and stop taking over responsibility. This, of course, will be a challenge.

DEVELOPMENT TOOL

Many families have a designated "patient" who messes up constantly, sees him- or herself as a victim, and constantly needs rescuing. At the same time, most families also have a designated "rescuer," who posts bail, makes the overdrawn checking account right, calls the office when the family "patient" can't make it to work, and generally goes around making life work for the irresponsible patient. The result, for the rescuer, is a sense of being put-upon by the patient or victim, which serves to infantilize and paralyze the patient even more, thus creating yet more dependent behaviors. Often, this extends outward from the family so that the rescuer—whom one can picture often beating his or her chest in one of those "Why me?" laments—begins to appear in the office, the classroom, and the relationship. Let's do a bit more homework, then, in order to help you identify when this is happening so you can retool yourself and step down from the throne before you get too accustomed to it—or before you are deposed.

The Family

Here's where the problem begins, so let's begin here too.

1. There is probably someone in your family who's always asking for a favor or a handout. The next time it happens, tell them the bank's closed. Offer a suggestion for how they can get the funds they need or who else might do the favor. Be pleasant—*but don't cave in.* You may hear the familiar lament, "But you're the only one I can ask," or "I don't know where else to turn." Dismiss them; if they conduct themselves this way repetitively, you can be sure they're working on your guilt, and *you* need to eliminate that guilt. Their financial (and general) well-being is not your responsibility.

2. Think of one of your habitual knee-jerk reactions to offering help in the family (this will work in your close circle of friends as well). Unless it's a medical emergency, force yourself to wait for an hour or a day while you consider how else—not involving you—the situation might be handled. People can be remarkably resourceful when they need to be.

3. If there's a role that irks you because it limits you to a rescuer position, opt out for the day—and say that's what you're doing. Tell your spouse or partner that today you're not the Mommy or Daddy, and today you're not the ever-patient big sister who listens endlessly to whining or the ever-present big brother who rescues weaker family members after they've picked a fight.

The Office

You've heard of the "office wife"? Both men and women bring these roles into the office and, in many ways, try to mirror their home life there.

1. Your boss has always assumed that you will sit at your desk through your lunch hour each day while you finish whatever job is current. He expects

it on his desk when he returns from lunch. Let him know that you've begun a special fitness program and you walk during your lunch hour. Be flexible—certainly there are emergencies and unexpected deadlines now and then—but also be firm. Make yourself get up from your desk for that stroll each day; you'll be a better worker and a happier person if you charge your batteries at lunchtime most days.

2. Do you make coffee each day so that everyone has it when they come in? Help yourself by setting up a rotating schedule so that everyone gets to participate in this activity.

The Relationship

Here we have the "girlfriend/mother" and the "boyfriend/father" role. Power is central and ruling is everything.

1. The next time the love of your life seems to be making a decision that isn't something you would decide to do, take the opportunity to remain silent. If you're pressed, consider offering helpful suggestions so your opinion isn't the only one imaginable. It's nice to feel omnipotent, but it doesn't make for a balanced relationship. Do you want a soulmate—or an overgrown child?

2. When an activity is suggested, don't always present *your* favorite activity as the only one for the two of you. Compromise and begin to find new *mutual* interests.

3. Rather than picking up after your partner (in whatever way you typically do so, whether physically cleaning up messes around the house or emotionally trying to save him or her from feeling distress), declare tomorrow "Adult Day"—and back off. You're both fully functioning adults on this day, so do not pick up his socks, do not rescue her when the tire she was supposed to replace goes flat for the fifth time, and do not cook him a separate meal from what everyone else is eating just because he doesn't like what you made. While you're at it, don't feel guilty for your behavior on Adult Day!

Taking Care vs. Taking Over

Remember, we're not talking about not caring for others; instead we're talking about *not taking over care* of others. There's a big difference. You can still be nurturing, loving, and giving—and in fact you'll have more energy and desire to be these things because you won't be dissipating your energy by solving everyone else's problems.

It's not only all right to step back from taking ownership of others' problems; it's the most nurturing, loving, and giving thing you can do, because it encourages others to stand on their own, grow, and take flight.

PRESENT TENSE

You will discover, trying out the above exercises, that in some ways it's easier than you might have expected to change how you handle the issue of responsibility, and in other ways it's more difficult. It can seem easier because the results are typically so profoundly satisfying and sweeping. All sorts of changes will occur, many that are unanticipated, particularly when you refuse to take on the responsibility for others. You will have more time, as a bottom-line outcome, but as I noted above, you'll also have more energy, more opportunities for interacting with others in new and exciting ways, as well as less anger, resentment, and frustration. On the flip side, the difficulties will come primarily as a result of others' reactions to the change. It is at least initially inconvenient, annoying, and frustrating for others when you refuse to take care of them anymore.

OBSTACLES

If giving up the throne—taking on responsibility for yourself while giving up responsibility for others—has such magical results, why is it so difficult to do? There are plenty of reasons, obstacles that stop you in your tracks even as you make a commitment to give up the throne. Perhaps the most significant is that it is hard work—or harder work, anyway—to take responsibility than to abdicate it. Among other things, taking responsibility for yourself means:

- Admitting to the truth

- Finishing your work

- Fixing your mistakes

- Apologizing for your screw-ups

- Feeling incompetent or embarrassed

- Knowing your strengths and weaknesses

- Making things right when you've made them wrong

And giving up responsibility for others means:

- Giving up your power over them

- Being proven wrong

- Watching as others take longer, make mistakes, and sometimes suffer

- Experiencing frustration when you think you could do things better

- Acknowledging that you don't corner the market on the right answers

- Watching as others surprise and surpass you at times

- Admitting that you're not superior to others

Most of us don't want to admit that we have trouble with these things since it doesn't make us sound good if we're unable to admit to mistakes, give up our power, and the rest. In fact, the obstacles can make you sound like a cross between an irresponsible child, an egomaniac, and a control freak! It's hardly a personality type you or I want to admit to, is it? Be kind to yourself, though; if you add negative self-judgments to the guilt, brand new lessons, and other elements involved in making this change, you're going to set yourself up for failure. I guarantee it.

The way to make any change, including this one, is to treat yourself well, to recognize that you deserve congratulations and admiration for the hard work you're doing. Beating yourself up by believing that you must have been a pretty awful person to begin with if you need to make this change, or by believing that you aren't making the change fast enough, brilliantly enough, or just plain *enough*, will make the process of change unpleasant for you. It will also remove the rewards that come in the form of pride in your new skills and choices. This pride is one of the chief benefits of making *intra-* and *inter*personal changes, but there are others as well. We'll detail some of them below, so you can recognize the power in giving up the throne—and the power in making any of the other changes we've discussed.

BENEFITS

When you give up the throne, despite an initial "rocky" period that may occur, you will also begin to notice *significant changes in your relationships.* These changes are the result of the growing authenticity in the relationships. *Because you are growing as a person*, the relationship naturally changes.

Also, *you grow in skill* as you take on new responsibility in your life, and you watch *others grow in skill* once they are no longer inhibited by your caretaking. Because the power balance shifts in your relationships as a result of not taking on a parental or otherwise in-power role, *intimacy increases with others.* This is partially the result of the fact that *you can now be more honest*—and as a consequence, *you will begin to see more honesty coming from others* with whom you have relationships.

I'm sure you can identify other benefits as well, and certainly you'll do so as you begin to give up the throne. Watch for these benefits, because they are the rewards for the sometimes difficult work you're doing.

CONCLUSION

On the loftiest throne in the world
WE ARE STILL SITTING ONLY ON OUR OWN RUMP.

Michel de Montaigne, Of Experience: The Essays

Perhaps the throne doesn't occupy such a mighty space after all. Whether perching on the throne translates to believing yourself superior to others because of your frequent rescues, or believing that you're not responsible for your choices and behaviors, the end result is the same. Your relationships lack authenticity and intimacy, you experience tremendous frustration and a host of other negative feelings, and you inhibit yourself and others from growing individually and together because of the lack of authenticity the throne demands. Give up the throne and you'll see that you won't lose your inheritance. Instead, you'll gain the potential for true power and intimacy.

On Your Way

THINGS DO NOT CHANGE; WE CHANGE.

Henry David Thoreau

When I set the first words of this book upon paper, I had in mind several ideas, each forming a hope for you. I've been invited into the most hidden corners and intimate areas of my client's thoughts, feelings, failures, and successes for the twenty-plus years I've been a psychologist. As a result, the first thing I hoped for you and wanted to share with you was what I've learned—often from my clients—about *how to live successfully*. To me, success has never been about money, status, and other similar, fleeting symbols of achievement, although you can find plenty of books that are based on that very premise. Such books will claim that they can make you a millionaire overnight, or they will offer "surefire" methods for getting the big promotion, winning friends, vanquishing enemies and becoming the most popular person in town. That's not what I wanted to write about, in part because I don't believe in the formulas, the one-size-fits-all, ten-steps-to-success approaches. Those methods only work in the most predictable of situations, and since you're neither an automaton nor a clone, few of the challenges that you face are predictable. You are *you*, an incredibly complex, unique, and special individual, and because of that, your challenges are complex and unique—and that leads to the second idea, which is interlaced with the hope I had as I began writing.

The second thing I wanted to pass along is what I've learned not only about how you can live successfully, but how you can do so *without giving up your distinct character*. Unfortunately, what I have found far too often as I've worked in the field of psychology is that traditional therapy, supposedly designed to nurture and celebrate your individuality, often does just the opposite.

Traditional therapy has a bad habit of quashing your power, denying your truth, and overlooking your self-knowledge. For these reasons, I developed a system of self-therapy over the years as I worked with individuals, and I taught it to my clients so that they could complete their work with me and go on to serve as their own therapists. This then, is my third hope for you: I want to share this system with you and step back and watch it work, as I have with so many of my clients. In my work I came to realize that teaching this system to as many people as I could reach could loosen the stranglehold that traditional therapy has on our society. At the same time, it could strengthen self-esteem, develop a powerful self-concept, and eliminate the hopelessness and despair that is so sadly rampant in our society.

It is a gift to be allowed to walk beside people during their deepest pain, to celebrate with them at the times of their greatest joy, and to contribute in even small ways to their triumph over the slings and arrows of life. Taking that walk with others has challenged and shifted my definition of success, and I believe that setting out on this journey with yourself will do the same for you. Whether you travel alone or with others, you open the door to many things you might not otherwise see in yourself: courage, strength, and triumph come easily to mind. I have applauded as a woman once paralyzed by insecurity and shyness spoke confidently before an audience of a thousand. I have watched as a man unable to sustain a relationship—if you could even use the word *relationship* to describe his desperate and brief attempts at intimacy—joyfully celebrated 15 years of a deeply satisfying and intimate marriage. I have seen regular people, *just like you and me*, make the decision that they were not going to be miserable, or intimidated, or fooled, or dependent, or too scared to risk love—and I have seen them carry those courageous decisions through to success.

Ultimately, success is what I wish for you, and it is about finding and exercising your personal strength, accepting yourself as you are, even as you continue to strive to be ever more authentically "you" and looking at the difficulties in life as challenges rather than obstacles. You've learned how to do these things. You've learned that achieving success means *facing reality*; it means *allowing yourself to make mistakes*, and plenty of them, *without whining*, without criticizing, and certainly without going into hiding from the shame of your mistakes. There *is* no shame in making mistakes; the only thing worth hanging your head over is a failure to *live dangerously* and to live fully. *Learning to live as a full adult, standing up for yourself* and *challenging authority*—these are also all essential parts of living successfully. *Taking chances, giving up the useless work of being responsible for others* while taking on the critical work of *being fully accountable and responsible for yourself* are equally important. When you make the choice and commitment to *change your behavior, the belief in your own abilities and strengths will follow.*

I want you to live successfully, as a complex, unique individual—and I want you to be able to do so *authentically, powerfully, and joyfully.* If you use the 10 tools in *How to be Your Own Therapist*, this wish will become your reality.

As you continue along your journey, I'll leave you with one other hope, a final wish I hold for you, one that I know will be fulfilled as you become your own therapist, your own parent and teacher and friend. Henry David Thoreau said it, and I echo it from this day on: *I hope that you live on good terms with yourself and the gods.*[1]

Notes

Chapter One

1. Carol Burby and Adrienne Kirkey. Community health: working the puzzle." *Behavioral/Mental Health.* 1999; 77–86.
2. Gerald L. Klerman, and Myrna M. Weissman. Increasing rates of depression. *Journal of the American Medical Association.* 1989; 261 (15):2229–2235.
3. William E. Narrow, Donald S. Rae, Darrel A. Regier, et al. The de facto mental and addictive disorders service system. Epidemiologic Catchment Area, prospective one-year prevalence rates of disorders and services. *Archives of General Psychiatry.* 1993; 50(2):85–94.
4. William E. Narrow, Donald S. Rae, Darrel A. Regier. NIMH epidemiology note: prevalence of anxiety disorders. One-year prevalence best estimates calculated from ECA and NCS data. Population estimates based on U.S. Census estimated residential population age 18 to 54 on July 1, 1998. Unpublished, cited on NIMH web-site at http://www.nimh.nih.gov/publicat/numbers.cfm
5. http://www.nimh.nih.gov/publicat/numbers.cfm
6. "Psychology in Daily Life: Get the Facts." In *Managing Traumatic Stress: Tips for Recovering From Disasters and Other Traumatic Events,* American Psychological Association. Sept. 2001.

Chapter Two

1. Quoted in: Irving Klotz, *Bending Perception.* Book review. *Nature.* 1996; 379:412 (1).

Chapter Four

1. Jonathan D. Rankin, "The Modern, the Postmodern, and George Kelly's Personal Construct Psychology," *American Psychologist.* 2001. 45 (4): 368–369.

Chapter Five

1. Judith Wurtman and Richard Wurtman. Carbohydrates and depression. *Scientific American* (January 1989).
2. Benton T Donohoe. The effects of nutrients on mood. *Public Health & Nutrition* (September 1999).
3. Linda Carroll. Infatuated with Chocolate. MSNBC (March 13, 2000).
4. Donald E. Super and Branimir Suerko, eds. *Life Roles, Values, and Careers.* San Francisco: Jossey-Bass, 1995.
5. Robert A. Josephs, et al. Protecting the self from the negative consequences of risky decisions. *Journal of Personality and Social Psychology.* 1992; 62 (1):26–37.
6. Romin W. Tafarodi and William B. Swann. Self-liking and self-competence as dimensions of global self-esteem: initial validation of a measure." *Journal of Personality Assessment.* 1995; 65:322–342.
7. J. W. Thibaut and H. H. Kelley. *The Social Psychology of Groups.* New York: John Wiley & Sons, 1959.
8. John Locke. *An Essay Concerning Human Understanding.* New York: Digital Classics, 1995, book 4, chapter 19.
9. Kahlil Gibran. *The Prophet.* New York: Alfred A. Knopf, 1976.
10. G. R. Weeks and L. L'Abate. *Paradoxical Psychotherapy: Theory and Practice with Individuals, Couples, and Families.* New York: Brunner/ Mazel, 1982. Also: J. Haley, *Uncommon Therapy: The Psychiatric Techniques of Milton H. Erickson.* New York: W.W. Norton, 1993.

Chapter Six

1. Julian B. Rotter, "Generalized Expectancies for Internal vs. External Control of Reinforcement, *Psychological Monographs* 80/1 (whole no. 609), 1966.

Chapter Eight

1. From "The Serenity Prayer," sometimes attributed to Reinhold Niebuhr, though may be ancient in origin. Date unknown.
2. Cathy Stapells. "She's a Real Barbie Doll: Cindy Jackson Transformed by Cosmetic Surgery." http://www.caldercup.com/Health9902/05_ makeover.html (from *Toronto Sun*, February 5, 1999).
3. Jeff Langley, "Plastic Surgery Will Make Barbie Fatter, Flatter," http://www.texasonline.net/langley/columns/barbie.html (copyright 1997).

Chapter Nine

1. Edward Hoffman, *The Right to be Human*. New York: McGraw-Hill, 1999, p. 1.
2. http://www.geocities.com/beyond_stretched/holmes.htm.

Chapter Ten

1. Irwin Altman and Dalmas Taylor. *Social Penetration: The Development of Interpersonal Relationships*. New York: Holt, Rinehart & Winston, 1973.
2. Martin Seligman, *Learned Optimism*. New York: Simon & Schuster, 1991.

Chapter Eleven

1. Blanche Wiesen-Cook. *Eleanor Roosevelt*. London: Bloomsbury Publishing Ltd., 1993, p. 16.
2. Peter Biskind, "Kazan: The Master Director Discusses His Films," July 18, 1999, http://www.newmarketpress.com/title.asp?pid=385.

Chapter Thirteen

1. *Columbia World of Quotations*. New York: Columbia University Press, 1996.
2. Erich Fromm, *Escape from Freedom*. New York: Rinehart & Co., Inc., 1941.

Afterword

1. Letter, February 16, 1843, to Ralph Waldo Emerson. In *The Writings of Henry David Thoreau*, vol. 6. Boston: Houghton Mifflin, 1906, p. 62.

Index